GLOBALIZATION AND NORTH EAST INDIA

Books for NEICSSR

- Reorganisation of North East India Since 1947
  —*B. Datta Ray* and *S.P. Agrawal*
- Sociological Constraints to Industrial Development in North East India
  —*B. Datta Ray* and *Prabin Baishya*
- Changing Agricultural Scenario in North East India
  —*Bimal J. Deb* and *B. Datta Ray* (Eds.)
- Development Priorities in North East India
  —*Bimal J. Deb* (Ed.)
- Guwahati: The Gateway to the East
  —*K. Alam, N.C. Das* and *A.K. Borah*
- Agenda for North East India
  —*B. Datta Ray* (Ed.)
- Linguistic Situation in North-East India
  —*Mrinal Miri* (Ed.)
- Martial Traditions of North East India
  —*S. Dutta* and *B. Tripathy* (Eds.)
- Population, Poverty and Environment in North East India
  —*B. Datta Ray, H.K. Mazhari, P.M. Passah* and *M.C. Pandey* (Eds.)
- Education in North East India: Experience and Challenge
  —*Biloris Lyndem* and *Utpal Kumar De*
- Perspective of Security and Development in North East India
  —*S.K. Agnihotri IAS* and *B. Datta Ray*
- Ethnic Issues, Secularism and Conflict Resolution in North East India
  —*Bimal J. Deb* (Ed.)
- Globalization and North East India
  —*Bimal J. Deb, Keya Sengupta* and *B. Datta Ray*

About the Editors

Bimal J. Deb is Professor of Political Science at North Eastern Hill University, Shillong and is having a number of prestigious publications on North East India. He is also Executive Council Member of the Indian Institute of Public Administration at New Delhi.

Keya Sengupta is Professor of Economics at Assam University, Silchar. She is currently Dean of the School of Social Sciences in the University.

B. Datta Ray is Secretary, North East India Council for Social Science Research and has pioneered outstanding works which have been nationally and internationally acclaimed.

GLOBALIZATION
AND
NORTH EAST INDIA

Edited by

Bimal J. Deb
Keya Sengupta
B. Datta Ray

In Collaboration with

North East India Council for Social Science Research

Published by

CONCEPT PUBLISHING COMPANY, NEW DELHI-110059

Cataloging in Publication Data—DK
Courtesy: D.K. Agencies (P) Ltd. <docinfo@dkagencies.com>

Globalization and North East India / edited by Bimal J. Deb, Keya Sengupta, B. Datta Ray.
p. cm.
Papers presented at a national seminar organised by the North East India Council for Social Science Research at Shillong.
Includes bibliographical references.
Includes index.
ISBN 13: 9788180695100
ISBN 10: 8180695107

1. India, Northeastern—Economic policy—Congresses. 2. Globalization—Economic aspects—India, Northeastern—Congresses. 3. India—Economic policy—1991- —Congresses. I. Deb, Bimal J. II. Sengupta, Keya, 1955- III. Datta Ray, B. (Basudeb), 1925- IV. North East India Council for Social Science Research.

DDC 338.954 1 22

ISBN 13: 978-81-8069-510-0
ISBN 10: 81-8069-510-7

First Published 2008

Published and Printed by
Ashok Kumar Mittal
Concept Publishing Company
A/15-16, Commercial Block, Mohan Garden
New Delhi-110059 (INDIA)

Phones : 25351460, 25351794
Fax : 091-11-25357103
Email : publishing@conceptpub.com

Preface

Reforms are 16 years old. They have taken roots and seem irreversible in coming years. The New Economic Policy adopted by the Government of India in 1991 had the objective of integrating the Indian economy with the global economy. The major policy instrument consists mainly of providing all opportunities to private sector for launching new industrial undertakings by removing all kinds of Government controls which had been the characteristic feature of planned Indian economy since 1950. Dismantling of public sector units by way of denationalisation and disinvestment process and extending patronage and encouragement of the private sector have been the main policy focus of New Economic Policy. The major objective of these policy issues is to raise the Global competitiveness of Indian products by effecting cost and price efficiency and thereby create Global demand for Indian products. India made a series of efforts to explore and extend the Global markets but she had also opened her domestic fields to foreign players being a member of World Trade Organisation. Encouragement to international trade is one of the policy instruments of New Economic Policy. International trade becomes liberalised. At this time of upsurge of market forces all round integration of markets across the countries got facilitated by the radical advancement of information and communication technology. This facilitated the process of Globalisation.

Till now the New Economic Policy has marginal impact on the people of North East India. This is due to backwardness of the region with its semi-feudal anarchy in agricultural front. In urban areas new aspirations among emerging middle class have created a climate for all kinds of consumer durables. As a result the traditional skills in the field of weaving and bell and metal cottage industries are being adversely affected. Small men and women in civil societies are being pushed to the periphery. Tea and silk industries are losing ground in the world market. The New Economic Policy has brought uncertainty in our economy. It needs to be reviewed.

16 May, 2007

B. Datta Ray
Secretary, NEICSSR

Contents

Introduction

The New Economy Policy introduced in July 1991 was basically aimed at making the Indian economy vibrant, dynamic and internationally competitive as a prelude to its integration with the world economy behind the façade of structural adjustment, inherent in the very reform process itself, lay the compelling force of neoliberal policy perspective which could hardly be ignored by Indian planners and policy makers. Ostensively, higher level of economic growth was the desirable end but it was inconceivable without releasing trade, commerce and industry in particular from shackles of bureaucracy.

Liberalization, Globalization and Privatization are the three facets of New Economic Policy which together provided a market oriented direction to the Indian Economy away from the myopia of mixed economy which failed to deliver and had virtually taken the economy to the brink of collapse. The reform process initiated by the New Economic Policy soon engulfed industrial financial, and service sectors alike and over a period of time the basic thrust in the approach resulted in high growth rate of GDP, and per capita GDP. In general, there there was heightened rate of industrial production apart from fall in inflation rate and fiscal deficits.The most remarkable thing has been a spectacular rise in foreign direct and portfolio investment which has had the effect of making the economy more growth oriented than ever before. The NEP in the past fifteen years has also triggered positive changes, though inadequate, in different facets of human development, involving level of living, employment and wages, literacy and education, nutrition and health. However, its impact on agriculture and rural development has fallen short of the expectations.

North East India presents a resource abundant economy which continued to remain backward in comparative perspective with other regions. However, backwardness of the economy could be attributed as much due to geo-political constraints as to retrograde policies pursued by the constituent states, a fact which impeded the process of transformation of traditional economy to one having the semblance of a modern one. Tradition and identity issues had lulled the region to a zone of complacency and inaction and the only grace point was the safety net of the region which operated through the community based socio-economic structure prevailing in the tribal areas.

An agricultural economy with shifting cultivation predominating, together with total absence of infrastructure and restrictive land market militated against the development process in the region and as a result, when the NEP came into being the requirements of change could hardly be made applicable to the economy in a radical manner. In the region as a whole, there was no long term perspective of development, notwithstanding the creation of North Eastern Council. Further, internal security scenario was not conducive either to development. The concept of tribal development had also made no dent in the situation. The region despite massive flow of Central resources continued to lay behind in basic infrastructure, power generation, mineral development, cross border trade and agricultural productivity.

The NEP has now opened up great opportunities to bring about structural changes in the economy, although the challenges are daunting as well. The State Governments of the region have started showing the requisite political will to surge ahead by reaping the benefits of NEP. Significantly since 1996 several bold initiatives have been taken by the Central Government by augmenting Central investments in different spheres of the economy with primary focus on the region's infrastructure in order to bring about perceptible changes in economic governance of the region. In fact, state intervention in the economy of the region has become more strident to prepare the ground for absorption of market oriented economic reforms. In the past one decade, central packages, new industrial policy, creation of non-lapseable pool of central resources, upgradation of DoNER from department to a Ministry and revamping of the North Eastern Council have created the required springboard for developmental leap forward. Winds of change can very well be seen to be in operation in the economy's response to the imperatives of NEP. Indeed the success of India's Look East Policy hinges on the overall development of the region as a whole. However, one has to guard against lopsided planning and faulty implementation. Time has come to initiate proactive measures to address issues like militancy, political extremism and insurgency by evolving a region specific community participation in the process of development. The tremendous manpower potential of the region will then get meaningful channels of productive pursuits.

To accelerate the pace of industrialization and development of the region, the Centre has announced the North East Industrial and Investment Promotion Policy, 2007 (NEIIPP). The policy ensures continuance of 100 per cent excise duty exemption in respect of finished products made in the North East. Capital subsidy would be enhanced from 15 per cent of the investment in plant and machinery to 30 per cent. Further, the limit of automatic approval for capital subsidy has been announced to be Rs. 1.4 crore from Rs. 15 lakhs. Again, for grant of capital investment subsidy higher than Rs. 1.5 crore but up to a maximum of Rs. 30 crore, the decision would be taken by an Empowered Committee. What is noteworthy is the eligibility of new as well as existing units to enjoy incentives for a period of 10 years. The industrial units could be located anywhere in the region and there would be no distinction between thrust and non-thrust industries as it existed earlier. Besides 100 per cent income tax exemption, there is provision for eligibility for reimbursement of 100 per cent insurance premium. The inclusion of service sector, bio-technology and power generating industries within the policy framework is likely to bring about a qualitative change in the pace of industrialization.

The New Economic Policy has undoubtedly opened up the possibilities of harnessing immense potentials of the North East region for developmental imperatives which had hitherto remained illusive in the absence of economic infrastructure and strong political will. Evidently, the decline in agricultural growth rate and retrograde industrial policies only contributed to a stagnating situation. No doubt, the idea of regional planning was invoked in early seventies with the establishment of the North Eastern Council but it made no headway whatsoever.

Of late, a new realization has dawned on the political leadership that the region can emerge as a vibrant economic zone on the strength of exclusive and proactive central initiatives which prominently include non-lapseable pool of resources and industrial and investment promotion policy. In addition, Look East Policy expectations have generated a positive outlook in favour of making the region a prominent hub for international trade and commerce. Significantly, the Eleventh Five Year Plan has focused on the exploration of huge resources of the North East for economic development of the region. A step in the right direction has been on highlighting public-private partnership in investment in the field of road and air connectivity, power generation and mineral development. The improved security scenario in the region and the all-out effort of the DoNER Ministry is all set to bring the benefits of globalization to the region's doorsteps to get over the skewed development profile.

The book is a pioneering attempt to assess the prospects and constraints facing the region in absorbing the New Economic Policy in its political economy. This is clearly seen in the in-depth and penetrating analysis of the contributors covering all possible issues and dimensions of the development scenario.

The Contributors

Amalesh Banerjee, Retired Professor of Economics, Rabindra Bharati University, Kolkata.

Anjanjyoti Borah, Mendipather Collage, Mendipathar, Meghalaya.

Ashok K. Roy, Scholar in National Foundation for India, New Delhi.

B.C. Pradhan, Department of Political Science, S.S. Collage, Hailakandi.

B. Datta Roy, Secretaty, N.E.I.C.S.S.R, Shillong.

B. Francis Kulirani, Superintending Anthropologist, Anthropological Survey of India, Shillong.

Bibhash R. Choudhury, Retired Head of the Department of Economics, G.C. College, Silchar.

Bimal J. Deb, Professor of Political Science, North Eastern Hill University, Shillong.

Biswajyoti Dasgupta, Investigator, NSSO (FOD), Silchar.

D.R. Das, PSO and Head, RO. MNRE (NER) Guwahati.

Dolly Phukan, Centre for Women's Studies, Dibrugarh University, Dibrugarh.

E. Nixon Singh, Lecturer, D.M. College of Commerce, Imphal.

G.P. Prasain, Department of Commerce, Manipur University, Imphal.

Ganga Rani Das, A.D.P. College, Nagaon, Assam.

Gorky Chakraborty, Department of Economics, Dibrugarh University.

Hiranmoy Roy, Department of Economics, Karimganj College, Karimganj.

J.B. Ganguly, Former Vice-Chancellor, Tripura University, Tripura.

Kaustubh Lahiri, Surendranath College for Women, Kolkata.

Khorshed Alam, Retired Professor of Economics, Gauhati University.

Kingshuk Adhikari, Karimganj College, Karimganj.

Malabika Das Gupta, Professer, Centre for Urban Economic Studies, Calcutta University.

Manoj Kumar Singh, Lecturer, People's College Mokokchung, Nagaland.

Mithilesh Kumar Sinha, Department of Economics, Nagaland University, Nagaland.

N. Tejmani Singh, Department of Commerce, Manipur University, Imphal.

Pabitra Giri, Professor of Economics, Calcutta University, Kolkata.

P.C. Dutta, Department of Statistics, S.S. Collage, Hailakandi.

P.J. Goswami, Reader, Department of Commerce, Assam University, Silchar.

P.M. Passah, Retired Professor of Economics.

R.P. Bhattacharjee, Deputy Registrar, North Eastern Regional Institute of Science and Technology, Naharlagam, Arunachal Pradesh.

Sakiya Khan, Department of Economics, Gauhati University, Guwahati.

Surojit Sen Gupta, Department of Economics, St. Edmund's College, Shillong.

Th. Binapani Devi, Lecturer, G.P. Women's College, Imphal.

Th. Jitendra Singh, Research Scholar, Department of Commerce, Manipur University.

1

North East India in the Context of New Economic Policy

B. Datta Ray

India adopted the policies of globalisation, liberalisation and privatisation and market economy in the wake of economic crisis of 1991 which arose due to collapse of Soviet Union and East European Socialist economy and the gulf war which resulted in global economic power imbalance. The immediate cause is the serious balance of payment crisis, fall in exports and in the decline in domestic production of crude oil, agriculture and industrial outputs. The new economic policy was a desperate response to the crisis of confidence. The Government of India adopted an adjustment programme that was directed towards stabilization and structural reform to dilute the philosophy of planned development prospect, a modified socialistic pattern so far followed since 1950 modelled on Mahalanobis formula of economic development in India. Stabilization effort brought some kind of restoration of foreign confidence and improved foreign exchange reserve following the devaluation of rupee and tightening of fiscal management such as cutting down of public expenditure particularly non-planned ones. Industrial and trade liberalisation was targeted to attract foreign investment. Some foreign capital inflow surged in demanding immediate deregularisation of industry and trade, liberal exchange rate regime and drastic reduction of state economic activities by privatising public enterprises. These conditionalities directed and guided by International Monetary

Fund and World Bank asked for free flow of foreign investment in all sectors including service sectors, reduction and removal of controls, privatization of public sector units. India opted for this soft way of survival. The argument was that this would expand production, increase employment and export and there would be prosperity in the countryside.

The New Economic Policy launched by the Government of India in 1991, had the clear objective of integrating the Indian economy with the rest of the World. The policy instruments consist mainly providing all facilities to the private sector for starting new industrial ventures by removing all kinds of government restrictions which had been a characteristic feature of the Indian Economy from 1950. Dismantling of public sector units through disinvestment and denationalisation and providing encouragement to the private sector, have been the main focus of the New Economic Policy. Raising competitiveness of the economy through quality production, cost and price efficiency, so that Indian products become globaly competitive, have been the major objectives of these policy issues. In an effort to create global demand for our products, India not only had to make serious efforts to explore the international markets, but she had also to open up her own markets to foreign products. In other words, most of the trade restrictions had to be liberalised to encourage international trade as one of the policy instruments related to the New Economic Policy.

As India embarked upon the market oriented economic reform programme the process of economic globalization also started gathering greater momentum. The factors that facilitated the process are resurgence of market economy worldwide, coming of the WTO regime and advancement of information and communication technology. At this time of upsurge of market forces all-around, integration of markets across countries got facilitated. Consequently, inflow and outflow of goods, services and capital across countries have expanded expediting the process of globalization.

India has now travelled the path of New Economic Policy for 16 years, numerous hurdles and obstacles notwithstanding. The results achieved so far are not much encouraging. So far, it has failed to make a viable economy where the benefits, if any, of economic globalization percolates down to the small person in the village and of the town. The result achieved so far is not much encouraging. Non-agricultural growth rate never exceeded 8 per cent. The agricultural growth rate is dismal, being 1.7 per cent during 1999–2004-05. The National Income increase is marginal. The employment growth rate is nearly stagnant. The growth in industrial sector has been at the cost of social sector like health, education, shelter, food and medical care. There has been no decline in the proportion of poor since mid-80s. Liberalisation has not led to any improvement in the life style of the masses. This trend shows that the low agricultural growth and near stagnation is not a serious constraint to non-agricultural and service sector growth of 7 per cent. The failure of agriculture is not considered as important factor in the post-liberalisation economic growth, the benefits being reaped by a small section of neo-rich. Special Economic Zones (SEZ) fits in such an analysis of post-liberalization situations in India. Poverty line is fixed at Rs. 264.00 per capita per month for urban areas and Rs. 228.00 per capita per month for rural areas at 1992-93 prices. The Planning Commission based its findings accepting Professor Lakdawala methodology.

We have major constraints like low capital, low level of technology, millions of small and marginal farmers, and wide-spread rural unemployment. There should have been genuine radical land reforms in rural India pursued prior to present day globalization and economic liberalization providing some infrastructure and human resource development. Without this pre-condition fulfilled, the present day policy of liberalization and globalization might reduce India to a stunted growth of Argentina, Brazil and Peru variety. In these countries, liberalization, privatization and globalization have created the worst form of concentration of national wealth in the hands of few and poverty is widespread in severe form for the majority of the people.

In the name of globalization, we are allowing foreign capital in labour intensive industrial areas like small scale sectors and in consumer goods and retail sectors. In the name of liberalization, we are allowing foreign capital to enter our market even without any promising green technology transfer. It is true we need foreign capital and import of eco friendly technology in infrastructure building sector. But it cannot be an entry of outdated technology discarded elsewhere.

The process of liberalization has not helped social sector development in the country. The private sectors are seldom anxious in investing in fields of education and health care for the poor masses. With globalization, the farming sector is being thrown up in the name of Special Economic Zones to multinationals and to agricultural big business.

Till now the New Economic Policy has marginal impact on the people of North East India. This is due to economic backwardness of the region with its semi-feudal anarchy in land relations which is the basic anchor of the economy of the region. But in urban areas, new wants and new aspirations among the neo-middle class are being created. An active consumer culture is coming up in urban societies. As a result, the traditional skills of women of North East India in the fields of agriculture, weaving, etc. are being adversely affected. The opening of market economy led to commercialization of agriculture and new technology penetrated in the traditional fields and small scale industries. New land owning classes are emerging. The small men and women are pushed to the margin.

The policy of globalization has brought some adverse effect on the region's tea export to the world market as the competitiveness of tea industry is marginal. There is a possibility that India's tea may face challenges even in domestic market from Sri Lanka and from East Africa. They may market quality packet tea in India's market. The traditional silk industry of North East India is facing challenge from China in home market.

The possibility of foreign and domestic investment in a big way for North East India's economic development is not so bright. Investment if any is likely to be limited to the service sector. Under these circumstances, the present stagnant social and economic scenario is likely to continue which is inconsistant with the philosophy of liberalization and globalization. An active social welfare state has still an important space to lift the masses from the current semi-feudal anarchy. The state has still a commanding place to take economic initiative for social and economic development of North East India. The economic transition is not so visible. The neo-liberal strategy of the New Economic Policy cannot provide employment growth in North East India for the jobless persons. They would be on the doles increasingly by the anti-poverty programmes of the Central Government.

2

North East India and its Council for Development

Bimal J. Deb

With the inclusion of Sikkim in the reconstituted North Eastern Council, the region virtually encompasses as many as eight states, although elementary requirement of a viable economic region does justify without any shadow of doubt, the inclusion of North Bengal in its fold for conceptualizing any development thrust and making it operational in the real sense of the term. Be that as it may, the new-look forum on the strength of its much orchestrated elevation to a regional planning body from its earlier advisory status was doubtless a step forward in the right direction to effectively address geo-political distinctiveness of North East and its economic backwardness, inherent as much in the natural topography and terrain which traditionally sustained large scale shifting cultivation as in lack of infrastructure and isolationist policies of the colonial past.

Alongside, the region also witnessed sociological constraints and apprehensions to the concept of development and its concomitants, a situation compounded by crisis of internal security arising inevitably out of sustained militancy, insurgency and xenophobia. All this seen in the background of overall economic deficiencies of the region present considerable hurdles, though not insurmountable, to much needed exploitation and management of resources for development.

True, there may have been a time when the Central policies of indifference had created popular resentment and fostered regional sentiments in North Eastern states. One can only recall, without any fear of contradiction, as to how the demand for second refinery in Assam in mid-sixties was brushed aside despite availability of crude oil and its reserves. Indeed, there was but little concern for economic development of the region and public anger and agitation surfaced on issues ranging from extension of broad gauge line to denial of job opportunities to sons of the soil. A clear metamorphosis of the Centre's attention to the sensibilities of emerging middle class elite in North East was more than evident in the seventies and eighties leading, among other things, to creation of small states not necessarily economically viable, upgradation of Union Territories to the status of full-fledged states and attempted conflict resolution through constitutional resilience and accords. The inventive policy was further enriched in the succeeding decade by the mechanism of cease-fire of the sovereign state with the rebel groups in search of peace and stability however elusive it, at times, appeared to be.

Constitutional Resilience

Significantly, the accommodative gestures of the Centre produced strikingly positive results in several parts of North East India. A fact of extraordinary importance was the installation of a Mizo rebel leader in the corridors of power without having to undergo the electoral process. The success of the move could be measured from the subsequent emergence of the state of Mizoram as a zone of peace which was inconceivable at one time. No less important is the contemporary readiness of the present political leadership in the state to act as peace broker in the region. This recent granting of Z-plus security to NSCN (IM) leader while in India is another example of constitutional resilience par excellence. Again, North East India also witnessed as to how a regional formation, riding on the success of its struggle against the presence of foreigners romped in power, although it was another story why its idealism faded in the whirlpool of shortsighted political expediency. In another development, not long ago, the electoral process went unheeded in Nagaland in course of thirteenth general election to the Lok Sabha despite boycott announced by the undersigned rebels. On the whole, a spectacular growth of liberal democracy in the tribal areas of the region is unmistakably visible outside the shell of what the Sixth Schedule of the Constitution intended to promote.

A turning point in the development strategy of a landlocked and peripheral region came in 1973 with the establishment of North Eastern Council having the declared purpose of addressing its special needs and requirements, including those relating to security in response to a new political reality taking shape as a fallout of successive reorganisations of Assam. The whole approach was unconventional being a deviation from the Indian planning process and with its anchorage in the arm of the Ministry of Home Affairs it was justified in defence of coordinated regional development and security through the expertise of an advisory body as it was then meant to be as per the letter of the law.

Counter Productive Role of NEC

Though unique in many ways, the declared goal of the Council from the very beginning remained undirected as well as uncertain. No doubt, the resource base of the region was identified but a clear absence of focus loomed large in its confused perception and muddled understanding of the basics of regional planning. Predictively, the counter-productive orientation of the Council became all the more glaring when it arrogated to itself no doubt with Centre's blessings, the status of an intermediary funding and disbursing body, an open-handed role that unleashed the floodgates of mutual bickerings, acrimony and accusations among the resource starved constituent states on developmental priorities resulting in lack of consensus, demands and counter demands about equitable distribution of funds and worst still, the process of politicisation started rolling out when the Chairmanship of the Council became a contentious issue in mid-nineties culminating in the lowering of its creditability.

The inevitable climax was yet to come and it did come sooner than expected in an inexplicable form when the Secretary of the

Council was placed under suspension and inquiry ordered leading ultimately to his exit. The Council resembling the proverbial ship without a radar was in the brink of a collapse and the realization that lack of monitoring and evaluation mechanism had stalled the execution of a number of Council funded projects precipitated the crisis further. In fact, at no stage, timely implementation of the sponsored schemes could ever become the key word in its lexicon.

Over the years, successive Council meetings had persistently advocated higher fund allocation as an essential prerequisite of its supposed ability to deliver and strangely enough, shortfall on its demand was highlighted disproportionately to proper utilisation of sanctioned resources. Even the fifty-third meeting of the Council held recently emphasized this in full chorus unmindful of the track record.

Looked at closely, the funding pattern of the Council from the very beginning, was without any sound rationale as it sought to cover as many areas as demanded by political leadership of the States. Each of the member states preferred to remain desperately keen to highlight its own potentials and requirements conveniently forgetting the concern that brought them together on a common platform. The deliberations of the various meets invariably left the concept of regional development as volatile as ever. One has to appreciate the fact that it was never the intention of the framers of the Council to empower it the capability to trigger development initiatives in all conceivable fields.

More credible role would have been for the Council to act as a repository of expertise, nay a think tank, to articulate the implications of special category status accorded to the region in modification of the Gadgil formula or North East industrial policy or non-lapseable pool of Central resources by suggesting norms for project formulation, monitoring and evaluation within the overall framework of the Indian planning process. It is a sad story that notwithstanding the functioning of the Council for more than three decades the contours of development in North East India remain by and large unaddressed. The much declared regional development goal has conveniently been pushed under the carpet and one wonders how a forum is able to justify its existence only on the basis of piecemeal measures and that too without any perspective plan of unifying development priorities.

Vision Plan in Abeyance

The worsening situation warranted prime ministerial attention and concern in early 2005 underlining the necessity of a vision plan to set in motion the process of development. Ever since, rhetorical outbursts aimed at creating a euphoria became the be all and end all of Council leadership which started assiduously publicising the on set of an imminent paradigm shift in its planning approach involving people's participation in the formulation of development plan. The prospective vision document, it was made out, would lead the region along the garden path and bring about albeit coordinated and comprehensive socio-economic development of the region. What is more noteworthy is that two full time septuagenarian members of the Council instead of finalising the draft found it appropriate in their wisdom and contemplation to abdicate their responsibility and entrusted the job to a private consultancy firm. Revealing as it may appear, the publicity studded Vision: 2020 is yet to see the light of the day even though long two years have been over in anticipation.

It is an enigma as to why Vision: 2020 even after its declared completion has been kept in abeyance but its redundancy stands out clearly following the inclusion of a separate chapter on North East in the approach paper of the Eleventh Five Year Plan envisaging a blue print of development for the region. In this connection, one cannot but concede the inspiring role of the very idea of vision in the formulation of regional planning but sadly enough the same spirit is yet to percolate the mind of political leadership. For each one of them the bottom line is demand for fund to address the specific requirements of the state. Even the Centre's sound policy of releasing project fund out of non-lapseable pool through the Council is not readily acceptable to the states. This apart, there is also a demand from Arunachal Pradesh, which has the distinction of receiving eighty-five per cent of its total expenditure from the Centre, that geographical area of the State instead of population should be the basis of the funding pattern. Strange as it may sound, in total disregard of all that the Council stands for, a political dignitary of the region wanted the forum to take up inter-state border disputes which have defied all solutions so far. Further, the persistent use of the Council platform by political leaders of the region to popularise the pet theme to have insurgency problem in their respective state declared a national issue is no more than a shortsighted strategy aimed at mere fund-grabbing rather than a genuine desire to set their house in order. What is inexplicable is the alleged diversion of development fund in the region to insurgent coffer. In this connection nothing can be more forthright than the recent lamentation of head of a state in the region on slippages of development fund which undoubtedly presents a great challenge to all those who stand by North East's development.

Intriguingly, the Council has taken too long time to recognise the vital fact that communication and power hold the key to the development of the region. It is pertinent to note that the Council's role in this respect touches only the tip of the iceberg. Out of the total investment of Rs. 7000 crores since 1972, as much as Rs. 1867 crore has gone for road network of 97 roads with a total length of 7700 km. and Rs. 142.12 crore for airports upgradation. As per the policy the Council funded up to 60 per cent for the upgradation of airports in the region in collaboration with Airports Authority of India. Besides there is also subsidy to Alliance Air for providing services of four ATR aircrafts.

The heart of the matter is that Shukla Commission's recommendations relating to infrastructural development in the region was not given the importance it deserved. Development challenges cannot be solved in one stroke and hence one of the priorities of the Council should have been to facilitate private investment or public-private partnership in core sectors in order to sail in post-liberalisation era. Instead of developing consensus on this emerging area, political leadership of the region has ruled out its long-term feasibility. Only recently, a major initiative in this regard has come from National Highway Authority of India in the form of North East Express Highway covering a length of over

3,000 km. of national highway and 600 km. of Council funded road involving an investment of Rs. 19,235 crore in various projects in next forty-two months. The Asian Development Bank too has shown interest in roads for urban development in the region.

Power Generation

As regards power generation the picture is anything but satisfactory. It was widely accepted earlier that the estimated hydro-power generation potential in North East was over 30,000 MW. Significantly, the Central Electricity Authority has estimated phenomenal hydro-power potential of Arunachal Pradesh alone at 55,000 MW. So far, participation of NHPC and NEEPCO has been nominal and in the absence of any long-term policy with the Council, the power house status of the region is bound to remain only a matter of theoretical interest. A big stride outside the involvement of the Council has now triggered a silverlining in Arunachal Pradesh with its Government signing memorandum of understanding with National Hydro-Electric Power Corporation and National Thermal Power Corporation for generating an ambitious 15,000 MW of electricity at a cost of approximately Rs. 41,457 crore. Again a small non-industrial state like Meghalaya has over the years remained a power deficit state having been able to develop roughly one-tenth of its potential. In Manipur the fate of multi-purpose Tipaimukh dam, initially mooted four decades back continues to hang in the balance despite the foundation stone having been laid because of local opposition centring displacement of tribal villages. Further, nobody has yet learnt any lesson from the acute crisis of management apparent from the accumulated loss of State Electricity Boards of the region which has now reached a staggering figure of Rs. 33,000 crore.

There is little to cheer about industrial growth in the region even though the states concerned had formed a joint front to put up in vein a credible image to the prospective investors to allay their apprehensions about security and sustainability. The North Eastern Industrial Development Policy (NEIDP) launched in 1997 and later extended to other special category states provided for incentives to entrepreneurs in the form of transport subsidy and tax exemptions and it could attract no more than Rs. 1268 crore in the region in course of seven years as compared to Himachal Pradesh which drew Rs. 7010 crore in just one year. The policy having proved to be a damp squib for the North East during its life span of ten years, the states of the region are now engaged in an all out offensive in favour of an alternative package with additional incentives exclusively for the region. Little wonder then that the Council's resolve in February 2006 to accord due importance to industrial pace through launching of innovation schemes was too unconvincing to create any flutter among the investors.

The inclusion of a separate chapter in the plan document for the region is by itself not going to be rejuvinative in its stretch and orientation unless the States concerned express their explicit commitment to the developmental process. To say the least, what is also needed is internal resource mobilization in order to be able to bear the minimum expenses in reaping the benefits of Central assistance or in warding off debt burden. Interestingly, the literacy drive called Sarva Siksha Abhiyan initiated by the Centre is a pointer and as matters stand, the states of the region are reluctant to contribute mandatory ten per cent in order to receive remaining ninety per cent as grants under the scheme, a fact which inevitably means non-participation in a critical area of enhancing social infrastructure. In the Council meeting as well, the states of the region have been vociferous in demanding revival of the earlier funding pattern having components of ninety per cent grant and ten per cent loan as was applicable to special category states. However as a concession and in defiance of the Finance Commission's recommendation, the Centre has now decided to pass on external assistance to such states in the grant-loan ratio of 90 : 10 which may reduce their debt liability in the event of such offers forthcoming.

Look East Policy

Of late, the Centre's Look East policy initiative, though in its formative stage, generated considerable interest in the region.

However, a hard look at the ground realities is indeed needed to assess the possibility ever of economic integration of the region with South East Asian countries even though the former DoNER Minister and erstwhile Chairman of the Council was bent upon building castles in the air as if the expectations would operate in a self-propelling manner. What is even lacking currently is the absence of a comprehensive policy governing international trade with the eastern neighbours through the North East which shares nearly 5,000 km. of border with Bangladesh, China, Myanmar and Bhutan. No one can hide the fact that at present the region only has unorganised and weak formal trade with the neighbours to the east. If the volume of total official export and import through the region has remained more or less static over the years, informal trade went up by leaps and bounds and hence any attempt at reversal of the trend may prove to be a daunting job. Admittedly, beyond its border, the South East Asian economies are in a booming phase unlike the backward economy of the region with its total lack of trade infrastructure worth the name. It is well known that there existed historical trade linkages, though extremely limited, of the region with countries of South East Asia. But, today's situation warrants organised, comprehensive and uninterrupted trade and not just the show of it.

The states of the region have, of late, been exhorted by the Planning Commission to increase the volume of trade with the neighbouring countries in line with Centre's Look East policy. Absence of infrastructure apart, any regional trading hub or headquarters is conspicuous by its absence. Nor is there any composite check post anywhere in the border area of the region drawn from customs, immigration and narcotics. More importantly, in the ultimate analysis vibrant border trade is basically coterminous with friendly relations between neighbours.

As a matter of fact, the hard reality is that Bangladesh is not very keen to have any comprehensive border trade with Meghalaya, although in the pre-partition days the districts comprising the State had viable trade relations. Elsewhere in the region, Nathula pass border trade between Sikkim and China got reopened after a lapse of more than four decades, but items included in the list do not suggest any promising turnout, a fact when combined with poor road connectivity will only have the effect of marginalising the expected benefits. Besides, security considerations which are of uppermost nature may not suggest an all out liberal policy.

In the same manner, Stilwell road reopening would only bring about partial relief in the stagnant economy of the region largely because of inaccessible isolation and remoteness from the possible centrally located trading hub. In the absence of a massive transport subsidy such a venture may turn out to be self-defeating. Further, real trade is contingent upon road reconstruction of 1,726 km. basically with Chinese initiative as the Indian side covers only a stretch of 60 km. from Ledo to Pangsau. Again, in Manipur, the existing border trade through Moreh in Chandel District bordering Myanmar is restricted to 22 selected items although unauthorized trade knows no bound.

In order to boost border trade, there is a proposal to develop infrastructural and other facilities for the Myanmarese port of Settawe which is 200 km. from the nearest Indian border in Mizoram. What is however discouraging is the tough and in-hospitable terrain leading to Zakhawthar in Champai district of Mizoram and Rih in Myanmar and further beyond which by itself is restrictive of the volume of trade. About the financial viability of the move, the less said the better.

It may not be out of place to mention here that the constraints of road connectivity has actually stood in the way of border trade materialising in an effective manner even after two decades of Mizoram Accord incorporating and underlying its importance in principle. At present, a temporary trade agreement regulates trade centring 22 exchangeable goods and that too without a check post worth the name. Quite inevitably, the region has to continue to depend largely on land route and in the absence of Bangladesh playing any role in easing connectivity problem the facilities offered by Kolkata Port, even though situated at a distance of 900 km. from nearest point in North East, appears to be a better option.

Non-Lapseable Pool

More significant than economic development in the region is actually the politics revolving round non-lapseable pool of central resources created in October 1998 to replace successive aid packages offered earlier more on expedient basis than on any long-term perspective. The fund, unique in its very conception, is undoubtedly a national commitment in the true sense of the term, to generate and boost economic activities in the backward North East out of mandatory ten per cent contribution of various Ministries of Government of India barring defence and a few more, in support of viable projects proposed by the states and approved by a committee of experts of the Planning Commission with its member secretary as its chairman. As a matter of abundant caution, the committee is provided with teeth to streamline the flow of fund and quite expectedly to assess and prioritise the projects, recommend phased allocation of fund, monitor and review the progress within the overall objective of time-bound implementation. The mechanism when mooted was expected to generate an amount of rupees fifteen hundred crores annually.

For the North Eastern states central packages were more welcome than non-lapseable fund as the former was to be given to the states concerned against identified projects without the intermediary role of the Council. The result was lack of enthusiasm and in 2003 Parliament was informed that only Rs. 1,318.66 crore of the Rs. 5,806.07 crore deposited in the pool between 1998 and 2002 had been released. Thereafter the DoNER Ministry with its elevation from earlier departmental status could not also come to the rescue of the states and North East MPs' Forum expressed nothing more than concern about lack of developmental projects.

It is too obvious that the states of the region have not been proactive in getting central funds under the pool and this is revealed from in fact that even in 2005-06, the spending was less than eight per cent of the budgets of central ministries. The existence of huge shoftfall in spending to the tune of more than Rs. 1,700 crore in five key sectors of development has only confirmed the failure of the states to rise to the occasion for reaping the benefits offered by this innovative avenue of development. Against this background, it is difficult to explain the failure of the States concerned to submit a single project under National Rural Health Mission envisaging Rs. 370 crore for the region.

It would have been appropriate for the Council to formulate a framework of developmental priorities and provide all necessary inputs to give a sense of direction to the central pool and enhance its operational dynamics. The Council cannot be oblivious of its catalytic role so as to dispel opinions about Centre's apathy and neglect towards the region. Such a role will not necessarily convert the Council to a super state in the region. At least it would be in consonance with its status as a regional planning forum.

The failure of the States of the region to utilise the allotted fund from the Council is more than apparent if one only reviews the utilization record of the concerned departments. An example from Assam goes to substantiate the point. Assam, being the largest recipient of the Council fund, is also looked upon with envy by the less fortunate ones but the peak of non-performance has been displayed by the Irrigation and Water Resources departments by not being able to spend even a penny so far against the amount released by the Council under its Tenth Plan. Taking a few other departments, against a release of Rs. 428.17 lakh, the amount remaining unspent is Rs. 59.48 lakh. As regards a small state like Mizoram, the Council Secretary two years back had to call for proper utilization of funds with a reminder that its departments had failed to spend sanctioned fund amounting to Rs. 569.54 lakh.

The crux of the matter is how to make the best use of non-lapseable Council fund. The onus is clearly on the eight State Governments and to start with, both technical and managerial competence of the development personnel has got to be upgraded in skill and orientation along with their accountability and transparency to cope with the challenges of tribal development. Otherwise they will have to rest content with improper utilisation of funds, a fact which may also give rise to intra-regional disparities. As a matter of fact, since June 2004 till date 187 projects worth Rs. 1,681.44 crore have been sanctioned by the Centre out of non-lapseable fund without however applying the yardstick of regional development which so far has remained more as a slogan than a strategy. The accumulated amount in the pool therefore remains mounting.

Fund Diversion

The bogey of resource crunch impeding development in North East and highlighted too often turns out to be a myth if one decides to take a cue from the recent statement of Union Minister Jairam Ramesh in Shillong who without minching words dumfounded all critics by stating that an amount as high as Rs. 15,000 crore every year from various governments at the Centre has not been enough to move the wheels of development in the North East. Such lamentation is candid but rare at the same time and we get its echo in Meghalaya Governor's observation that the Centre had allocated Rs. 58,000 crore for the various development projects in the region in the past decade. By all account, these are revelations brutally frank and expressive but silently supportive of the Prime Minister's repeated concern over lack of governance and development in the region.

The regretable fact is that the Council could neither create any benchmark for performance not put the process of development in the centre stage of the region. All along it was only holding the wrong end of the stick. A crisis of management is more evident in the inability of the Council to bear recurring expenses of Rs. 200 crore in maintaining institutions of regional importance set up with its initiative such as Regional Institute of Medical Sciences at Imphal, Regional Dental College in Guwahati, North East Police Academy at Barapani, B. Barooah Cancer Institute in Guwahati and Lokpriya Gopinath Bordaloi Mental Hospital in Tezpur. The recent decision to hand them over to State Governments concerned subject to their maintaining regional character is bound to stall professionalisation in such institutions. The modalities are being worked out keeping an eye on their upkeep from the non-lapseable fund which however does not permit recurring expenditure in support of established institutions. It may be remembered that an amount of Rs. 200 crore earlier given to Bodoland Territorial Council from non-lapseable fund had to be adjusted from some other source in the face of political outcry from the region.

Security Scenario

Against this background it would have been suicidal to involve the Council in the security domain of the region. This very fact had guided the Ministry of Home Affairs to which the Council was attached in its earlier incarnation to keep the provision in cold storage as the Council was ill-equipped to review measures taken by the States for internal security in the backdrop of militancy, insurgency or terrorism and hence not competent to recommend anything worthwhile. In early nineties, a sterile debate started on the linkage between security and development in the working of the Council following which the Director General of Assam Rifles was designated ex-officio security adviser of the Council, a provision which was only of cosmetic nature and not intended to make any material difference whatsoever on the ground. Even the initial enthusiasm which guided the creation of Regional Communication Centre with all the Director General of Police of the states in the region remaining in constant hotline with the ostensible aim of ensuring coordinated approach to security threats died down with the passage of time and the Ministry of Home Affairs had the better option of disbanding it.

Meanwhile, two crucial policy decisions has cast deep imprint on the security scenario in the region. The first one related to the abandonment of military solution as a policy option to the problem of insurgency and the second being an inevitable and significant follow up was directed towards bringing about political solution to long standing grievances and aspirations. In the present dispensation, no state in the region is keen to have internal security discussed in the Council meetings as it would do no better than opening up pandora's box given the complexities of the ongoing peace process. Nevertheless, intrinsic linkage between better security and faster development cannot be underestimated. It may not be out of place to reiterate that it was as much lack of security as infrastructural bottleneck which had cast negative impact on the flow of Foreign Direct Investment worth the name despite the Council's tantalizing missions projecting horticulture, trade and bamboo. Even the Centre's Look East rhetoric has failed to attract entrepreneurial activity in the region.

Since there is no alternative to development in the region, the Council cannot be allowed to become a white elephant and an unnecessary appendage to the planning process. The leadership of the Council has to extricate itself from the comfort zone so as to become instrumental in promoting a path of targeted development commensurate with availability of resources from the Centre. Apart from Arunachal Pradesh which topped the recipient status among the States of the region in support of their administrative and developmental costs, the Centre's shares for Nagaland and Manipur stood at 80 per cent, Mizoram 72 per cent, Meghalaya and Tripura 70 per cent, Assam 51 per cent and Sikkim 40 per cent. Against this background the North Eastern Council has only to deliver by addressing the challenges and opportunities facing the region in the wake of globalization.

3

Self-Help Groups, Micro Finance and Political Economy

Asok Kumar Ray

The neo-liberal economic reforms invited serious trade-off between the existing land-based livelihood system in the Afro-Asian countries through progressive de-peasantisation and labour substituting farm economy. In its extreme form this led to agri-business, corporate farming and bio-technology. This scenario systematically axed the tenancy mode of agriculture and the community mode of shifting cultivation. The neo-liberal reforms let loose a new chapter of poverty in the developing and the less developed societies. This led the political economists of neo-liberalism to contemplate on the "new poverty agenda for the 1990s by important institutional actors such as the World Bank and the UNDP".[1] There are two ways of looking at the "new poverty agenda":

One, the "strategic embedding of micro credit in the global political economy of poverty reduction serves as a safety net by containing resistance to neo-liberal economic policies. Analysts have pointed to the significant presence of micro credit and micro enterprise projects in relief packages specially the Emergency Social Fund, designed by the World Bank to contain popular agitation in the third world countries undergoing structural reforms ....Micro finance was promoted in Africa as the grassroots dimension of the human face of structural adjustment policies, which had created widespread unemployment and pushed up the cost of basic amenities."[2]

It also entails "soft pedalling of the role of the state and is marked by the conspicuous absence of the agenda of redistribution of economic resources and asset ownership. Micro credit programmes do not entail structural redistribution of non-renewable resources as land reforms programmes would and yet constitute an anti-poverty intervention of tremendous public visibility as they mobilize large number of the poor seeking access to credit, creating federation of rural and urban poor. We understand therefore the instrumental and strategic leverage that micro credit programmes offer to powerful global development actors who need to manage economic restructuring-related political and social tensions in developing economies and to respond adequately to studies that reveal increasing poverty levels."[3]

The World Bank's "framework for attacking poverty emphasized action on three inter-related fronts: empowerment (addressing inequalities that prevent the poor from influencing policies and interventions that influence their lives), security (addressing the risk and vulnerability that poor nations face in the global economy and that the poor within nations experience) and opportunity (creating condition for investment and sustainable economic expansion in which poor participate)."[4]

Extracts from the Aide Memoire of the UN Centre for Human Settlement found the cooperatives, savings and credit groups and micro credit as effective tools for poverty alleviation and economic development. Self-employment and household entrepreneurship with saving and credit mechanisms have drawn international support. The international NGOs and bilateral donors are eager to support savings and credit movements. The multilateral funding agencies are also increasingly eager to promote and fund micro credit or micro lending schemes. Access to credit is considered as an effective strategy for poverty alleviation. They argue that the poor remain enmeshed in poverty, firstly, because they are underpaid or earn an inadequate return for their time/labour if they are self-employed. Secondly, with little or no savings or assets of their own, the poor are cut off from conventional credit sources at market interest rates and are forced to borrow at higher interest rates from the landlords and informal sector/local money-lenders.

Any emergency also can plunge the poor into further debt, which further erodes their incomes.

Community based savings and credit groups emerged as an effective medium through which credit could reach the poor. Most of these community savings and credit schemes were pioneered by local and international NGOs. In the community based savings and credit schemes, the poor community members came to play the central role in accumulating the savings, setting the terms of credit and in guaranteeing that money borrowed is paid back. The solidarity that is developed through the successful functioning of the groups was expected to strengthen confidence and commitment of the individual members and to help them improve their livelihoods and lifestyles. It is also expected to feed their capacity for community development. However, in many other community savings and credit schemes the interest rates from the donor or organising institution are much higher than the market interest rates. This tendency to charge interest rates much higher than the market rates in the formal sector soon attracted the interest of international banks and finance institutions. This was reflected in the first privately organised development Summit on Micro credit held in Washington in 1997. Citicorp, Chase Manhattan and American Express, among others sponsored, it. Obviously, it drew attention of the international financial community that there are enormous profits to be won from micro lending where interest rate can range from 20 to 100 per cent. With more than a billion poor people in the world, the market for micro lending was found enormous. At the Micro credit Summit micro credit was presented as a win-win process in which investors can gain impressive profits and the poor can gain access to financial resources that enable them to help themselves.

Two, the advent of market economy directed the micro credit programme towards the business approach in which the poor could find trajectories for poverty alleviation. The Declaration and the Plan of Action of the Micro Credit Summit justified business approach to the alleviation of poverty. This metropolitan bandwagon impacted the policies of many recipient states in the world including India and accordingly micro finance as a 'strategy of poverty alleviation' was offically endorsed in the plan documents. Apart from the state, micro finance occupied the central place in the civil society, corporate and banking sectors in their poverty alleviation programmes. Taking out the millions of people from the core livelihood activities based on agriculture created serious loss of purchasing power of the poor community. This loss, as the new institutional economics of micro finance envisioned, might be augmented by increasing the same through the business model of micro finance. Therefore, the supporters of *commercially inspired* micro credit like the Consultative Group to Assist the Poorest (CGAP) of the World Bank saw micro lending as an end in itself (Italics mine). Following its all-out effort to get governments to repeal their respective anti-usary laws, CGAP has been urging countries to completely *privatize their micro lending institutions* and to remove all subsidies for banks that service the poor (Italics mine). The latter measure have been urged, the World Bank argues, because such subsidies place banks like the Grameen Bank at an unfair advantage over private banks in the market place. Many of the World Bank Group's client governments place a high priority on developing their indigenous private sector to participate in and lead future growth. A related and equally pressing issue is raising the ability of the self-employed and rural poor to sustain the economic activities essential to their survival. A diversified financial sector capable of meeting the full range of demand for financial services, including informal and small businesses, is needed to facilitate these objectives. The related current challenge in small and medium scale enterprise (SME) development is to build on the success of micro finance, establish good practices for SME finacing and the provision of non-financial services to SMEs. The World Bank found vast potential market for retail financial services among low-income clients, and a growing number of commercial banks have successfully entered this market. Compared with many existing providers of micro finance, commercial banks have potential competitive advantages in a number of areas, such as recognizable consumer brand names, existing infrastructure and systems, and access to capital. Given the differences between classic banking and micro finance, commercial banks need to view micro finance as a new business line and conduct the same kind of research that any company would be entering a new market. No bank should expect to make a "quick buck" from micro finance, but the evolving models are encouraging more banks to see the long-term business rationale.

According to ADB, given the increasing potential for the private sector to profitably and efficiently provide micro finance services, the scope for involving the private sector in micro finance development is expanding. Hence, ADB has to harness this opportunity. ADB's private sector operations pledged to make a concerted effort to enhance private sector participation in public sector projects that have potential for such participation, proactively seek equity investments to support new MFIs, transform NGOs providing micro finance services into regulated MFIs, provide technical assistance for such efforts, provide technical assistance to downscale operations of viable private commercial banks where clear commitment for such downscaling exists and consider direct support for developing micro finance industry infrastructure such as rating agencies and equity funds that support financial institutions involved in micro finance.[5] Accordingly, the Asian Development Bank has developed a development strategy for institutional micro finance covering the services provided by both formal and semi-formal sources. The strategy focuses on enabling policy environment; development of financial infrastructure; building of viable institutions and improvement of the Bank's own capacity in micro finance assistance.

There are obviously many organisations which are using savings and credit groups as vehicle not just for the provision of credit to their members but also for building members' solidarity, self-esteem, political awareness and organisational capacity to address their social, economic and environmental problems. Another feature of a savings and credit group is that it provides an organisational base in poor communities that can endure although community based organisations that were set up for implementing physical shelter or infrastructural development often fell apart once those goals were achieved. It is also claimed that groups organised around savings and credit have a continuing relevance to people's lives even when their economic situation has significantly improved.[6] This excerpt exposes the inner agenda of global capital behind self-help and credit. After globalization the SHG programme has gained tremendous popularity and policy support in the developing and underdeveloped countries of the world. In India also we have seen significant policy cooption of the SHGs in the institutional reforms process and eventually in the development process after globalisation. SHG, organized in the context of the global finance, has tremendous social, political and economic implications. In the larger background of the political economy of global micro-finance the two major propositions of the SHG, viz. building organizational solidarity and self-esteem of the community and addressing poverty through micro lending become problematic.

Under the global economy therefore the SHG needs to be viewed from the larger perspective of movement of capital. The movement of global capital took place in two directions. One is vertical movement that implied capital movement from the metropolitan countries to the colonies. It came in the shape of foreign direct investment and international aid by the global financial institutions including the World Bank. This vertical flow of capital hindered indigenous capital formation in the under-developed and developing countries and created a comparador bourgeois class that could facilitate the vertical movement of capital in such countries. The other is the horizontal movement of capital from the metropolis to the colonial population that came in the shape of micro-finance. In the first case the less developed and the developing countries became the market place of foreign capital and foreign direct capital and at the same time provided space to the investment regime. In the second case the poor and the disadvantaged rural community became the market place for micro finance. The Self-Help Groups provided the institutional space for micro finance market. To channelise global micro finance to the community, other country financial institutions like the banks were restructured with the mandate of micro finance and still other new institutions were made. The micro finance programme was also induced to different poverty eradication and self-employment programmes of the government. The micro finance programme gained a political legitimacy for a basically profit driven programme. Therefore, the politics and economics of micro finance became complementary to each other. The country's response to the global micro finance programme can be looked into from this perspective.

The Approach Paper of the 9th Plan accorded priority to agricultural and rural development with a view to generating adequate productive employment, poverty eradication, accelerating growth rate of economy, ensuring food and nutition security, providing basic minimum services of safe drinking water, primary health care facilities, universal primary education, shelter and connectivity in a time-bound manner, containing growth rate of population, ensuring environment sustainability of the development process through social mobilization and participation of the people at all levels and empowering the women and the socially disadvantaged groups like the SC/ST, OBC and minorities as the agents of change and development. The plan document, in this connection, intended to promote people's participatory bodies like the PRIs, cooperatives and the SHGs and to strengthen the efforts to build self-reliance. The plan document stated that every effort would be made to make the cooperatives work. They need to be liberated from higher bureaucratic control. SHGs, Association of Workers and Small Producers etc. are the other forms of institutions that would be encouraged. Government would seek active participation of the voluntary organizations in organizing and promoting these institutions.[7] The DWCD of the Government of India in its gender empowerment programme emphasized on organizing women in SHGs and making them agents of change. The Common Minimum Programme also expanded schemes for micro finance based on SHG. The holistic programme of micro enterprise development under SGSY emphasized on organizing the rural poor into SHGs and more into women SHGs. It is significant to note in this connection that unlike the individual beneficiary focus of its predecessor IRDP, the SGSY laid emphasis on social mobilization and group formation for financial assistance. The SIDBI, NABARD, RMK and many Zilla Parishads and not the least the NGOs emerged as important players in promotion of SHGs. Later the corporate bodies also became important players in it. The 10th Plan approach[8] added vigour to rural poverty alleviation through self-employment and wage employment programmes through SGSY that would shift to a process oriented approach in four stages including social mobilization for formation of SHGs; group saving and internal lending among the group members and the provision of revolving fund; micro finance and micro enterprise development.[9] Network of institutions that promote self-help movement would be created during the plan period and partnership would be forged between NGOs, community based organizations, government agencies and other financial institutions.[10] The 10th Plan approach also favoured promotion of a movement which enhances social capital and forges linkages with other formal and informal stakeholders.[11]

The Third Round Conference of Ministers in charge of Panchayati Raj suggested seven-point measures for empowerment of women in the panchayats. These include: women component plan; linkages with SHGs; training and capacity building; opportunity to the elected members to serve full time; Mahila Sabhas (or equivalent) to facilitate women's concern and priorities being raised in the gram sabha or ward sabha forums and separate quorum for women's participation in gram sabha and sub-gram sabha meetings.[12]

In the context of financial liberalization, micro finance is advocated as a panacea for poverty eradication and development. But as Kavaljit Singh argued, the success of micro finance depends on other development efforts undermined by the structural adjustment policy. Micro finance is no longer a localized activity. It has become global. From the World Bank to the citi-group everyone has jumped into micro finance bandwagon. For banks and financial institutions micro finance offered new avenues of profit making since interest rates and repayment rates are far above commercial lending. This economic logic made the poor more attractive to the banks and financial institutions but not *vice versa*. Even agricultural and consumer goods companies have jumped into micro finance bandwagon to penetrate the rural market.[13] He further said, the common criterion of success of micro finance programme is loan repayment rate which is higher than commercial lending. But this does not explain the qualitative impact of such programme in terms of increasing flow of income and level of employment. The more important impact indicator of micro finance is loan repayment rather than the economic empowerment of the poor. Peer pressure becomes more important for repayment rather than the collective responsibility of the group; loan repayment through loan recycling; increasing debt burden of the borrower; aggravation of social tension out of that; tapping the bigger chunk of credit by those in the SHG having better income; predominance of consumption need over-production; growing over-dependence of the micro finance institutions on donors and lesser sustainability of these institutions[14] are some of the critical problems not only of micro finance but also of the community that is conceived within the instituional form of SHG. Moreover, the cash-flow approach to poverty eradication through credit and IGP does not match with the structural inequality and mal-distribution of income. It may be noted that the micro finance is no substitute for social sector spending and anti-poverty programme. Cuts in social sector spending, soaring poverty, increase in total labour hour of women and shrinking public policy would not be compensated by micro finance.[15]

In line with the larger micro finance policy the banking sector reforms included newer institutional attempts to promote, develop and regulate micro finance sector in India. A new bill is introduced in the parliament in this respect. Apart fiom the nationalized banks private sector banks and foreign banks are also now interested in the sector of micro finance. Yes Bank approached the RBI for approval to set up a non-financial banking company to extend credit to the slum dwellers starting with those of Warli in Central Mumbai. The private sector banks like the ICICI Bank and foreign banks like Citi Bank, Standard Charterd Bank, ABN AMRO Bank also witness the emerging trends. They prefer to work in investment banking, retail and corporate banking, corporate affairs, global markets and micro finance. The ICICI has also moved to RBI seeking licence for non-banking financial company. The Grameen

Foundation US and the Grameen Bank of Bangladesh are the strategic partners for such initiative. ICICI Bank has also joined Grameen Foundation of USA and ITCOT consulting to set up Grameen Capital in India. Besides the concept of micro credit is further enlarged to include micro insurance and other financial services. In this way the micro finance institutions are now emerging on a large scale on the rural financial landscape.[16] In order to promote micro finance institutions in a big way, the RBI issued guidelines on outsourcing of financial services and non-financial services by banks to various agencies. These guidelines proposed use of two types of intermediaries, namely business facilitators and business correspondents by banks for extension of banking services towards financial inclusion. As per the guideline of the RBI of 25 January, 2006, the eligible entities and scope of activities of business facilitators and business correspondents are given. The eligible entities include intermediaries such as NGOs/ Farmer's Clubs, Cooperatives, Community Based Organisations, IT enabled rural outlets of corporate entities, Post Offices, Insurance Agents, well functioning village Panchayats, Village Knowledge Centres, Agri-Clinics, Agri-Business Centres, Krishi Vigyan Kendras and KVIC/KVIB Units. The scope of activities include: identification of borrowers and fitment of activities, collection and preliminary processing of loan applications including verification or primary information/data, creating awareness about savings and other products and education and advise on managing money and debt counselling, processing and submission of application to banks, promotion and nurturing of Self-Help Groups/Joint Liability Groups/Credit Groups/others and follow up for recovery. In the Business Correspondent model, the eligible entities include NGOs/MFIs set up under Societies/Trust Acts, societies registered under Mutually Aided Cooperative Societies Acts or Cooperative Societies Acts of States, Section 25 of the Companies Act and Post Office. The scope of activities of Business Correspondent include: disbursal of small value credit, recovery of principal/collection of interest, collection of small value deposits, sale of micro insurance/mutual fund products/pension products/other third party products and receipt and delivery of small value remittance/other payment instruments.[17]

The Micro Finance (Development and Regulation) Bill, 2007 needs a critical review in this connection. The horizontal spread of finance capital now needs promotion, development and orderly growth of the micro finance so as to offer an enabling environment to ensure that the disadvantaged sector has universal access to micro credit and micro finance organizations. Hence, the bill intends to regulate the micro finance organizations through a legalized structure of micro credit and micro finance organizations.[18] This bill intends to make the distinction between micro finance institutions as the profit oriented ones and the non-banking financial companies and companies registered as non for-profit organizations under Section 25 of the Companies Act. The NBFC and the companies registered under Section 25 of the Companies Act deal with 90 per cent of the micro finance and by virtue of this they are the major players in this. The micro finance organizations on the other hand deal with only 10 per cent of the same. The Act intends to regulate societies, cooperative societies and trusts under the state law and micro finance organizations. In this way this bill excludes NBFC and non for-profit companies and tends to promote and regulate the micro finance institutions that are small players. This is done in view of the rapid growth and fear of less than credible institutions dealing with the poor and the illiterate people. The promotion of MFI therefore trivializes the SHG model.[19]

Institutional reforms in the retail financial services now go beyond the SHG model and the government through this bill intends to comply with the ADB's mandate of promoting regulated micro finance institutions. This opportunes many NGOs providing micro finance service to transform into micro finance institutions and the private money-lenders to "register as MFOs". Giving the existing market forces' challenges the SHGs face and also given the fluid state policy to provide adequate safety net to SHG entrepreneurship, promotion of MFIs would challenge the poverty alleviation bandwagon and expose the inner contradiction of global finance between retail finance economy and redistribution. It is on record that the MFIs in Krishna district of Andhra Pradesh imposed a non-transparent, flat rate interest, instead of simple interest on the diminishing principal amount. The periodicity of repayment was weekly instead of monthly and the insurance policy of MFI was such that premiums were collected without giving any policy and they used methods of recovery that were demeaning to women, including making them stand in hot sun, locking up their homes and even advising them to commit suicide. The raids on local offices of some of the MFIs operating in the district seized signed cheques, blank signed plain sheets of paper and home site *pattas* and land deeds.[20]

In the wider context of macro economic policy, we see job-losses in formal sector, closure of public sector units, decline in state's role in social sector development, growing unemployment and jobless growth. Moreover, the serious problem is that of marketing of the SHG products and denial of the state to provide safety net to the SHG producers in the face of the big business houses and the transnational corporations. Advertising, branding, selling and marketing by the latter overpowers the micro enterprise of the SHG members. The shift of policy towards powerloom discouraging handloom on which many SHGs bank is another serious cause of concern. In such a context, self-employment jargon appears to be a distant dream that would ultimately make the poor responsible for their own fate as micro finance philosophy throws the onus of poverty to the poor. This is the greatest hypocrisy of the micro finance philosophy. As we know, in a country like India poverty issue can be addressed largely through redistribution of land and emancipatory social policies. But in the changing political economy, the corporate sector and the multinational players are grabbing land. They make conspiracy to vacate lands owned by the poor and the latter are thrown to the debt trap of micro finance from which they can hardly come out without surrendering the meagre means of livelihood that they might possess.

It is to note in this connection that the instrumentality of micro finance in addressing poverty apart, the "concerns of vulnerability and risk mitigation have themselves become central to the development discourse" and micro finance finds itself upheld as the key route by which poor households may avoid downward descent into immiserisation. Indeed the valorisation of micro finance as a household level risk management strategy has gained importance at the time that 'risk management' and 'vulnerability reduction' have emerged as the catchwords of international development community concerned over the possibility of an increase in the vulnerability of the population across the globe in response to the inception of structural adjustment programme, economic reforms, globalization process and international and regional financial crises.[21] The community thus organized in Self-Help Groups for micro finance and micro business is not essentially an inclusive group and certainly does not include the extremely poor community into its fold. Self-Help Groups, therefore, stand as exclusive interest groups that organize on the principle of thrift and credit and then on that of trust, faith, neighbourhood cooperation and neighbourhood network. As both economic and social groups, the Self-Help Groups within the micro finance mode create division within community and fracture the same as a collective mass. In order to address the serious problems of the extremely poor within the community, another concept distinct from micro finance has come up which is known as Nanofinance.[22] Nanofinance creates community within the community. On one count micro finance constructs the community and on another count breaks it and throws the community into the fold of Nanofinance.

Secondly, the Corporate Social Responsibility (CSR) initiative of the Oil India Ltd. also banks upon community to respond to the company's development initiative through involving the SHGs and also involving them in the process of social audit of the CSR initiatives.

The SHGs thus formed with the women members become artifactual communities either through state supported or through the other donor supported activities and eventually get tied with the programme mandate of the latter. Many multilateral agencies, international development NGOs and donor governments make taller claim that micro credit is a panacea. But this is not so. It can hardly be a palliative.[23] Once the SHGs are created as per the policy direction (like the SGSY), the oppressed class is divided between those who are in the SHGs and those who are outside these. The SHGs in this context are organized as *'bio-regional'* communities. In most cases the identities of the SHGs are those of 'beneficiaries' under the schemes of poverty eradication. This also fractures the oppressed class. In some other cases the SHGs work either as parallel bodies or are institutionally and functionally linked with the Panchayati Raj institutions (as the SHGs in Andhra Pradesh or Kudumbasree in Kerala). In the latter case, the SHGs loose the identity as independent and autonomous community organizations and become the policy created ones. Now that the community question is factored into the political economy of micro-finance, the strategic role of such social formations is to invest the community that can act as bridge between the global micro finance and the people and can at the same time also become significant market place for global micro finance. Both construction and deconstruction of the community have taken place under the finance capital regime. The micro finance bill deconstructs the artifactual communities at one point of time, still remains so in the horizontal flow of capital. But the corporate content of SHG is taken over by other institutions called micro finance institutions. SHG as the "romanticized other of modernity, came to supplement capital and was in turn constituted through the performativity of capital,[24] is now being destroyed and de-enacted. This lets loose the central dilemma of political economy of horizontal capital.

NOTES

1. K. Kalpana, Shifting Trajectories of Micro Finance Discourse, *EPW*, December 17, 2005.
2. *Ibid.*
3. *Ibid.*
4. *Ibid.*
5. Finance of the Poor Microfinance Development Strategy of the ADB, Micro Finance in Asia and Pacific Regions.
6. Aide Memoire, United Nations Centre for Human Settlements, Community Development Programme for Asia, Supporting effective and equitable financial services for the Urban Poor in Asia, 1-3 April, 1998, Bangkok, Thailand.
7. The Approach Paper of the 9th Five Year Plan, Vol. I, Planning Commission, Government of India.
8. Poverty Alleviation in Rural India—Strategy and Programme, 10th Five Year Plan, GoI.

9. *Ibid.*
10. *Ibid.*
11. *Ibid.*
12. Third Round Table Conference of Ministers in charge of Panchayati Raj, Ministry of Panchayati Raj, July-December, 2004. A Compendium of Resolutions of Seven Round Tables, PRIA, New Delhi.
13. Kavaljit Singh, *Questioning Globalization,* Madhyam Books, New Delhi, 2005.
14. *Ibid.*
15. *Ibid.*
16. Small Change, *Microbusiness Monthly,* Vol. 2(6) November 2006, Gurgaon. Also see *Yojana,* Planning Commission, GoI, August 2006.
17. *Ibid.* Also see *Yojana,* Planning Commission, GoI, October 2006.
18. Self-Help Doubts, *Frontline,* March 23, 2007.
19. *Ibid.*
20. *Ibid.*
21. K. Kalpana, *op. cit.*
22. In micro credit, savings and other financial services are offered to the non-tax paying poor section of the society. It restricts vulnerable non-poor to 'fall below poverty line. In Nanofinance tiny grants, credit, savings and other welfare services are offered to the BPL poorest and deprived section of the society. It can eradicate extreme poverty. Nanofinance is subsidized funding for addressing extreme poverty. Subsidized Welfare Schemes through NGOs, Social security funds, grants, interest-free loans etc. with special government investment in health, education and infrastructure development can help raise the level of the extremely poor. The Nanofinance Model, Small Change, *Micro Business Monthly,* Vol. 3, November 2005, Gurgaon.
23. Microcredit, NGOs and Poverty Alleviation, *The Hindu,* November 15, 2006.
24. Mirinda Zoseph, *The Romance of the Community,* University of Minnesota Press, London, 2002.

4

Implications of New Economic Policy for Development of North-East India

Pabitra Giri

I. Introduction

To understand the impact of New Economic Policy on the economic development of North-East India it is useful to outline the changing overall scenario prior to economic reform[1]. India followed the path of mixed economy. The state is supposed to control and direct the economy as much as possible. This has been done through regulatory policies, affecting the private sector production and investment decisions, and direct public investments in infrastructure and in production and supply of goods and services, in which the Planning Commission along with various Central Government departments played an important role. The external trade as well as internal trade in many commodities were controlled and directed by the state. In the various financial markets the state wielded its control through public sector financial institutions. This has resulted in a largely regulated and administered economy. The other characteristics of the pre-reform regime is that the economy is much less open, partly due to the emphasis on import-substituting economic policies and various incidental policies of import restrictions.

The New Economic Policy summarily speaking consists of changes in policies aimed at internal and external liberalization, providing more space for private sector, both internal and external and accordingly adjusting regulation and controls in various fields. The New Economic Policy is aimed partly to accommodate the need of global capital. Therefore alongside the gradual roll-back of the state allowing market and private sector more space to function, there is competition from the outside world and greater in-road of the globalisation process in various parts of the national economy.

In a federal structure with strong Central Government, Central Government's intervention played a crucial role in the evolution of the regional economies within India. Most of the controls and regulatory policies have originated from the Central Government. Though the state governments also imposed controls and regulations in their own jurisdiction, almost in an imitative manner, these had limited scope compared to those of the Central Government.

The Central Government's intervention in the regional economies has been through (a) industrial licensing policy; (b) Planning Commission's allocations; (c) major public sector investment decisions and (d) administered pricing (for goods and services) and credit policies. Further, the neglect of export-oriented growth to pursue the inward-looking import-substitution policy has a bearing on realizing the external trade potential of the regions. With the gradual weakening of the centrally administered system, it is natural that the development path of the regional economies would depend more and more on the regional initiatives and comparative advantage. Since comparative advantage is given in a dynamic world, the changing economic environment would usher in both opportunities and challenges before the regional economies.

Following the abolition of industrial licensing system[2] the state governments can take initiatives for the industrial-urban development using the advantages of the respective state, which is an opportunity. A state, can utilize its resource base to create comparative advantage of its own by making suitable investment.

However, this is true for every state. There will be competition among states for attracting investment from outside. Those states are likely to be more successful who have favourable initial conditions in terms of infrastructure and resource base.

In the early stage of development, for utilizing its natural resources and region specific advantages, a backward regional economy requires investment in basic infrastructure, that too from outside. But the private investment, always in search of assured and quick profit, is unlikely to come forward for such projects. In fact in underdeveloped regions the ground for private profitability is laid by state investments. In the regime of New Economic Policy that advocates for a roll back of state, the flow of central Government investment in the development-inducing infrastructure is likely to shrink in the backward area, at least relatively, unless strategic reasons dictate the contrary. Thus the New Economic Policy throws before the backward states the challenges of mustering adequate investments in basic infrastructure, which is a pre-condition for attracting private investments from outside. With macro-economic streamlining of state government budgets, it is a difficult task to successfully face the challenge.

The other opportunity opened by the New Economic Policy is the greater scope for external trade. However, it also increases the threats of foreign competition.

The above analytical discussion is more general in nature. Each region has its own specificities. Below, in Section II, we outline the regional specificities of the North-East region and the development scenario prevailing there prior to New Economic Policy. In Section III we discuss about trade possibilities in North-East under New Economic Policy and the development. Section IV examines the issues related to strengthening the supply-side of the North-East economy. Section V discusses about the role of state and institutional adjustments in the context of economic reform. Section IV summarizes the main points with a brief reference to the observed trends in the North East.

II. Pre-Reform Development Policy in the North-East

The North-East, a land-locked region,has geography mostly unfavourable. A major portion, more than two-thirds of the area consists of hilly terrain while plains are limited to Brahmaputra, Bank (in Assam) and Imphal (in Manipur) valleys and some flat lands in between the hills of Meghalaya and Tripura (Sachdeva, 2006). Majority of the rural and urban settlements are small and poorly connected (Table 4.1). As a result in large parts of North-East India market is small and fragmented. The North-East region has borders with different nations (Table 4.2). Except the case of border with Bangladesh, on the both sides of the border there are mountainous areas, with height ranging from three thousand to six thousand or more above the sea level. Thus apart from the political border, the geography also serves as a barrier to trade and exchange. Further the multiplicity of the neighbouring countries, each having different political complexity, makes the trade relations difficult.

Table 4.1: Infrastructure in Villages of North-East India in 1981

States	*No. of villages with percentage of irrigated area to cultivable area*				*Percentage of villages having approach by pucca road*	*No. (and percentage) of villages having population <200*
	≤5%		*≥50%*			
	No.	*%*	*No.*	*%*		
Arunachal Pradesh	2973	100.0	0	0	3.73	2402 (80.8)
Nagaland	960	100.0	0	0	9.17	334 (34.8)
Manipur	1667	83.6	231	11.9	13.30	976 (50.1)
Mizoram	—	—	—	—	—	—
Meghalaya	4503	100.0	—	—	7.29	3191 (69.6)
Tripura	3347	70.8	530	11.2	8.76	2993 (63.3)
Sikkim	—	—	—	—	—	—
Assam	18952	85.3	1294	5.8	19.55	56159 (25.27)

Source: Census of India (1987), Study on distribution of infrastructure facilities in different regions and levels and trends of urbanization (Occasional Paper 1 of 1986), Office of the Registrar General of India, New Delhi.

If we look back into pre-independence period, the development in the North-East was along the line of colonial interest. The construction of railway lines, the growth of plantation industry, the construction of sanatoriums and summer resorts all fell in the same line. The purpose was to exploit the natural resources and appropriate the surplus. From these activities some people obtained some benefits but overall development of the people at large was not the target. The process has been described as 'people around the development' as distinguished from the process of 'development around the people'.

Table 4.2: States and Border with Neighbouring Countries

States	*International Border with*	*Internal border with*
Arunachal Pradesh	China, Bhutan, Mayanmar	Assam, Nagaland
Sikkim	Bhutan, Nepal, China	West Bengal
Nagaland	Myanmar	Assam, Arunachal Pradesh, Manipur
Manipur	Myanmar	Assam, Nagaland, Mizoram
Mizoram	Myanmar, Bangladesh	Assam, Tripura
Meghalaya	Bangladesh	Assam
Tripura	Bangladesh	Assam, Mizoram
Assam	Bangladesh, Bhutan	All states of North-East India except Sikkim and West Bengal

In the early part of the post-independence era, till the border conflict of 1962, North-East India did not receive much attention. Though the region has long border with the neighbouring countries and network of local trade and transportation with across the border over a long period of history, most of these links were disrupted in the post-independence period for political reasons.[3] The land-locked region was thrown into isolation except the links with rest of India by rail and roadway through a land corridor of only 40 km. wide between Assam and West Bangal. It is only after the Indo-China conflict in 1962 that the North-Eastern region gained importance. The Central Government took initiative to increase accessibility of the region primarily from strategic point of view, investing in road and rail infrastructure. Though the road and rail links have improved over time yet many parts are quite inaccessible. Futher the region is politically divided into eight states, of which only seven are physically contiguous (Sikkim, the new member of North-Eastern Council, is the exception).

The growth of population, through natural growth and migration, put pressure on the local economy. Available economic opportunities proved inadequate for the population growth. Further, with the spread of education, there is rising aspiration among youth for white-colour jobs and better economic opportunities. This growing mismatch between aspirations and opportunities gave rise to the ethnic movements and conflicts, which have affected the North-East region, while terrorism that has followed the ethnic conflicts proves to be inimical to development itself.

The development policy that has been pursued in case of North-East India is aimed at an *endogenous* or *from-within* development process, but the approach followed is basically a top-down approach. The essence of this approach is to make investment in major infrastructure, large projects and upstream development activities with the assumption that development impulse so generated will spread or trickle down to the bottom. The assumption has not been fulfilled. In fact it is less likely to be fulfilled in North-East India than anywhere given the diverse ethnic composition of its population. The communities not only have different cultures and languages, but also are at different stages of evolution and change. A bottom-up approach that would have been participatory in nature and possibly ensured integration of indigenous people with the development process has never been emphasized that much. But one should recognize that top-down approach and bottom-up approach to development are not mutually exclusive rather the two are complementary in nature and need proper coordination.

This top-down approach has been linked with various problems that appeared in the context of development efforts. The most important of them are relatively poor linkage and multiplier impact. The substantial import of labour and human resource inputs in the North-Eastern India, consequent remittances from North-East India and slow expansion of the regional market (Trivedi, 1990, p. 128) are partly a result of inadequate emphasis on the bottom up approach. Another problem of such development strategy is the large-scale exclusion of the local people from the development process and their alienation from land and other natural resources. The restrictions on the land and property transactions are aimed to prevent such alienation,[4] though it has had an adverse impact on the overall development of the North-East economy.

This is the development scenario in the North-East when Government of India adopted the New Economic Policy. The three tenets of New Economic Policy, namely, privatization, liberalization and globalization—all imply that the regional development will be more open to the market forces—market forces from outside the region and market forces from across the border. The opening up of trade opportunities across the border is considered as one of the major market forces that would drive development of the region.

III. New Economic Policy, Trade and Development

In view of the 'Look East Policy' of the Government of India and her participation in various trade agreements in South-East Asia[5] following liberalization and globalization, there is high expectation that it would have a positive impact on the North-East's economy. From an analytical point of view, this expectation is based on the following agruments. First, trade extends the market and is a source of additional demand. Expanding export market increases the scope for full and better uilisation of resources, particularly in the sectors that are not facing competition from imports. Second, trade may lead to development by easing the supply-side constraints when it facilitates cost-effective imports of raw materials, fuel and investment goods.

The great expectation that trade following liberalization would accelerate the pace of development and transformation in the North-East does not take the trouble to articulate whether it relies most on demand or supply-side impact. However, the repeated reference to the traditional trade routes across the borders and historical evidence of local trade in the region suggests that the weight is on the demand or market expansion. Implicit is the belief that there is ample scope for trade between the North-Eastern India and the neighbouring countries like Bangladesh, Myanmar, Nepal, Bhutan and China. And this trade possibilities have not been realised so far because of the following reasons: (a) the geo-political hostility has snapped the rad links; (b) absence of adequate development infrastructure—transport, communication, banking, insurance and custom facilities which are required for expanding trade in modern context; (c) India's overall inward looking economic policy, along with (a) above has also contributed to the lack of initiative to improve the situation with respect to (b). In the backdrop of globalization and its pressure, as India is going for a liberalized economy it has to find new areas of trade expansion, and advocate earnestly for 'Look East Policy'. It is participating in various regional trade blocks and as a result trying to establish or strengthen trade links with the neighbours including those on the North-Eastern border.

Now we consider ifs and buts. First, India being a vast country, one should be careful to note that her 'Look East Policy' is not necessary a 'Look East through North-East' policy. With respect to small land-locked neighbours, like Bhutan and Nepal, the two may be same but for other countries, having alternative trade routes through sea (for example Myanmar and China) or border with other parts of India (for example Bangladesh) the two policies need not be the same.

Second, is there a ready market across the border? Excluding the border with Bangladesh, the immediate areas across the border are mostly mountainous regions, with low population density. Given that the surrounding countries have low per capita income, market density across the border will not be very high. Therefore, any trade across the border, except the local trade on head load, would have to cover a distance no less than that of trade with the eastern states within India, namely Bihar, West Bengal, Jharkhand, and Orissa. If the trading by land route is not easy and cost-effective, even if the volume of trade between India and the South East Asia increases that may not be routed through the North-East India.

Of course, there is the talk of Trans-Asian highway passing through the North-East India and India being connected by land route with the South-East Asian countries including those which are not neighbours right across the border, like Philippines and Singapore. Associated with this, is a romanticised view that 'look east through north-east' would eventually be a sizeable component of India's 'look east policy'. However, this would be a reality only when the constraints of difficult, disaster prone terrain and related risk and uncertainties in trade could be overcome, which would be demanding in technology and investment, and the problems of establishing and operating trade routes across the multiple political boundaries could be resolved.

Third, while accessibility is important for trade, equally important is what can be traded and what are the current and future production possibilities in the North-East India. Even if it is accepted that there would be a big increase in the trade across the North-East border, it is important to distinguish between 'cross-border trade through North-East' from 'cross border trade of North-East'. The latter refers to the export of goods and services produced in the Norh-East and imports that are used in North-East, while the former consists of exports originating from and imports destined to rest of India and routed through the North-East. It is not that growth of trade through North-East would bring no benefit to the region but that would be only marginal, and give rise to the situation described as 'porter's economy.' To expand the 'trade of North-East' significantly, there is need to improve the supply conditions of the region along with trade related infrastructures.

Fourth, opening up of trade and improved accessibility involve not only opportunities but also threat of increased access from cheaper foreign goods. The remoteness and trade restriction provide certain protection to local industries and handicraft. With the increased access from across the border, the cheap foreign goods may price out the local produce, which would adversely affect the output and employment of the North-Eastern region.[6] From the foreign statistics of India (CNO, 1999) it can be seen that she is an exporter with Myanmar, Bangladesh, Nepal, and Thailand, but net importer with respect to China, Malaysia, and Singapore. The all-India trade figures are not really indicative of the trade of North-East India, yet it may not be an incorrect apprehension that the border trade with China would involve more threats than opportunities compared to the border trade with Bangladesh and Myanmar.

The strengthening of the supply condition is important because cross-border trade is not only a source of demand but also a source of competition from neighbouring countries. One important issue therefore is how to improve the infrastructure investments required for augmenting and diversifying the supply situation of the North-East which is not just same as the infrastructure investments made for facilitating the cross-border trade and accessibility. Further, improving supply condition in the region would need investment in both physical and social infrastructure.

Below we discuss the options for strengthening supply side in North-East under economic reform, while keeping in mind that it is important in itself whether there is trade or not.

IV. Economy of the North-East: Strengthening the Supply Side

To analyse the strengthening of supply aspects, we look at different components of the North-East economy. To go by the composition of state domestic product agriculture is the second most important sector after the tertiary or service sector. Manufacturing sector comes last and even there the share of large-scale manufacturing is negligible (Table 4.3). In terms of employment shares also these sectors have similar relative ranking.

Table 4.3: Sectoral Distribution of Net State Domestic Product for North-East States (at constant 1980-81 prices)

States	*1980-81*			*1995-96**		
	Agriculture	*Manufacturing*	*Others*	*Agriculture*	*Manufacturing*	*Others*
Arunachal Pradesh	36.91	6.51	56.58	31.89	6.91	61.21
Sikkim	Na	Na	Na	Na	Na	Na
Nagaland	27.53	2.06	70.42	18.05	7.89	74.05
Manipur	45.55	4.61	49.84	30.78	5.18	64.05
Mizoram	Na	Na	Na	Na	Na	Na
Meghalaya	37.75	3.22	59.02	21.08	4.54	74.38
Tripura	45.84	4.59	49.57	31.26	6.30	62.44
Assam	44.21	6.53	49.26	35.07	5.58	59.35

* Figures for Manipur, Nagaland and Tripura relate to the year 1993-94.

Source: *Economic and Political Weekly* Research Foundation, 1997, *National Accounts Statistics of India 1950-51 to 1995-96,* Mumbai.

Agriculture

Though agriculture is the largest sector and is providing occupation of a large majority of the population in almost every state in the North-East region, it is not vibrant. Most of the villages have very negligible irrigation facilities. In 1981, the proportion of villages having no more than five per cent of cultivable area under irrigation varied from 83 per cent (Manipur) to 100 per cent in most of the states excepting Tripura (71 per cent) (Table 4.1). It is not surprising therefore that in the North-Eastern states the growth of output of food grains is unstable and has experienced deceleration since 1980s and if this trend prevails there would be growing food-shortage in the region (Khundrakpam, 2000). While attempts should be made to increase the food grain output and enhance food security, diversification of agriculture and switch over to high value crops are necessary. Cultivation of harbal and medicinal plant utilizing but without adversely affecting the rich bio-diversity of the region, may be another possible source of increasing income and employment in the region.

Therefore not only to feed the growing population but also to take development opportunities through opening up of trade, there should be investment in agriculture, not only for growth but also diversification of agriculture. The new economic policy, which asks for reduction of subsidies in agricultural imputs, like seeds, fertilizer and irrigation, is unlikely to bring out agriculture from its deceleration. Moreover, given the macro-economic constraints on the state expenditure it is unlikely that sufficient fund will be available for infrastructure related investments in agriculture.

Industry

To talk about industrialization in the North-East, we should remember constraints on large-scale manufacturing based industrialization. Large manufacturing sector means large volume of production, for which inputs have to be procured and the final products to be marketed outside the local/regional markets, and these will involve transportation and logistic costs that may adversely affect the competitiveness of the large units located in the North-East. Consequently, the share of North-East in the large-scale manufacturing sector in India is negligible (as seen from 1999-2000 data), and that too is mostly accounted by Assam, only state having sizeable plain lands[7]. Given that North-East is a land-locked region interspersed within and surrounded outside by the terrains that cause transportation difficult, uncertain[8] and costly, and the existing major centres of market concertration being far away, large-scale manufacturing sector is unlikely to be the major plank of development in the North-Eastern states, at least in major part of the regions.

As the industrial licensing policy has been withdrawn, the reform regime provides more room for state government initiative to attract industrial investments. As every state can take such initiative, the states of North-East would have to compete with other states of India. There is the Central Government incentive packages for industrial location in the hilly North-Eastern region but this does not help much because similar facilities has been extended to other hill states, namely Himachal Pradesh and Uttaranchal. Besides the reform regime is not much in favour of such incentive schemes, as they are contrary to the free free market principle[9]. In respect of industrial development the North-Eastern states are in a disadvantageous position compared to many other states of India for their three common difficulties: (a) inadequate infrastructure, (b) small and fragmented markets (because of small and poorly connected settlements and ethno-cultural differences), and (c) social unrest and terrorist activities. To compensate for these disadvantages, there might be competition among the North-Eastern states themselves to give tax concessions and incentives to large industries, which would put pressure on the already strained state budgets. This would be far from being a right strategy for industrialization in view of the inherent constraints of the Noth-East with respect to the location of large-scale manufacturing industries. The state should focus on medium and small-scale industrial activity, for which they might create comparative advantage and thereby play a positive role for strenghtening the supply conditions.

Service Sector

Moving from agriculture and industry, one may turn to the service—the third component of the North-East economy. Service sector is a relatively labour intensive sector. In service sector it is consumers who move rather than the producers. Therefore, in areas where transportation of goods in large scale is difficult one can think of developing suitable service sector—which mostly need transportation of human being and transmission of information. Because of revolution in information and communication technology though cost of information transmission has declined sharply. There is opportunity to build comparative advantage in selected service activities exploiting the natural and climatic resources of the North-Eastern states.

We briefly mention some service activities in which North-Eastern states may gain comparative advantage given suitable investments.

Health and summer resort : In may be noted that some of the urban centres in the North-East were established as sanatorium and/or summer resort of British people. Therefore taking the advantage of cold climate and scenic beauty of the region, North-East may set up health complexes and export such services.

Tourism and Eco-Tourism: Tourism and particularly eco-tourism is another such sector, which if properly developed can be a sustainable source of income generation.

Education: It is possible to develop good educational facilities that may be availed not only by students from other states of India but also from neighbouring countries. The climatic conditions may be helpful for such developments.

IT and ITES related services: Information technology and infromation technology enabled services are another area for which one can have a close look.

The above potentialities are always there. As yet apart from tourism activity[10] which involves implicit export[11], there is not much of export-oriented service sector[12] in the North East. However, in view of the emerging scenario following New Economic Policy, the state can take initiative to realize these potentialities. As service sector development is closely linked with the human resource development, it would require a coordination of bottom-up and top-down development initiatives. In developing such coordination, one needs changes in institutional arrange-ment, which is discussed below.

V. Role of State and Institutions

The New Economic Policy implies a change in the role of state. The neo-liberal economic philosophy underlying the New Economic Policy demands a rollback of the state. The state would withdraw from the market as a party to exchange process (privatization), minimize intervention in economic activities in the from of control and regulations (liberalization) but remain active as a facilitator for the development and widening of the market.

The emphasis on external trade is linked to this emphasis on the market-induced development. Such development strategy will call for promotion of markets in various factors of production, like land and property, capital and labour and for integration of fragmented local markets into a single regional market. However, the process of development of markets in various spheres and integrating indigenous people to such markets are not easy and fraught with various constraints.The market development process should be carefully sequenced and designed such that the local people get themselves fit into it. Otherwise the process may result in large-scale alienation of local people from resources, employment and livelihoods. In fact, from such an apprehension presently there are restrictions on the market for land, one of the most important resources.

As mentioned above, New Economic Policy would make it imperative for the state governments to take initiative for strenghening supply conditions. But state governments would have to face other problems also. One is the growing problem of intra-state and inter-state inequality that would come with trade and market oriented development. There are states which are geographically constrained or not yet integrated. Another is the compulsion for the North-East states to work in unison to solve their common problems and to avoid intra-region inter-state rivalry, as they have to compete with other relatively advanced states of

India. Thus there is need to develop infrastructure and institutions that would ensure both inter-state and intra-state integration in the region[13].

Governance refers to the institutional arrangement and process through which the social needs are fulfilled. New Economic Policy implies that there will be more of market forces. People and governance have to be adjusted to such a situation gradually. Social change is a slow process. Sudden introduction of market forces alienates people who are not ready for such changes in terms skill and network. Therefore, governance in North-East should be carefully designed. The existing restrictions on market forces should be relaxed gradually and preferably in limited zones. For such gradual changes in the socio-economic parameters and related bottom up development approach, it is necessary to strenghten the local government institutions in North-East India.[14]

Augmenting inter-state and intra-state transportatiom (by rail and road) and communication facilities in the North-East India (not just accessibility across the internal or external border) is a necessary step but not sufficient by itself for bringing the majority of indigenous people in the fold of development process. These are more in line with the top-down approach to development. Alongside there is need for micro-level development initiative so that the local people can integrate themselves with the development process—the bottom up approach. There is a need for synthesizing the top-down and bottom-up development initiatives. The governance system comprising of central and state governments is not enough for bringing in such synthesizing. A dynamic, forward-looking local level participatory governance system has to be developed.

VI. Conclusion

To conclude we must admit that many of the points raised above are just possibilities. Because, economic reform process is always constrained by political considerations, and there is often difference between the ideals of economic reform and what actually happens. Given the geo-political importance of North-East India, the tenets of New Economic Policy may not flower in their fullest form for the region.

There is no doubt that the role of trade and market forces will be increasingly important over time. But one should be cautious in projecting the possibilities and consequences of trade.The nature of trade in the North-East, the constraints on the expansion of trade of North-East, and how far these would trigger an inclusive development process need to be carefully examined.

The trade and external market-oriented development through the economic reform process may cause further increase in social and political tensions in the region. It is imperative therefore that the botttom-up development process be given immediate emphasis and other development measures should be coordinated with it. Trade is one route of development but not the only one. Nor should it be the dominant development scenario of North-East given its socio-ethnic realities. Therefore, the promotion of trade should not be at the cost of other development initiatives. Rather, trade should be properly integrated to the development trajectory of the North-East.

Various existing institutional arrangements that restrict market forces should not be dismantled abruptly for facilitating development of market. This would benefit mostly those who are well endowed in terms of resources and networks, but not the mass of indigenous people. What would be appropriate is a gradual and selective removal of restrictions, giving opportunities to the indigenous people to adjust with economic and social processes that would unfold under New Economic Policy and have links beyond the small villages and towns of the North-East.

The New Economic Policy has been pursued since early 1990s. Whatever be the shape of economic reform in North-East, the data for last one decade does not reflect a bright economic performance of the region. The North-Eastern economies have grown in general at a slower rate compared to the economy of India—the share of the North-Eastern economies in total all-India economy declined from 3.00 per cent in 1993-94 to 2.72 per cent in 2002-03. Except three states, namely Mizoram, Sikkim and Tripura, for all other states relative per capita income (in respect to all-India per capita income) has declined (Table 4.4).

Table 4.4: Per Capita Net State Domestic Product and Net State Domestic Product Across the States of North-East India

States	*Per capita net domestic product at current prices (Rs.)*		*Net state domestic product at current prices (in Rs. Crores)*		*Index of per capita income (India = 100)*		*Percentage share in Indian economy*	
	1993-4	*2002-3*	*1993-4*	*2002-3*	*1993-4*	*2002-3*	*1993-4*	*2002-3*
Arunachal Pradesh	8733	15589	812	1744	113.6	82.1	0.12	0.09
Nagaland	9129	18911	1251	3664	118.7	99.6	0.18	0.18
Manipur	5841	13658	1141	3238	76.0	71.9	0.17	0.16
Mizoram	8319	22207	618	2027	108.2	117.0	0.09	0.10
Meghalaya	6893	16803	1309	3976	89.6	88.5	0.19	0.20
Tripura	5634	18676	1619	6085	73.3	98.4	0.24	0.30
Assam	5715	12074	13477	32583	74.3	63.6	1.96	1.63
Sikkim	7550	20456	337	1139	98.2	107.7	0.05	0.06
NE India			20564	54456			3.00	2.72
India	7690	18988	685912	2003282	100.0	100.0	100.00	100.00

Source: Government of India, *Economic Survey 2005-2006*.

NOTES

1. In this paper the term 'economic reform' is used interchangeably with 'New Economic Policy'.
2. Licensing system of the central government designed to direct private investment to chosen sectors and location was considered appropriate for the balanced development of the national economy. In reality the system perhaps only partially modified the location decisions of private investment but failed to direct it to the backward region. Most often the licensing system had served central government's political consideration rather than the economic objective of regional equality. This centralized control of location of large-scale private industry had left little room for state (regional) government's initiative for urban-industrial development.
3. Most of the historical links with the region were through the erstwhile East Bengal (now Bangladesh), and these links were disrupted first after the partition and severed completly after Indo-Pakistan war in 1965.
4. An indirect evidence of such restrictions is proportion of urban households living in the hired occupation which is more than all-India average (34 per cent). The percentages for North-Eastern states are as follows: Arunachal Pradesh (66), Assam (42), Manipur (12), Meghalaya (60),

Mizoram (41), Nagaland (65), Tripura (28), Sikkim (78). (*Data Source*: Central Statistical Organisation,) 1999, Statistical Abstract, India, p. 515).

5. After the liberalisation of external trade, under the pressure of increased competition emanating from globalization, Government of India is looking for promotion of trading arrangements in the from of Preferential Trade Agreement (PTA) or Favoured Trade Agreement (FTA) with the countries in South and South-East Asia. This is known as 'Look East Policy' of Government of India. It is expected that such measures will increase the cross-border trade of the North-East with its neighbouring countries.
6. Improved accessibility would increase competition from the other regions of India also.
7. To go by net-value added North-Eastern states accounted for only 1.12 per cent in 1999-2000 of which 1.10 per cent is accounted by Assam alone. While in terms of employment North-Eastern India accounted for 1.55 per cent of total organized sector employment in India and Assam accounted for about 1.39 per cent.
8. The uncertainty is caused by two factors: (a) Iandslides during the rainy seasons; (b) law and order problem arising from terrorist activites.
9. Reported in *Ananda Bazaar Patrika,* 5 May 2007. (In news item related to Finance MInister of India on p.10).
10. It might be noted that tourism is not identified as an industry or separate sector in the national income accounts or in industrial classification.
11. Implicit export means goods and services are sold to the non-resident consumers. Service sector exports are often implicit exports.
12. This refers to export outside the North-East, i.e. either to rest of India or to other countries.
13. In fact those who argue for integration as the key issue for the development of North-East Region (NER) talk about four dimensions of integration and put 'integration amongst its constituent units' as the foremost agenda, while the other dimentions are, in order, integration between North-East region and the rest of India, NER and South East Asia and NER and a Greater Asia (Rajarentnam, 2006).
14. Whether the Autonomous District Councils are the right sort of arrangement should be reviewed.

REFERENCES

Barua, P.E. (ed.), (1990), *Development Planning of North-East India—Agriculture, Economic, Environmental, Financial, Industrial, Manpower and Rural,* New Delhi, Mittal Publication.

CSO, (1999), *Statistical Abstract,* India; New Delhi, Central Statistical Organisation, Government of India.

Khundrakpam, J.K., (2000), 'Foodgrain Production in North-East India 1970-71 to 1996-97', *Review of Development and Change,* July-December, pp. 185-208.

North-Eastern Council, (1990), *Plans and Programmes for Regional Development,* Shillong North-Eastern Council (Ministry of Home Affairs, Government of India).

Rajaretnam, M., (2006), 'North-East and SE Asia connecting over *chai,' The Statesman,* 27 November, 2006.

Sachdeva, Gulshan, (2006), 'India's North East Rejuvenating: A Conflict-Riven Economy', in www.stap.org affiliated to the Institute for Conflict Management.

Trivedi, P.H., (1990), Economic Environment in the North-Eastern Region, in Barua, P.C. (ed.), *Development Planning of North-East India—Agriculture, Economic, Environmental, Financial, Industrial, Manpower and Rural,* pp. 127-139.

5

Recent Developments for Boosting Development of North East India

J.B. Ganguly

Since 1996-97 consecutively three Prime Ministers—Deve Gowda (June 1996 to April 1997), A.B. Vajpayee (from 1988 to 2004) and Dr. Manmohan Singh (since 2004)—took some bold decisions on augmenting central investments in different spheres, including the region's infrastructure and bringing about structural changes in economic governance of this region. Excepting for a few, all the Central Ministries are required to expend 10 per cent of their respective budget allocations for this region. All unutilized budget provisions of the ministries go to the non-lapseable pool created for the NER. In 2001 DoNER was established for formulating and implementing and coordinating the programmes of development of this region. The NEC and the NEDFI have been brought under this Department. DoNER has since been upgraded into a separate Union Ministry. Several important projects for development of the region's infrastructure have been under execution such as construction of the East-West Corridor from Gujarat to Silchar, building of Bagibil bridge over the Brahmaputra, Subansiri and Kameng Hydro-electric projects, etc. A massive road development programme with an estimated investment of more than Rs. 12000 crore has been undertaken which is expected to encourage investment for industrialization, expansion of the trade and transport sector and increasing employment opportunities. Under the National Highway Development programme the second phase of the four-lane North-Eastern Corridor of 678 km. in length has already commenced (*The Statesman,* Kolkata, 5-10-06).

Prime Minister Dr. Manmohan Singh has been vigorously pursuing the Look East Policy for the accelerated pace of social and economic development by expanding the volume of transborder trading activities. On his first visit to this region in November 2006 the Prime Minister told the eight states that since money was no problem they should come up vigorously with development proposals.

Revitalization of the BIMSTEC (Bangladesh, India, Myanmar, Sri Lanka and Thailand Economic Cooperation) and building of the Asian Highway may be also expected to boost import and export trade of the region with the neighbouring areas entailing lower transport costs and minimum hassles.

The Central Government has decided to build up a port in Srot town in Mizoram by connecting it with Kaladani river of Myanmar. This port will be the major outlet for exporting the products of NEI and importing goods from outside. It will take about three years to complete the project at an estimated cost of 103 million dollar. The Government of Myanmar has rented out the use of the river to the Government of India. When functional this port will be India's main centre of business with South and South-East Asia. A direct link will be established between Mizoram's highway network and the port of the Kaladani.

Data about NEI's border trade with neighbouring countries are gross underestimates mainly because of inadequate infrastructure that accounts for such trade being of informal nature. According to the NE Newsletter of the Ministry of Home Affairs this region accounted for exports valued at Rs. 391.85 crore in 2004-05 as against imports from international market amounting to Rs. 30.35 crore only (*Newsletter,* Vol. 9, No. 6, June 2006).

An important recent development relates to the efforts of the region's opinion-makers to put pressure on the Central Government for liberalising the terms and conditions of providing central assistance for development projects implementable by the State Governments.

In August 2006 the forum of parliament members of this region led by P.A. Sangma and Reisang Keising met the P.M. to press for central assistance for implementing all the development schemes announced by the Prime Minister in the ratio of 90 : 10, i.e. 90 per cent grant and 10 per cent loan. They have also urged the Central Government to implement the PM's development package without delay. The P.M., according to press report, has agreed to accept these proposals and has assured them that the industrial policy for the region will be simplified and infrastructure developed for augmenting investment for industrial development. Of late the prospects of mobilizaing foreign aid for development of the individual states have brightened. According to 'back to back' policy on administering such loans the State Governments will have to repay fully the loan amount plus interest thereon. For utilizing foreign aid the NE States have been urging the Central Government to undertake this obligation by providing grant to cover 90 per cent of the repayable amount and 10 per cent as loan for the State Government to meet. In the beginning the Planning Commission did not accept this demand. Ultimately on 21 December, 2006 the cabinet decided to extend 90 per cent of external assistance to special category states including those in the North East as grants. This would further boost the development process through increased utilization of external investments.

At a meeting of Prime Minister Manmohan Singh with a delegation of the North East Students' Organization (NESO) on 18 June, 2006 Prime Minister declared the North East India as a Special Economic Zone (SEZ).

As a consequence of the increased volume of investments total output will rise as the region has idle resources. But the problem of ensuring equity in the distribution of the flow of benefits to different sections of population will remain unless the problems of unemployment, poverty, food and health insecurities are directly tackled by implementing the employment guarantee scheme, and strengthening the public distribution system and anti-poverty programmes for providing social safety net for all sections of population. Some parts of the region are quite unquiet on account of continuing insurgency, terrorism, corruption, extortions and an environment of intractable insecurity. But the development process cannot be sustained or accelerated, unless peace prevails in the region.

Social and economic progress achieved by these States can be assessed by the Human Development Index prepared by the Government. The HDI for these States are given in Table 5.1 below.

Table 5.1: Human Development Index

S.No.	*States*	*Ranked with Respect to All India 32 States/UT*
1.	Arunachal Pradesh	29
2.	Assam	26
3.	Manipur	9
4.	Meghalaya	24
5.	Mizoram	7
6.	Nagaland	11
7.	Sikkim	18
8.	Tripura	22

Source: *Yojana,* January 2007, p. 91.

Human Development Index of the North-Eastern States indicates that the ranks of some states such as Arunachal Pradesh, Assam, Meghalaya, Tripura and Sikkim are not far below the national average. Compared with other Indian states, levels of socio-economic development of North-Eastern states do not lag far behind. But there are also areas of failures, such as, universalization of elementary education in the age-group of 6 to 14 which has not yet been achieved. Food, health-care and safe drinking water securities have not been ensured for all sections of population. The goal of achieving "inclusive" and equitable growth still remains unfulfilled. The problems of poverty and unemployment causing human suffering and misery need to be addressed in right earnest.

6

New Economic Policy and Assam's Economic Performance

Khorshed Alam

The new economic policy regime in India was created by effecting a number of drastic economic reforms in mid-1991 in order to tide over the acute economic crisis faced by the country caused by deteriorating balance of payments position, rising fiscal deficits, low rate of economic growth, dismal performance of public sector enterprises. The main thrusts of the economic reforms are liberalisation, privatisation and globalization. The reform process initially touched industrial sector, financial sector, trade, foreign investment etc. The major reforms that have been brought about are decontrol, debureaucratisation, deregulation of industry and service sector, disinvestments of public sector undertakings, opening the economy for foreign investment and integration of the economy into the world economic system.

These reforms are expected to put the sagging economy in the right direction, help overcoming the crippling economic problems besetting the economy and help the country to attain a high growth rate of GDP and per capita GDP. It is gratifying to note that the economic reforms effected since 1991 have resulted in a sharp increase in economic growth rate, rate of industrial production, fall in inflation rate and fiscal deficits, remarkable rise in foreign direct and portfolio investment, disinvestments of public sector undertakings.

New Economic Policy or economic reforms were introduced in 1991 at the national level. Therefore, naturally critical study or analysis is made to measure the impact of these economic reforms on the national economy. Nevertheless, it is expected that the impact of these economic reforms would fall also on the economy of the individual states. However, the rate of economic growth and the concomitant growth in various economic sectors or aspects of the economy would naturally vary from state to state. Economic reforms, in the long run, serve as a means for harnessing the vast underutilised resources of a state for accelerating GDP growth rate. The individual performance of a state in this direction depends largely on the state's ability to provide an environment conducive to the new economic policy. Such an environment can be provided by a well developed socio-economic infrastructure including well developed transport and communication system, adequate power supply, availability of skilled manpower and above all, peaceful law and order situation. In such a state there would be no dearth of investment flow both domestic and foreign. Thus, it is the economically advanced states having a growth friendly environment buttressed by well-developed infrastructure that have benefited most by the economic reforms. On the other hand, the states where infra-structural development during the initial or pre-reform period was not favourable, have failed to take advantage of the opportunities opened up by the economic reforms for taking their economies to a higher growth path.

Now let us take the case of Assam, the most important state of the North East India for an intensive study of the impact of the new economic policy on its economy. The economic performance of the state in the perspective of the new economic policy would be judged on the basis of some important criteria of economic development, viz. annual rate of growth of State Domestic Product, Per Capita State Domestic Product, Structural Transformation of the Economy, Poverty Elimination.

First we would show in the following table the annual rates of Growth of State Domestic Product (GSDP) of Assam during two periods—pre-reform period and post-reform period. In order to highlight the growth lag of Assam, we have given the corresponding growth rates of some of the advanced states for comparison.

Table 6.1: Annual Growth Rates of GSDP of Assam and some Richer States

(in per cent)

State	*Period*	
	1980-81 to 1990-91	*1991-92 to 1997-98*
Assam	3.26	3.23
Rajasthan	6.60	6.54
Tamil Nadu	5.38	6.22
Karnataka	5.29	5.29
West Bengal	4.71	6.91
Gujarat	5.08	9.57
Maharashtra	6.02	8.01

Source: For Assam: estimated from data given in Economic Survey, Assam for relevant years, for other states: M.S. Ahluwalia (2004).

The above table clearly shows that the GSDP growth rate in Assam was very low in comparison with the advanced states during both the pre-reform and post-reform periods. It indicates that economic reforms had little impact on the economic growth of Assam. According to Economic Survey, Assam (2002-03), the annual compound growth rate of Net State Domestic Product (NSDP) of Assam at 1993-94 prices during the period from 1993-94 to 2000-01 is as low as 1.99 per cent. Again, the annual growth rate in NSDP at constant 1993-94 prices was 2.37 per cent in Assam as against 7.30 per cent in all-India in 1994-95. In 1997-98, the respective growth rates became 1.63 and 4.80. In the next year, Assam recorded a negative growth rate of –0.87 per cent as against all-India's 6.50 per cent. In the subsequent years, the performance of Assam has slightly improved. Thus in 2004-05, Assam showed a growth rate of 5.76 per cent as against India's 7.50 per cent.

Now let us give the picture of another important indicator of economic growth, that is annual rate of growth of per capita Gross State Domestic Product (GSDP) during pre- and post-reforms period in Assam and some advanced states in Table 6.2.

As is evident from Table 6.3, in case of per capita SDP also Assam's performance during both the periods was very disappointing. This is highlighted when we compare the scenario

Table 6.2: Annual Growth Rates of GSDP

(in per cent)

State	*Period*	
	1980-81 to 1990-91	*1991-92 to 1997-98*
Assam	0.98	0.74
Rajasthan	3.96	3.96
Tamil Nadu	3.87	4.95
Karnataka	3.28	3.45
West Bengal	2.39	5.04
Gujarat	3.08	7.57
Maharashtra	3.58	6.13

Source: M.S. Ahluwalia (2004), for Assam, estimated from data given in Statistical Handbook, Assam for relevant years.

with the richer states. Thus Gujarat and Maharashtra have recorded remarkable increase in the rate of growth of per capita GSDP as a result of economic reforms. The rise in the case of West Bengal is particularly noticeable. This is a clear indication of which states have benefited most by the new economic policy. Assam's performance in this respect has been very poor. Thus economic reforms have failed to make a dent in Assam's economy. This finding would be further strengthened when we compare the progress of per capita income of Assam with that of all-India over the post-reform years. The following table provides the necessary data.

Table 6.3: Rise in Per Capita Income (at constant 1993-94 prices): Assam and All India

Year	*Assam (Rs.)*	*All-India (Rs.)*
1993-94	5715	7698
1995-96	5760	8499
1997-98	5796	9288
1999-2000	5785	10067
2000-01	5867	10254

Source: Economic Survey, Assam, 2005-06.

Table 6.3 clearly shows that while per capita in all-India has registered a steady rise over the post-reform years, the amount of per capita of Assam has remained more or less stationary. Moreover, the gap in the per capita income between Assam and India has progressively widened. Thus while Assam was behind all-India in per capita income by Rs. 1983 in 1993-94, the gap increased to Rs. 4387 in 2000-01. This also indicates that the new economic policy has had little impact on Assam's economy.

Structural Transformation of the Economy

Structural transformation of the economy is concomitant with the process of economic growth. Growth-driven structural transformation occurs in mainly two aspects of the economy—change in the sectoral contribution of the economy of GDP and change in the sectoral share of the labour force. Now let us make an assessment of the structural transformation of Assam's economy in the era of new economic policy. The following table shows the first aspect of the sectoral structure of GDP of Assam and all-India over the years.

Table 6.4: Percentage of GDP by Industry of Origin

Year	*Primary Sector*		*Secondary Sector*		*Tertiary Sector*	
	India	*Assam*	*India*	*Assam*	*India*	*Assam*
1980-81	39.6	53.8	24.4	11.8	36.0	34.4
1991-92	32.0	48.0	27.3	13.4	40.7	38.6
1995-96	28.8	45.0	29.2	12.0	42.0	43.0
2000-01	27.0	42.8	24.1	9.9	48.9	47.3

Source: Government of India, Economic Survey, 2005-06; Government of Assam, Economc Survey, Assam, 2005-06.

We know that when economic development takes place, there is significant fall in the relative contribution of primary sector to the generation of GDP followed by sharp rise in the relative contribution of secondary and tertiary sector. The above table shows that the decline in the proportion of contribution of primary sector to GDP in Assam was not at all significant. Even ten years after in 1991, this proportion has remained above 40, as against 27 for all-India, which should have been below 10, as we find in the case of the developed countries of the West. On the other hand, the relative contribution of secondary sector, instead of increasing, fell from 11.8 per cent in 1980-81 to 9.9 per cent in 2001-02, as against 24.4 per cent and 24.1 per cent in the case of all-India. The tertiary sector only showed a significant rise in the proportion of contribution to GDP from 34.4 in 1980-81 to 47.3 in 2001-02. But the importance of secondary sector should have preceded that of tertiary sector in the process of economic development of the state. But this did not happen showing the limited impact of economic reforms on the economy of Assam.

Next we would assess the sectoral share in employment of labour force over the years. The table below will give the necessary information for Assam and all-India.

Table 6.5: Sectoral Share in Employment of Labour Force in Assam and All-India

Year	*Primary*		*Secondary*		*Tertiary*	
	India	*Assam*	*India*	*Assam*	*India*	*Assam*
1981	68.8	69.2	13.5	4.8	17.7	26.0
1991	66.8	64.1	12.7	5.5	20.5	30.4
2001	59.9	59.1	17.2	6.0	22.9	34.9

Source: Census Reports of 1981, 1991 and 2001.

We know that in the course of economic development the proportion of labour force engaged in primary sector falls sharply, while that in secondary and tertiary sector rises. But as is evident in the table above, over the long twenty-year period 1981-91-2001, there is only 10 pecentage point decline in the share of primary sector in both all-India and Assam, the percentage increase in secondary sector in Assam is almost insignificant. In the case of tertiary sector, there is 9 and 5 percentage point decline in the share of labour force in Assam and all-India respectively. The relative share of the sectors in labour force engaged over the twenty year period remained almost the same for both India and Assam—

primary sector coming first followed by tertiary and secondary sectors. In the case of Assam, the proportion of secondary sector is not only very low but also comparatively much smaller than that of all-India. Thus based on this criterion Assam and also India, as a whole still remain agricultural economies.

According to the development theory, in the process of economic development of any country, there is a proportionate decline in the importance of primary sector and increase in the importance of secondary and tertiary sectors. As is evident in the given tables, although with the rise in the growth rate of GDP over the years, there is a change in the sectoral contribution to the GDP, but the proportion of contribution of primary sector did not come down significantly low as is required to attain economic growth. The above tables show that although agriculture's contribution has registered a decline, it still engages large proportion of labour force, thereby weakening and impoverishing the primary sector. Again, it can be observed that the structural change in employment has lagged behind the structural change in income generation. Thus there is a phenomenon of structural lag in the process of economic growth in Assam and also all-India.

From an analysis of the Tables 6.4 and 6.5, showing the two aspects of structural change, we can conclude that there is no basic change in the economic structure of Assam in the perspective of new economic policy. Thus the new economic policy could not give any momentum to the development process in Assam and failed to take the state to a higher growth trajectory.

Problem of Poverty and Its Elimination

Economic growth and social justice are two inseparable objectives of our economic efforts. Therefore, apart from growth acceleration poverty elimination is another important criterion to be studied to judge the positive impact of the new economic policy on an economy. Higher growth rate of the economy does not mean economic development in the real sense of the term. Because in a poverty stricken economy, higher economic growth is not meaningful, when a large section of the people suffer from acute poverty which manifests in poor quality of life, deprivation from basic amenities of life, malnutrition, illiteracy and low human resource development. Thus economic reforms aim not only at a higher rate of economic growth but also at tackling the problem of poverty and unemployment. The table below gives the changes in the poverty ratio over the years in all-India, Assam and some of the advanced states of the country.

Table 6.6: Poverty Ratio at the State Level

States	*1973-74*	*1993-94*	*1999-2000*
Assam	51.21	40.86	36.09
Gujarat	48.15	24.21	14.07
Karnataka	54.47	33.16	20.04
Maharashtra	53.24	36.86	25.02
Punjab	28.15	11.77	6.16
Tamil Nadu	54.94	35.03	21.12
West Bengal	63.43	35.66	27.02
All-India	54.88	35.97	26.10

Source: M.S. Ahluwalia (2004).

As is evident from Table 6.6, in contrast to all-India and the richer states, Assam's record in poverty alleviation is quite dismal. Thus during about 25 year period from 1973-74 to 1999-2000, the reduction of poverty ratio in Assam is by 15 percentage points only, while in all-India and the richer states shown in the table, the rate of poverty reduction is much higher. It would be disconcerting to estimate that at this rate poverty can be totally eliminated in Assam not before 50 years time, unless appropriate measures are taken towards this end with honesty and sincerity. In some of the richer states particularly Gujarat and Punjab, poverty ratio declined significantly. This relative success in this respect is due not only to higher growth, but also effective implementation of various poverty alleviation and employment generation programmes and also PDS programmes, successful land reforms measures, empowerment of Panchayats and also human resource development.

Now a study of Poverty Prevalence Ratio by Rural-Urban Locations gives some interesting results. We would use the following table for this purpose.

Table 6.7: Percentage of Population below Poverty Line

(in per cent)

State	*Rural*		*Urban*	
	1993-94	*1999-2000*	*1993-94*	*1999-2000*
Assam	58.25	61.78	10.13	12.45
Gujarat	28.62	26.22	28.86	21.70
Karnataka	37.73	38.50	32.41	24.55
Maharashtra	50.21	50.00	33.52	32.16
Tamil Nadu	37.27	39.27	37.83	29.82
West Bengal	54.15	56.16	20.97	16.74
All-India	39.36	36.35	30.37	28.76

Source: M.S. Ahluwalia (2004).

The above table gives some interesting results. Compared with all-India and the selected states, rural poverty ratio is much higher in Assam, and instead of a fall, it has increased by 2.53 percentage points over the years. However, in contrast, the urban poverty ratio in Assam in significantly low compared with its rural counterpart, in spite of a small increase of 2.32 points during the period under survey. Moreover, in all-India and the richer states, the urban poverty ratio is much higher in both the years than that in Assam. This may be due to the small ratio of urban population in Assam, only 13 per cent as against 28 per cent in all-India according to 2001 Census, lesser exodus of rural population to urban areas and job opportunities for available workforce.

From the analysis of economic performance in terms of various criteria of economic development so far made, it is found that Assam's pace of economic growth in the new economic policy regime has been indeed very dismal. Thus it is obvious that Assam has failed to take full advantage of the economic reforms for revitalising its sagging economy. In contrast, the states like Karnataka, Maharashtra, Gujarat, Tamil Nadu, West Bengal,

Punjab and a few other states could utilise the opportunities thrown up by the economic reforms and have been able to lift their economies to a higher growth path. This difference in economic performance has widened the inter-state economic inequality during the first two decades of economic reforms.

Now taking the case of Assam, it would be a worthwhile exercise to make an in-depth study of why new economic policy has failed to make a dent in Assam's economy. In other words, we have to find out the constraints and impediments in the state's growth path, the aspects where the Government of the state has failed to take appropriate action in the light of the new economic policy, the extent of the role of the Central Government in accelerating the rate of economic growth of Assam and the appropriate measures to be taken to speed up the development process in the state. We would restrict our study to mainly industrial sector, as the major thrust of the first phase of the economic reforms was on this sector at the national and also state level.

Industrial sector in Assam has all the potentialities to play the role of catalyst in the economic development of the state. Assam had a great legacy of modern industrial development and globalization, albeit in limited directions creating an enclave economy. As more than 150 years prior to Independence, European tea planters established tea gardens in Assam beginning from 1835 and tea was exported to England and other countries. At present there are about 900 tea gardens in Assam producing 50 per cent of tea produced in India. Along with tea, oil refinery, incidentally the first one in India, was established in Digboi in 1901. Coal mines were developed in Ledo-Margherita area. Simultaneously river, road and rail communication was developed mainly to serve the purpose of the nascent tea industry. But this small industrial sector maintained a exclusive character and therefore, the overall economy of Assam remained more or less a traditional one.

During the post-independence plan period, a number of major industries based on the rich mineral and forest resources of the state were set up under the central public sector, viz., Oil India Ltd., ONGC, Guwahati and Bongaigaon Refineries and more recently Numaligarh Refinery, Fertiliser Industry (Namrup),

Cement factory at Bokajan, Paper Mills at Jagiroad and Badarpur etc.

The Partition of the country in 1947 hit hard the prospect of industrial development of Assam and the entire North-Eastern region was turned into a land-locked region with access to the mainland through a narrow corridor of 22 kms. or so via Siliguri in North Bengal. It created serious transport bottleneck for Assam. Another serious impediment of industrial development in Assam is lack of infrastructural facilities like transport and communication system, power supply, banking system etc. It is the responsibility of the State Government to develop roads, power, education and health facilities. But funds for development programmes are inadequate for a financially poor state like Assam. The state's limited financial resources are mostly exhausted for non-plan administrative expenditure leaving only a little for development projects. There is growing imbalance between government revenue and expenditure resulting in fiscal deficits. Incidentally, reduction of fiscal deficits is one of the major objectives of economic reforms. But Assam Government's record in this respect is very poor. Thus the budget deficit of Assam Government which was Rs. 10.28 crores in 1990-91, increased to Rs. 369.68 crores in 2000-01, Rs. 2465.53 crores in 2004-05 and Rs. 1448.74 crores in 2005-06. Moreover, the debt outstanding against the Government of Assam has also been increasing alarmingly. Thus debt outstanding as per cent of GSDP was 31.98 in 2000-01, 35.53 in 2003-04 and 40.21 in 2005-06 (Economic Survey, Assam, 2005-06). The main reasons for this worsening financial crisis are burgeoning administrative expenditure, security related expenditure, leakage in revenue collection due to tax evasion and rampant corruption etc. Another important cause of financial burden of the State Government is the losses incurred by many of the state public sector undertakings. There are 48 state public sector undertakings in Assam. Out of these, only 5 are earning profits, 7 are incurring losses, but improving recently and the majority are irretrievably in pathetic condition. In the true spirit of the new economic policy, these should have been closed or privatised. This measure would have relieved the state from huge financial burden.

Another serious impediment to the development process in Assam is law and order problem of the state, which has stood in the way of the flow of investment both domestic and foreign into the state. Law and order situation has begun to aggravate from 1980s with the movement spearheaded by the students against the foreigners. Later on due to the emergence of several extremist outfits in the state, fear of security has gripped the mind of everybody. There is rampant extortion, abduction and killings for money. The problem has been more compounded by frequent bandhs and strikes called by various organisations. This is one single reason why industrial investment has been insignificant in Assam for the last more than two decades.

Role of Central Government in Accelerating Economic Development in Assam

A common allegation made by the people of Assam, rather the entire North-Eastern region is that the Central Government has not paid adequate attention for speeding up the development of their region. Although the allegation is not completely baseless, the Central Government took various measures from time to time for accelerating the growth process of the NE region. And a part of this region, Assam has been a beneficiary of these measures. For example:

Special Category Status to Assam

Assam is no doubt one of the major states of India, yet to ease the financial problem of the state, Assam was given special category status along with financially poor hill states of NE India during the rule of the V.P. Singh Government. Because of this status, Assam now enjoys a favourable grant-loan composition of the central assistance for state plan as 90 : 10; for other states, this composition is 70 : 30. Moreover, the special category states are allowed to divert 20 per cent of their plan allocation to meet non-plan expenditure to ease the problem of finance caused by rising interest burden, burden of subsidy payment and rising administrative costs. Another sop given recently to the fund starved states of the NE relates to the funding pattern of the central schemes for rural development. So long these schemes were funded according to 75:25 ratio. Now the Central Government has taken the decision that from the next plan period, for the centrally sponsored rural development schemes, the pattern of funding would change from 75:25 to 90:10 for the North-Eastern states including Assam. This would give great financial relief to these states.

NE Industrial Policy of Government of India

In pursuance with the policy of helping NE region in their endeavour to develop industrial sector, Government of India formulated a broad-based Industrial Policy for the NE region for ten years from 1st April, 1997 to 31st March, 2007. Through this Industrial Policy, Government of India provided a package of incentives to investors for setting up industries in these states. But this policy did not bring about the desired industrialisation of the state of Assam as expected. Because the same package of incentives had been given to several other states like Jammu and Kashmir, Haryana and Uttaranchal and also for other reasons like better law and order situation, better infrastructural facilities like power and transport system and nearness to mainstream market, domestic investors have shown their preference for these states for investment. As a result, the investment made due to the NE Investment Policy of 1997 in the entire NE region amounted to only Rs. 1067 crores as against more than Rs. 20000 crores in Haryana alone. This is true in the case of foreign investment also. As a result of the Centre's NE Industrial Policy, only a few medium enterprises were established by taking advantage of the package provided in the 1997 Policy. Unfortunately, not a single large scale industry came up in the region, rather during the period from 2001 to 2005, as many as 19,940 small industries were closed down due to various reasons including lack of Governmental help. The exception is the coming up of the much-awaited Gas-Cracker Project in Assam. It is to be noted that the Assam Accord of 1985 included a clause for establishing a Gas-Cracker Project to utilise the huge amount of gas coming out with the crude oil from the ONGC wells being burned for absence of any gas cracker unit to utilise it. For the last 20 years no serious efforts were made by the Central Government to realise the dream of the people of Assam for a Gas-Cracker Project, which has tremendous potentialities of generating employment, both direct and indirect. Fortunately, after long years of efforts, Rs. 5,460 crore Assam Gas Cracker Project is coming up in Assam. It would be a Joint Venture Company with equity participation of Gas Authority of India Ltd. (70%), Oil India Ltd. (OIL), Numaligarh Refinery Ltd. (NRL) and Assam Industrial Development Corporation (AIDC) each having 10 per cent of equity share. The proposed Integrated Petro-Chemical Complex at Lepetkata in Upper Assam will be completed within 5 years period. The Complex will have the capacity to produce 2.20 lakh tons per annum of ethylene and 60,000 tons per annum of propylene with natural gas and naphtha as feed stock. A host of downstream industries based on the products of the Gas-Cracker Project are expected to come up in the state. It has been estimated that 500 plastic processing industries are likely to set up in the State. It has the potentiality to generate as many as 1 lakh indirect jobs apart from 600 direct employment in the Project. Considering the immense employment potentialities of this Gas-Cracker Project, the Central Institute of Plastic Engineering and Technology (CIPET), an Institution under the Union Ministry of Chemicals and Fertilisers has established a campus near Guwahati to give long-term and short-term training in plastic engineering so that trained manpower is made available to man the downstream industries of the Gas-Cracker Project.

The Role of DoNER

Another important step taken by the Central Government to facilitate the economic development of Assam or the entire NE India was the creation of the Department of Development of NE Region (DoNER) in 2001. To enable it to play a more effective role, it was given the status of a ministry. But in actual practice it had to work under certain handicaps, as a result of which it did not prove to be of much help in accelerating development process in the North-Eastern states. Because of the absence of technical cell in the ministry, clearance of development projects for the region and the consequent fund allotment took inordinately long time. As a result, the NE states have failed to get the finance from the Non-Lapseable Central Pool of Resources. It may be mentioned that 10 per cent of the budgeted fund in the various ministries is earmarked for the NE states and this amount does not lapse with end of the financial year.

Economic Development of Assam—A New Strategy

From the analysis made so far, it has been found that during the last more than one and a half deade of efforts after the launch of new economic policy, Assam could not succeed in speeding up the development process in the state. The major reasons have also been explained in some details. It is obvious that the existing strategy of development has failed to take the state's economy to a higher growth path. It seems that the strategy of development has to be reoriented, particularly by taking into consideration the historical developments that took place after the Partition. The Partition of the country in 1947 geographically isolated the entire North-Eastern region from the mainland of India. The region since then is connected with the mainland only by a narrow strip of land called the North Bengal corridor. It is surrounded on all its sides by foreign countries. The total length of the border between the North-East and the neighbouring countries, viz., China, Myanmar, Bangladesh and Bhutan is 4600 kms. which forms about 98 per cent of its border with these countries. This geographical isolation has grievously affected the economy of the region in various dimensions. In particular, it has lost the mainland market for its products. Moreover, as the region depends on the mainstream Indian economy for its requirement of many of the consumer and capital goods, people of the region have to pay higher prices for these products because of higher transport costs and uncertain supply.

However, we can follow a new development strategy, by which this geographical handicap can be converted into an economic opportunity by opening the borders for trans-border trade with the neighbouring countries. There is a strong basis of trade with these countries because of the existence of complementarities in respect of production between the North-Eastern region and its neighbouring countries. There is also a vast scope for expanding border trade with these countries. In 1994, only 2.87 per cent of India's total exports went to these countries.

'Look East Policy' of the Government of India

In order to pave the way for cross border trade between NE states and the South East Asian countries, Government of India announced the 'Look East Policy' in the early 1990s. This policy is expected to lead to a steady expansion of India's trade and investment links with the East and the SE Asian countries like Myanmar, Thailand, Malaysia, Indonesia, and Singapore etc. NE region is expected to be the most important beneficiary of the LE Policy because of the geographical contiguity of the NE region with the SE Asian countries. NE region would be the India's gateway to this vast ASEAN region and a free trade relation is expected to be established between India and the ASEAN countries. It is significant that the third India-ASEAN Summit held on November 30, 2004 formulated a long-term plan for expanding trade, investment, tourism, culture and sports. This possibility has raised the prospect of economic development of Assam, nay the entire NE region.

Another important development in pursuance of the Look East Policy is the creation of Bay of Bengal Initiative for Multi-Sectoral and Technical Co-operation (BIMSTEC) in June 1997 consisting of the littoral countries of Bay of Bengal like Bangladesh, India, Myanmar, Sri Lanka and Thailand. BIMSTEC is working for Free Trade which therefore has the potential to be the centre of future trade activities. For this purpose, connectivity of the NE region with the ASEAN countries will have to be developed mainly through road and railways.

Cross border trade will play the role of a catalyst in speeding up the development process in Assam. It will provide vast market for the products of existing industries and also for the prospective industries of Assam. Moreover, it will also rejuvenate the traditional village, cottage and small industries.

REFERENCES

Assam Beyond 2000, Asom Prakalpa, *The Assam Tribune.*

B. Datta Ray (ed.), *Agenda for North East India,* New Delhi, 2002.

Census Reports, 1981, 1991 and 2001.

Draft Economic Agenda of Assam Pradesh Congress Committee, 2001.

Government of India, Economic Surveys for relevant years.

Government of Assam, Economic Surveys of relevant years.

M.S. Ahluwalia, *Economic Performance of the States in the Post-reforms Period, in Indian Economy since Independence,* New Delhi, 2005.

P. Bordoloi, North East: Revive Old Routes, *The Telegraph,* 15th February, 2002.

P.M. Passah (ed.), *In Defence of Regional Economic Development in India: A Case for the North East,* New Delhi, 2006.

Rao, Barua and Das, India's Border Trade with Select Neighbouring Countries, New Delhi, 1996.

Statistical Handbooks (Assam) for relevant years.

The Indian Economic Association, 80th Conference Volume, Hyderabad, 1997.

The Indian Economic Association, 83rd Conference Volume, Jammu, 2000.

The Indian Economic Journal, Indian Economic Association, Vol. 54, No. 1, April-June, 2006.

Transforming the North East, Sukla Commission Report, 1997.

Uma Kapila (ed.), *India's Economic Reforms,* New Delhi, 1996.

7

Market-oriented Reforms in the Health Care Delivery System and the North East

Malabika Das Gupta

Introduction

Improving the availability of health care facilities of a region is extremely important for enhancing the quality of life of its population. Improved health care facilities can better the health status of its population, reduce its overall mortality rate and arrest the spread of communicable diseases like tuberculosis, malaria, HIV-AIDS and so on. Improved health care facilities can curb poverty in a region by reducing the likelihood of prolonged illness or premature death of household members that have a devastating and permanent impact on household incomes. Improvements in health care facilities in a region can also contribute to the quality of education by improving attendance of students and lead to improvements in the productivity and income-earning capacity of future generations.

The availability of health care facilities in a region depends on the health care delivery system, which in turn depends on the health care personnel and the health care institutions and infrastructure that are available in the region.

Health Care Delivery System in the North East

As shown in Table 7.1, the health care delivery system in the North East is more or less dominated by the public sector. The number of allopathic hospitals run by the State governments and the local bodies exceeds the number of allopathic hospital run by the private sector and voluntary organisations in all the states of the region barring Manipur and Sikkim. According to Table 7.1, Manipur and Sikkim had the same number of allopathic hospitals run by the State governments and local bodies on the one hand and the private sector and voluntary organisations on the other. Among the eight states in the region, the number of hospital beds in private hospitals and in voluntary organisations exceeded the number of hospital beds in the government sector and in local bodies only in Sikkim according to Table 7.1.

Table 7.1: Number of Allopathic Hospitals and Beds According to Ownership

State	*Reference period*	*Government*		*Local bodies*		*Private and Vol. Orgs.*		*Total*	
		Hos-pitals	*Beds*	*Hos-pitals*	*Beds*	*Hos-pitals*	*Beds*	*Hos-pitals*	*Beds*
Arunachal	1.1.2002	14	1236	0	0	1	182	15	1425
Assam	1.1.1999	141	9687	47	982	80	1992	268	1266
Manipur	1.1.2001	4	753	1	881	4	100	19	1734
Meghalaya	31.3.2000	7	1243	0	0	0	0	7	1243
Mizoram	31.3.2001	7	688	0	0	4	344	11	1032
Nagaland	31.3.2000	17	964	0	0	0	0	17	964
Sikkim	1.1.2002	1	300	0	0	1	400	2	700
Tripura	1.1.2001	17	1697	0	0	10	76	27	1773

Note: Hospitals exclude Community Health Centres.
Source: Health Information of India 2002, Director General of Health Services, Ministry of Health and Family Welfare, Government of India.

The states of the North East have a poorly developed health care delivery system both in terms of health care personnel and health care institutions and infrastructure especially in rural and tribal areas. Table 7.2 shows the population served per doctor, per hospital bed, per hospital and per bed in all allopathic establishments[1] in the different states of the North East and compares the last three sets of figures with the corresponding all-India averages. The table shows that the population served per doctor is quite high in all the states of the North East. It also shows that compared to the all-India average, the population served per hospital bed is higher in four out of the eight states of the North East, namely Tripura, Nagaland, Megalaya and Assam. According to the figure given in Table 7.2, in all the eight states of the North East, the population served per hospital is higher than the all-India average and the population served per bed in all allopathic establishments is higher than the all-india average in Tripura and Assam.

Table 7.2: Population Served Per Doctor, Per Hospital Bed and Per Hospital in the North East

State	*Population served per doctor*	*Period to which data relate*	*Population served per hospital bed*	*Population served per hospital*	*as on*	*Pop. served per bed in all allo. estabs. on 1.1.02**
1	2	3	4	5	6	7
Arunachal	3755	31.12.1999	880	83600	1.1.2002	475
Assam	11980	1.1.1999	1782	84183	1.1.1991	1410
Manipur	2820	31.12.1991	1378	125737	1.1.2001	931
Meghalaya	5581	31.12.1990	1958	347714	31.3.2000	738
Mizoram	10360	1.1.1999	863	81000	31.3.2001	465
Nagaland	6292	31.12.1991	1747	99059	31.3.2000	848
Sikkim			834	292000	1.1.2002	449
Tripura	4693	1.1.1999	1800	118185	1.1.2001	1420
All India			1503	66758	1.1.2002	1124

Note: Hospital exclude community health centres and refer to allopathic hospitals only.

* Includes all allopathic establishments—hospitals, dispensaries, CHCs, PHCs, Sub Centres, sanatoria and TB clinics and other health establishments.

Source: Col. 2, Health Information of India 1999, Director General of Health Services, Ministry of Health and Family Welfare, Government of India, Col. 4, 5, 6, 7—Health Information of India 2002, Director General of Health Services, Ministry of Health and Family Welfare, Government of India.

Table 7.3 shows that most of the people of the states of the North East live in rural areas. It also shows that even if the poverty ratio of Assam is assumed to prevail in all the states of the North

Table 7.3: Data on the Rural Population of India and the North East

States/India	*Arunachal*	*Assam*	*Manipur*	*Meghalaya*	*Mizoram*	*Nagaland*	*Sikkim*	*Tripura*	*All India*
Percentage of people living in rural areas in 2001	79.59	87.28	76.12	80.37	50.5	82.26	88.9	82.95	72.2
Percentage of rural population below poverty line in 1999-2000	40.04	40.04	40.04	40.04	40.04	40.04	40.04	40.04	27.09
Estimated CDR per 1000 population per annum in rural areas, 2001	6.00	9.90	4.80	9.90	5.20	N.A.	5.20	5.60	9.10
CDR per 1000 population per annum in urban areas in 2001	2.3	6.6	6.1	3.9	3.4	2.6	5.2	5.2	6.3

Note: Poverty ratio of Assam is used for all North Eastern states.

Source: Percentage of people living in rural areas in 2001—Census of India, 2001.

Percentage of population below poverty line in 1999-2000—Government of India, Planning Commision.

Estimated CDR per 1000 population per annum—Health Information of India 2002.

East, the proporation of population living below the poverty line in the rural areas of the states of the North East is higher than the all-India figure. Table 7.3 also shows that the health status of the rural population of the North Eastern states seems to be worse than that of the urban population of these states as the CDR per 1000 population is higher in the rural than in the in the urban areas of the eight states of the North East.

Yet, from Table 7.4 it is evident that there is an urban bias in the number of hospital beds and number of hospitals in the region. The table shows that the number of urban allopathic hospitals is higher than the number of rural allopathic hospitals in all the states of the region with the exception of Assam, Nagaland and Manipur and the number of allopathic hospital beds is higher in the urban areas as compared to the rural areas in all states of the North East. As shown in Tables 7.5 and 7.6, both the health care personnel and health care infrastructure in the rural areas of the North Eastern states display shortfalls when the latter is defined as the difference between the requirement according to certain norms and the number that are actually in position. As shown in Table 7.7, the number of PHCs in the rural areas of the states of the North East with a single doctor, no doctors, no laboratory technicians and no pharmacists is also quite singnificant. As shown in Table 7.8, the shortfall in the number of Sub-Centres, PHCs is also quite significant in the tribal areas of the states of the North East.

Table 7.4: Number of Allopathic Hospitals and Beds in the North East

State	*Reference*	*Rural*		*Urban*	
	Period	*Hospitals*	*Beds*	*Hospitals*	*Beds*
Arunachal	31.3.2002	0	0	15	1425
Assam	1.1.1991	151	3949	117	8712
Manipur	1.1.2001	14	695	5	1039
Meghalaya	31.3.2000	0	0	7	1243
Mizoram	31.3.2001	1	50	10	982
Nagaland	31.3.2000	9	146	8	818
Sikkim	1.1.2002	0	0	2	700
Tripura	1.1.2001	5	165	22	1608

Source: Health Information of India, 2002.

Table 7.5: Health Manpower in Rural Areas in the North East as on 31.3.2001

State	*Doctors at PHCs*		*Multipurpose workers (female)*		*Nurse midwife*	
	*Required**	*Shortfall*	*Required***	*Shortfall*	*Required****	*Shortfall*
Arunachal	65		338	37	205	134
Assam	610	0	5719	0	1310	886
Manipur	69		489	76	181	98
Meghalaya	85		498		176	64
Mizoram	58	9	404	19	121	13
Nagaland	46	17	348	186	109	89
Sikkim	24		171		38	38
Tripura	58		597		135	10

Note: * at the rate of 1 per PHC, ** at the rate of 1 each per subcentre and PHC, *** at the rate of 1 each per PHC and 7 each per CHC.
Shortfall means required minus in position

Source: Health Information of India, 2002.

Table 7.6: Shortfall in Health Infrastructure as per 2001 Population

State	*Sub Centres*		*PHCs*		*CHCs*	
	required	*shortfall*	*required*	*shortfall*	*required*	*shortfall*
Arunachal	253		43		10	
Assam	5082		849	237	2111	111
Manipur	470	50	78	9	19	3
Meghalaya	595	182	99	14	24	11
Mizoram	148	8	24		6	
Nagaland	531	229	88	42	23	14
Tripura	656	117	109	51	27	16

Source: Basic Statistics of North Eastern Region, 2002.

So, the availble statistics show that the health care delivery system is deficient in the region in general and in tribal areas of the region in particular. The need of the hour is to improve the health care delivery system in the region in general and in its rural and tribal areas in particular.

Table 7.7: Health Care Personnel in Position in PHCs

State	*PHCs functioning*	*No. of PHCs Functioning with*			
		one doctor	*no doctor*	*no lab tech*	*no pharmacist*
Arunachal	65	34	0	36	2
Assam	610	190	0	185	130
Manipur	69	42	4	42	9
Meghalaya	85	76	0	6	36
Mizoram	58	39	9	52	38
Nagaland	46	29	0	5	1
Tripura	58	16	0	10	0

Source: Bulletin of Rural Health Statistics (2002) reprinted in Basic Statistics of the North Eastern Region, 2002.

Table 7.8: No. and Shortfall of Sub-Centres, PHCs and CHCs in Tribal Areas as on 31.3.2001

State	*Sub Centres*		*PHCs*		*CHCs*	
	required	*shortfall*	*required*	*shortfall*	*required*	*shortfall*
Arunachal	550	277	73	8	28	8
Assam	804	463	121		31	
Manipur	263	42	41	4	7	1
Meghalaya	447	34	81		NA	NA
Mizoram	324		63	17	12	3
Nagaland	418	116	507	46	118	58
Sikkim	13		2		1	0
Tripura	275	25	30	2	14	8

Source: Health Information of India, 2002.

The Objective of the Paper

The objective of the paper is to examine whether the market-oriented policies in the health care delivery system that have been advocated with the onset of economic reforms in India since the 1990s can overcome the deficiencies of the health care delivery system in the North East and meet the health care needs of the people of the region in general and of its rural and tribal population in particular.

These questions are extremely topical as with the unleashing of economic reforms there is a widespread questioning not only in India, but all over the developing world of the ability of the public sector, which till now has played a dominant role in providing health care to the people of the North Eastern region, to deliver health care services to the population and especially the vulnerable population effectively.

The Case for Privatisation and Commercialisation of the Health Care Delivery System—The Viewpoint of the Pro-reform Lobby

The pro-reform lobby advocates two kinds of market-oriented reforms in the health care delivery system in the North East to overcome the problems facing it—commercialisation and privatization. Under the former kind of reform, a health care service provider is supposed to cover most or all of its costs directly from the individual or household service user. Reduction of subsidies for the provision of health care services by the public provider is the most common from of commercialisation that is advocated by the pro-reform lobby. The second kind of market-oriented reform that is suggested for the North East by this lobby is privatisation of the health care delivery system with private companies taking over some or all operations and responsibilities of providing health care services to the people and being compensated either through user fees or a fee-for-service by the government. According to this lobby the government's role in the health care system is to be restricted to ensuring robustness of competition and effective regulation of the private service providers.

According to the pro-reform lobby, commercialisation of the health care delivery system offers an economic solution to the problem of scarce resources plaguing the government sector. The pro-reform lobby advocates commercialisation of the health care delivery system in order to reduce the fiscal deficit of states by reducing subsidies. According to this lobby, the imposition of user fees also curtails the unnecessary use of scarce and expensive health care and diagnostic facilities. It also argues that while public health care service providers give subsidies that are often enjoyed by the non-poor also, user fees that are advocated by them are distributionally progressive because the income generated by the imposition of user fees on the affluent can be directed to services and used by the poor.

Privatisation is sought to be promoted by reformers who often point to the inefficient and poor quality of service provided by the public health care delivery system that is characterized by high rates of absenteeism by health care workers, inadequate supplies of medicines and equipment and poor infrastructure. They argue that this often forces the majority of the populaion to turn to largely unregulated private providers of health care services. The findings of the National Family Health Survey 2 conducted in 1998-99 with a sample coverage of 99 per cent of India's population corrobotates this belief[2]. As a part of the survey, the sample households were asked where they go for treatment when family members fall ill. Table 7.9 gives the percentage distribution of all the sample households in India by their main source of health care when household members fall ill according to the place of residence of the households and their standard of living index in 1998-99. It indicates that 69 per cent of the sample household in India used private health care services and only 29 per cent of them used public health care services under these circumstances. Reliance on the private medical sector was higher in urban than in rural areas. Though the use of health care services provided by different sources was strongly correlated with the standard of living of the households and the use of private sector health services increased with improvement in the standard of living, even among households with low standard of living, only one-third of the sample households typically used public sector services when a member of their household fell ill. The institutional rationale for privatisation characterises the private sector as being more competent, innovative and accountable than the public sector. According to the pro-reform lobby, the public health care delivery system is prone to political manipulation so that the rural and the marginalized population of the region like the tribals do not get the facilities they require. The most compelling argument provided for privatising the health care delivery system by the pro-reform lobby is that the government saves money by withdrawing from the provision of a wide variety of health care services that are primarily used by the rich. It can then direct those resources towards those who are more deserving as far as public services including health care services are concerned. The pro-reform lobby also argues that there are sheer economic and political compulsions for the government of poor countries to privatise their health care services emanating from the power of international donors that support the policy of privatisation. Throughout the 1990s and beyond, international donors like the World Bank and IFC have promoted market-oriented reforms including privatisation in the basic service sector including the health care sector.

Table 7.9: Percentage Distribution of Households by Main Source of Health Care According to Residence and Standard of Living Index, India 1998-99*

Source	*Residence*		*Standard of Living Index*			
	Urban	*Rural*	*Low*	*Medium*	*High*	*Total*
Public medical sector	23.5	30.6	34	28.3	19	28.7
NGO/trust	0.8	0.6	0.7	0.6	0.8	0.7
Private medical sector	74.8	66.2	62.5	69.3	78.8	68.6
Other source	1	2.5	2.8	1.7	1.3	2.1
Number of households	25243	65953	33064	40434	16640	91196

* Excludes Tripura

Source: National Family Health Survey 2, 1998-99.

Will Market-Oriented Reforms Imporve the Health Care Delivery System in the North East?

This section of the paper examines the possibility of bringing about an improvement in the health care delivery system in the region through market-oriented reforms. It points out that by and large, market-oriented reforms are not likely to achieve this objective in the North East because there are numerous difficulties associated with implementing market-oriented reforms in the region. Besides, market-oriented reforms are mainly centred round efficiency. Issues of equity and social justice are neglected by them or are treated as having secondary importance. So, a market oriented health care delivery system is not going to meet the needs of the rural and tribal people of the region.

A major stumbling block is likely to emerge in the privatisation process in the North East as very few private investors are likely to be interested in investing in the region. The lack of good infrastructure, a safe socio-political environment and a capable workforce will keep private investors at bay from investing in the health care sector of the region. Private firms in the health sector are nervous about risky investments and demand contractual guarantees from the government that virtually ensure profitability. Private investors demand tax and contract arrangements that minimize or even eliminate commercial risks. However, the North Eastern states may not be in a position to provide the same because of their financial constraints. To appease the concerns of investors, contracts are increasingly designed to minimize risk exposure for the private; investor-friendly polcies in the health care sector can have serious implications for the fiscal stability of the states of the North East, which ironically is one of the justifications for the privatisation of the sector. Even when private investment does take place in this sector in the region, as the private health care delivery system is geared to making profits, it is found that when private capital has financed health care facilities in the states of North East, it is targeted mainly at urban hospitals and clinics that serve customers who are able to pay commercial prices often for highly sophisticated services. Those with little or no income and cannot pay for the services provided by the private health care delivery system are excluded from access to services provide by this system. Rural and tribal areas do not attract investment by the private players in the health care delivery system because of the inability of the inhabitants of these areas to pay for the services and also because of the lack of infrastructural facilities there. As a result, health care services for semi-urban and rural people or people living in remote, inaccessible areas will have to remain almost exclusively delivered by the state and non-profit organisations. Regulation of privately provided health care services is required in order to protect the interest of the consumers. In the North East, the states are likely to be unable to monitor the service performance of the private players in the health care delivery system and consumers are likely to be vulnerable to over-pricing and low-quality service delivery because they are mostly weak states. In the absence of state regulation, private sector health care service providers propelled by the profit motive are very likely to make the uninformed and uneducated consumers of the North East undergo unnecessary medical procedures for earning high profits. If the private players take over the treatment of the rich and the public health care delivery system takes care of the needs of the have-nots, a two-tiered system of health care delivery system will emerge in Eastern India. Weaknesses in State provision have turned many governments in North Eastern states partly towards the private sector but there are considerable disadvantages in a fragmented two-tiered service. It promotes the exit of high-income service users from public provision. Pressure for reforming government service is possible only to the extent that vocal or influential citizens use these services. Yet, when these users are able to opt out of State provision, they lose any interest in holding the state to account.

So, ultimately, the states of the North East should be responsible for providing essential health care services even though voluntary agencies can and do pitch in with them. But providing essential health care services requires resources. Government with deficient services cannot promise access for everyone in the short term. However, they can articulate goals for progressively achieving universal access, and dedicate resources required for doing so.

For every developing country in the world and their constituent States, raising sufficient revenue from a resistant and largely impoverished citizenry is a key obstacle. People are unwilling to spend more of their income on a government that has already failed to provide basic services. More revenue is needed to improve and expand services, but improved and expanded services are needed to justify increased taxation.

International donors can help by financing investments like the construction of infrastructure. However to make universal service delivery sustainable the State must ultimately assume responsibility for covering recurring costs, ideally through general revenues and for certain kinds of consumption, possibly through user fees. By first expanding access and providing tangible benefits for excluded and neglected groups, the state can better justify higher levels of taxation provided that these services are run efficiently and do not become virtually defunct, existing just in name after some time.

This is not to say that the private sector has no role to play in the health care delivery system of the North East with suitable regulation by the state. The public-private partnership model may be tried out in the region for providing specialized health care services to the poor general public and the poor people of the region as well which the public sector cannot provide because of the huge costs involved. For example, government hospitals may not have enough funds to install the sophisticated gadgets required for CT scan or MRI. Private investors in the health sector may be asked to set up these units at government hospitals. However, the problem here will be one of ensuring a fair return on the capital invested by private players for providing the service while at the same time seeing to it that they provide affordable and quality health care services at government-approved rates to the poor. However, this may be in the realm of the possible because the private players may gain from having a steady stream of patients in the government hospitals that they might not have got if they functioned from private facilities but here again, the ability of the government to monitor the functioning of the private sector is questionable.

NOTES

1. All allopathic establishments include hospitals, dispensaries,CHCs, PHCs and Sub-centres, sanatoria and T.B. clinics and other health establishments.
2. The India Report of NFHS 2 is based on 25 of the 26 states since data collection in Tripura was delayed due to some local problems in the state.

8

People, Place and Potentials in the North East

Bibhash Ranjan Choudhury

Modulations of an economic policy, keeping the basic character unchanged, become an inevitable necessity to accommodate regional and sub-regional needs of a country and to facilitate, thereby, the development of all regions or prioritized sectors in unison. This is particularly true where a country is vast and marked by wide diversity. India is known for her unity in diversity but, possibly, it is not very widely known that there is a region, called the North-Eastern region in the country itself, where diversity is much more vivid and varied within a small spatial sphere.

The word 'diversity' ordinarily means differences, but here the word means something more than mere differences. It means collective differences, which distinguish one group of people from another. The difference may be ethnic, religious, linguistic and cultural. These differences apart, there are geographical differences among the sub-regions.

A striking feature of the region so far had been a tradition of accommodation and toleration leading to the emergence of a mechanism of co-existence of groups of people through functional interdependence. But the tradition is now threatened by not only insurgency but also by recurring ethnic conflicts in hill areas.

The relative backwardness of the region, in the context of the national economic setting, has been, amongst others, an important factor responsible for the unrest in plains and hills of the region.

The New Economic Policy, integrating the Indian economy with the rest of the world, has facilitated the expansion and growth of the market economy of the country, but the impact of changes thus caused has not been noticeable in the North East in view of its inherent weaknesses. People of the North East are the onlookers of the economic on rush of other regions of the country, but they cannot reap the benefits because of certain constraints, of which some are age-old and some are the consequences of improper planning.

It is in this perspective that a rethinking seems necessary to trace what actually stands responsible for the failure of the region to rise to the occasion *vis-a-vis* the New Economic Policy or to decide what should be the policy for bringing the North East abreast with the rest of the economy so that it may become responsive to new changes and avail itself of these changes for its own development.

An analysis of this state of affairs suggests that any new policy of uplifting the laggard North East will call for participation of people in the development process cutting across the boundaries of castes and communities or plains and hills. This may be possible if the policy is so designed as to ensure:

1. Comprehensive development of the region instead of developing a few irrationally favoured areas.
2. Development without disparities.
3. Sustainable development.

In this context, due attention and emphasis will have to be given and priority assigned to rural development and conservation of environment. Unplanned urbanization and industrialization must not be allowed to adversely affect the rural economy and environment, which hold the potentials for the development of the region.

The reason behind the inertia of the North-Eastern Region *vis-a-vis* the conditions created by the New Economic Policy for enhancement of economic activities may be attributed to the following factors.

Factors Working at Administrative and Political Level

1. The NE Region although divided into several states, has a separate entity in the country by virtue of its physical and situational features. States constituting the region have these features more or less in common. But the people at the helm of administration did not feel the necessity to treat the states as parts of a common geographical or economic unit for the purpose of their development in unison.
2. The failure to conceive the region as a broad economic zone led to the failure in ensuring the co-ordination of developmental efforts made by individual states. Each state took up its own programme independent of the programmes of neighbouring state. This has denied each of them the economics or services, which could be had from the neighbour. Sometimes, this has affected the cost efficiency.
3. While framing the developmental plans, economic and social considerations have not been of primary importance always, with the consequence that some areas have been irrationally favoured and areas deserving attention or priority remained overlooked.
4. There were no concerted efforts to grow a sense of oneness among the people of the region to make a collective effort possible which seemed very important for the development of this part of the country.

Natural Factors

It cannot be denied that natural factors have been largely responsible for impeding the process of development in the North-Eastern Region. But since no human hand was responsible for such factors like mountains, terrains, climate etc. human efforts could have been made to overcome them and to turn the disadvantages into advantages.

Economic and Strategic Factors

It is possibly here that we encounter the real constraints to development, namely, the lack of vision, lack of sense of appreciation of Nature and potentials latent in it, lack of innovative ideas and resultant absence of proper strategy and planning for development.

The consequence of the working of the factors at administrative level has been unplanned urbanization. This has met the needs of the present compromising the ability of future generations to meet their own needs. Prioritisation has been improper and environment's ability to meet present and future needs has been put to hazard. Neglect of the needs of those who deserved attention and priority has given rise to forces of secession and insurgency. The sense of oneness could not grow. That the emergence of Nagaland, Mizoram and Meghalaya as states, coming out of the fold of Assam has not been inimical to their interests is borne out by the fact that although the growth of population in each of these states has been much faster than the growth of population in Assam, the growth of Per Capita Net Domestic Product at current prices in these states has not been affected, rather the growth of Per Capita Net Domestic Product in these states has been quite fast in relation to corresponding growth of Per Capita Net Domestic Product in Assam. Between 1981 to 2001, there has been tremendous growth of population in North-Eastern states, but during this period Per Capita Net Domestic Product has increased 10 to 15 times. But Assam has lagged behind other NE states during this period.

Utilisation of Central Funds

The dismal performance of Assam is bound to give rise to the question: What is at the root of this poor show? The answer is not very far to seek. Assam lacks in the proper machinery and requisite conditions for her smooth development. Development potentials lie unharnessed or underharnessed. The Central Government can no longer be blamed for its apathy or aversion towards the development of the state. The data available from the Ministry of

Rural Development of Government of India show that during the Ninth Plan Assam with 69.25 per cent utilization of Central Funds available to it occupied 7th position among the 8 states of North East. The rate of utilization has been much higher in all other states, except Manipur. There has not been any improvement in the situation. On November 14, 2006, the Union Minister for the North East, while speaking in a meeting of NEC has observed that North-Eastern states have not been able to submit the project for health services in time and thus failed to avail the funds that were made available by the Union Health Ministry.

Reliability of Data

In fact, the estimated rate of utilization, too, may not be reliable everywhere. In Assam, the impact of utilization of Central funds for rural development and employment generation does not become much perceivable. Investigations show that in some places, funds distributed for IAY have not reached at all or have partially reached the beneficiaries-on-record. The same has been the case with the programmes for asset creation, infrastructure development, water supply, water shed development etc. in rural areas. A major amount of the funds made available by the centre for rural development is frittered away or eaten up by the pipe line itself. Thus, funds made available for the North East have failed to change the basic nature of the regional economy to attract private investments. This is because of the fact that the infrastructural development has not been given due attention over the past decades.

In the present state of affairs it is urgently needed to take up a strategy that will pave the way for development with its own potentials on the one hand and to facilitate the development of rural infrastructure simultaneously, on the other.

A New Approach

The problem of North East is not only composite but it is exceedingly complex, as well. Any measure of development will have to give emphasis on the maintenance of peace and harmony on the one hand and include on the other such projects or programmes of development for different areas as will be complementary in character.

Such programmes will promote interdependence among states and also among different communities. Ethnic conflicts in hills, a recent phenomenon, may be contained if various ethnic groups can be tied up by common economic interest.

The areas on which the emphasis will have to be given are many. Some may be referred to here.

- The newly conceived Bharat Nirman Programme aiming at the building up a proper rural infrastructure through the development of irrigation, rural water supply, rural housing, rural roads, rural telephone and rural electrification seems to have been formulated for areas like the North East. Such a programme will bridge up the gaps in the rural-infrastructure and will create conditions for accelerated growth of farm and non-farm sectors. Along with the aforesaid programmes, proper schemes of development and modernization of traditional village industries, particularly handloom industry, with new design and new technique will have to be undertaken.
- There is a vast scope for boosting up the production of foodgrains. This has to be exploited to open up the avenues for food processing industry in rural areas. It is needless to say that in this age of liberalization, these industries will be able to survive if quality control is effected through proper administration, research and development. Rural roads will have to be developed and inter-village connectivity promoted to widen the market and to expedite commercialisation of agriculture.
- Fisheries will have to be developed in low lying areas and in artificially created lakes between hills. Dry fish processing industry can be also viably developed in rural areas.

- Alternative land use pattern will have to be evolved to make agriculture more viable.

The measures indicated above will not produce the desired result unless there is collective effort of people in the society to promote development. This means, people's participation is indispensable to make the developmental effort effective. Once people's participation is ensured, incomes generated will get distributed more equitably creating conditions for further investments in the market.

These measures apart, serious efforts will have to be made to develop tourism. Tourism, if efficiently planned, can be the most viable industry of the North East. The Nature in the North East has generously gifted the region with such varieties of resources that the entire region can be converted into a paradise of International tourists. If Goa can be the richest state in terms Per Capita Domestic Product with practically no industry, why not the North East shall make similar endeavour, when the region is more favourably poised for the purpose.

Such an approach to development should make the development sustainable. And to make it sustainable the following objectives should be kept in view to guide our activities into the right direction. The objectives will include:

(a) revival and acceleration of growth,
(b) meeting the essential needs including the development of sanitation system,
(c) stabilization of population growth preferably at replacement level,
(d) conserving the resource base and environment,
(e) reorientation of energy, and
(f) enforcement of social justice.

The strategy of development indicated above has a rural bias. In fact, the development of the North East can be a real proposition only if the process of development is initiated from rural economy.

REFERENCES

Choudhury, B.R.: Some Reflections on the Strategy of the Economic Development of the North East India, published in K. Alam (ed.), *Planning in North East India,* 1985, Omsons Publications.

Economic Survey: Government of India 2003-04.

Economic Survey: Government of India 2004-05.

Kurushetra, October 2006, Editorial.

Misra R.P., *Urbanisation in India: Challenges and Opportunities,* Regency Publication, 1998, New Delhi.

Naik, S. and Singh, S.: North-Eastern States: A Rural Development and Poverty Alleviation Perspective, *Yojana,* March 2003.

Our Common Future, 1987 (A Report of WCED), reproduced under the title, Towards Sustainable Development in *Science Age,* August 1987, 30-38.

9

North-Eastern Region of India and the Economic Reform Programme

P.M. Passah

Introductory

The Economic Reforms Policy was enunciated in India in 1991. Yet after a period of fifteen long years, the policy does not appear to have had any impact so far as the North-Eastern Region (NER) of the country is concerned.[1] The socio-cultural and economic environment of the states in the region is in wide divergence with the rest of the country.

Hitherto the grievances of the people of the North East was that of neglect by the Union Government as being the cause of all the ills of the region. But now, especially after 1996, the problem is not of neglect but of lopsided planning and faulty implementation.

There is no dearth of funds to hasten the development of the region. But one does not know how much of these funds actually flowed down the development pipeline. The leakages of development funds in the Region have been at a higher level than it is in the rest of the country. The Region has still remained cut off from the national mainstream due to the absence of a coherent perspective on development.

The economic development of the NER has been one of the most formidable and complex processes right from the inception of planned development in India. Despite the nature's bounty bestowed on the region, its economy is growing barely at one-third of the national average. The few public sector enterprises set up in the region have hardly produced the benefits for the local population and the States' exchequer. The poor quality of infrastructural facilities have hampered industrial development. There is no denial that interminable violence due to militancy and insurgency has deterred many potential entrepreneurs both from within and outside the region. The agricultural sector tends to grow at a slower pace than manufacturing and services sectors. The credit-deposit ratio is as low as 35 per cent in Assam as against the national average of 62 per cent. It is far less in the remaining hill states in the Region. Therefore, this Paper aims at attempting the study of the prospects and impediments of economic development within the NER *vis-a-vis* the Economic Reforms Policy of the country.

Implications of Economic Reforms in NER

Liberalization

The policy measures adopted under the new economic liberalization do consist of measures to take care of the needs of the socio-economically weaker sections of the population during the short-run stabilization and adjustment period. This would take care of the capability building. But the measures did not envisage taking care of the interests and protecting the development prospects of less developed units of the country like the states in the North-Eastern Region. This should have been envisaged in the liberalization schemes considering the insurgency problem of the region. The implications of the liberalization policy in the context of insurgency have not been studied. Thus, the ability of the economic reform measures to create the needed peace dividend is yet to be known. In this context, it is doubtful whether the leadership in the region itself has been capable of appreciating the implications of the liberalization policy.

Globalization

It may be remembered that globalization has been driven by two main factors, namely (1) the rise of capitalism and its built-in urge to find new markets and extend the area of its influence, and (2) the advent of new technology in transport and communications which makes it possible to expand markets and to control these over a wide geographical area. This fact necessitates the opening up of every state's economy and society in the North East through the free and smooth road transport connectivity. It may be pointed out that the NEC Act amended in 2002 is still stressing or insisting on inter-state schemes except in case of Sikkim. But the weak points or areas of an individual state will have to be addressed while stress may be given to inter-state schemes and projects. Besides, development economics demands that one should be acquainted with socio-economic history of the Region, for development always takes place in a defined geographical space and for a given society. Such factors cannot be overlooked.

Privatization

The private industry is of the clear view that the existing units in the public sector need not necessarily be privatized. But new private units should be freely allowed to be set up and expanded as determined by the market forces of demand and supply. The efficiency of the public sector, it is truly believed, would certainly improve if they are exposed to competition, first within the country itself and later on, internationally. This principle would be more suitable to the NER.

Present Status of Development[2]

Industrial Base

A fairly extensive industrial base was laid in the NER by the British in the late nineteenth and early twentieth centuries. India's first joint stock company was started in Assam more than 160 years ago. The Assam (Tea) company was formed in 1839 and as many as eight companies were later established for running industries and transport services. The collieries are among the oldest in India. The tea industry was one of the country's top foreign exchange earners. The Assam Railways and Trading Company was formed in 1881 by the British to lay railway tracks up to the eastern extremity of the Brahmaputra's south bank where most of the industries they established were located. Two steamer companies were also formed in between 1847 and 1864 which operated steamer service on the Brahmaputra to and from Calcutta until Independence when East Pakistan (now Bangladesh) was carved out of India as part of an independent Pakistan. But after this partition, the entrepreneurial activities have been thwarted by a variety of factors mainly by the absence of critical minimum of infrastructural facilities. The inadequate rail and road transport services coupled with the virtual collapse of water transport after the partition, have hampered industrial development. The poor quality of highways is also a great hindrance to economic development. The interminable violence due to militancy and insurgency has, by and large, deterred many potential entrepreneurs both from within and outside the Region, from investing their skills and money. Some urgent and imaginative steps have to be taken to address the basic issues of security and development.

Agricultural Sector

The agricultural sector tends to grow at a lower pace than manufacturing and services sectors. The outmoded farming practices are still in vogue. In the hill areas, the destructive shifting method of cultivation still continues though to a lesser extent. The infrastructural constraints and recurring floods are major setbacks to the farm economy. The dominance of agriculture in the Region's economy defies the laws of economic growth as less than a quarter of the land is arable while it is about 60 per cent in the rest of the country. Worse still, less than 17 per cent of the cropped land enjoys the benefit of irrigation facilities as against 39 per cent of the all-India average. The estimated irrigation potential in Assam is over

4.8 lakh hectares but the utilization level is less than 25 per cent. Barely 21 per cent of the land under rice cultivation is irrigated in Assam as against almost cent per cent in Punjab.

In respect of credit facilities, the North Eastern farmers remain far behind the rest of the country. The monetary credit made available to Assam farmers is less than a third of the national average. The credit disbursement by the banks and financial institutions in the NER has shrunk over the years. In the decade 1989-99, the average sanction of credit was only Rs. 343.2 in Assam as against the all-India average of Rs. 592.4 (at 1980-81 prices), and the actual disbursement plummeted to Rs. 788.2. The credit-deposit ratio is as low as 35 per cent as against the national average of 62 per cent. The position in the remaining states in the Region is behind the Assam figure.

Inter-Sectoral Linkages

There is need for strengthening inter-sectoral linkages so as to give a thrust to industrial development in the Region. As of now, there is little perceptible structural change in the secondary sector in Assam and Arunachal Pradesh. In Manipur an improved coverage of the unorganized sector has helped to raise the secondary sector's share of the aggregate domestic product value in the state without any perceptible growth of manufacturing industries. In Nagaland and Mizoram, the expansion of construction industry has triggered the secondary sector's growth while manufacturing activities remain a non-starter. In Meghalaya, economic development has had a little impact on the secondary sector. Finally, in Tripura there has been a movement away from primary sector activities to tertiary sector.

Development Priorities[3]

Everywhere the infrastructural constraints coupled with inadequate plan allocations lie at the root of the economic inertia of the region. Each state in the NER should have well developed communication system. Assam should have broadgauge railway lines on both banks of the Brahmaputra river from one end to the other. Meghalaya should develop a Super Plateau Highway running from west to east, and from where lateral roads could be constructed to branch out northwards and southwards to the interior areas; conversely, any north-going and south-going roads would converge on this highway. The plateau highway would be the only road communication system that can open up the plateau economy of Meghalaya where railway construction is costly both in terms of finance and environmental damage. The existing north-south national highways will not be able to solve the transport problems of interior areas in the state.

Similarly, hill states like Nagaland, Manipur and Tripura should have each a Super Circular Highway from where roads can radiate to a central point at the capital city of the state. Mizoram has to convert its north-south Highway-54 into a Super Highway from where lateral roads could branch out eastwards and westwards to provide a well-developed transport and communication connectivity within the state. The remaining state of Arunachal Pradesh can think of achieving road transport networks and connectivity on similar lines.

After achieving a well-developed transport and communication network within each state, inter-state connectivity of road communication could easily be accomplished. Thus strong states would be able to make the North East a strong Region. But what is more important is the immediate need to perfect the links of the Region with the rest of the country so as to diffuse the benefits of natinal development freely covering the region as well.

The expansion of the GN Bordoloi Airport at Guwahati would be beneficial to the NER only if other state capitals are linked to it. The inland waterways along the Brahmaputra and the Barak rivers have to be fully developed. The development of both surface and water transport and communication systems would intensify the interactions within the Region and thereby release forces for further development in all other sectors of the economy of the NER.

The rich power potential of the Region has to be developed before the industrialization process can start in right earnest and be sustained. Although the North-Eastern Development and Finance Corporation (NEDFi) has been set up with Rs. 500 crores as capital for funding industrial and develpment projects within the region, yet scepticisms still prevail. Different voluntary organizations involved in industrial development in the region are of the opinion that the credit-deposit ratio would change only marginally unless the terms of conditions of banks and financial institutions in the region are made flexible to the advantage of the young entrepreneurs of the region. Their experience is that most of the banks are not even prepared to provide information on the different schemes offered by the Government.

Economic Integration of NER

One can notice that the economies of different states within the NER are far from integrated. The region has much to gain by integrating into one economy at the first instance as it moves towards integration with the national economy or towards globalization of the Region's economy. Hence the prospects and impediments of economic integration within the region need to be seriously analyzed. A larger market within the region can give it the advantage of the economics of scale facilitating the emergence of new and viable economic activities. As of now, the markets have been fragmented by a number of factors like the (i) underdeveloped communication network, (ii) high cost of moving men and materials within the region itself, (iii) lack of uniformity of tax structure among the states, and (iv) the absence of a shared vision among the different states. The differences in the local laws and customs also seriously hinder economic integration. The economic reform measures enunciated in the country cannot, therefore, be easily extended in the NER.

Conclusion

The foregoing analysis of the present economic situation of the NER has definitely shown that the region appears to be not ready to face the challeges of globalization process.[4] It is hoped that the leadership in the NER will evaluate implications of the liberalization policy measures and the fundamental weaknesses in the crucial sectors of the Region's economy. The leadership should see that not only the investment in the core sectors should be augmented but also the capability building of the people of the region is taken care of by the states and the Central Government. The Central authorities will have to think beyond liberalization, privatization or globalization and strengthen both the core sectors and the social sectors of the North-Eastern economy.

NOTES

1. P.M. Passah, "Economic Liberalization in India—Implications of NER" in Kousar J. Azam (ed.) (1997), *Economic Liberalization in India—Implications for Indo-US Relations,* Delta Publishing House, Delhi. Also P.M. Passah, "Implications of Economic Liberalization for NER" in Gurudas, *et al.,* (1998) *Liberalization and India's North East,* Commonwealth Publishers, New Delhi.
2. Most of the inputs for this Section is taken from P.M. Passah, "North-Eastern Region of India and the Look East Policy"—*A Paper* presented to the 8th Annual Conference of the North-Eastern Economic Association held on 16-17 December, 2006 in Mizoram University, Aizawl.
3. *Ibid.*
4. *Ibid.*

10

Globalization as a Model for Economic Development

Strategy for North East India

Hiranmoy Roy and *Kingshuk Adhikari*

Introduction

Liberalization, globalization and privatization are the three facets of new economic policy of India. The objectives of the new economic policy adopted by the Government of India are to achieve higher level of economic growth and development and making Indian economy vibrant, dynamic and internationally competitive not only by liberating the trade and industry from the unnecessary and unwanted bureaucratic controls but also through integration of Indian domestic economy with the world economy. Greater thrust has been given on the private sector and the role of the public sector has been gradually reduced.

The present paper makes an attempt to analyse the impact of globalization on North Eastern Region of India.

There are considerable discussion among the proponents and opponents of globalization. The advocates of globalization consider it as a wonderful contribution of capitalism to the world. Its critics perceive globalization as harmful, bringing about increased domination by developed nations over the underdeveloped countries. This divergence of views necessitates an urgent thought on the process of globalization from the viewpoint of less dominant countries of the world. There has already been much discussion on issues relating to the negative fallout of globalization. The globalization idea is itself a suspect. The empirical reality does not suggest any clear link between globalization and development. One picture reflects that globalization adversely affects the poor, and especially in poorer countries, while the other picture holds that it has supported poverty reduction (World Bank: 2002) particularly in developing and underdeveloped regions. Those who take a positive view of globalization consider it as a force of progress, increased wealth, freedom, democracy, and happiness. Its defenders present globalization as beneficial, generating fresh economic opportunities, political democratization, cultural diversity, and the opening to an exciting new world. From the opposite standpoint, it is perceived as a march of predatory capital subjugating the human race world over (Sen: 2002). Its critics see globalization as harmful, bringing about increased control by the wealthier over developed nations over the poor underdeveloped countries, thus increasing the hegemony of the "haves" over the "have-nots". In the midst of these opposing views, globalization may be defined as:

- A process of ever increasing economic interactions and trans-border migration of trade, technology and finance capital at the international level.
- Partial retreat of the state in regulating these flows and in intervening in the welfare of citizens.
- Ever increasing influence of the market forces in the economy (Baker, Epstein, and Polin: 1998).

Therefore, globalization can be defined as a process of ever growing economic interdependence of countries of the world which constitutes integration of national economies into the international economy through cross border transactions in goods and services, international capital flows and widespread diffusion of technology. This is the force that has shaped all of the twentieth century before being acquiring the current momentum during the last two decades.

Indian Experience

The dual effect of Globalization is manifested in case of India also. The balance of payment and foreign exchange crises in the country necessitated reforms in India in early 90s. Under such situation, India had to seek loans from international financial institutions and the conditions of reforms followed. Although it is too early to evaluate the long-run social and economic implications of the Policy of Economic Liberalisations adopted more drastically since the middle of 1991, there has been concern that some of the stabilization and structural reforms might have led to the erosion of living standards of the poor, increase in regional disparities in terms of industrial benefits, deterioration or, at best a sluggishness in employment opportunities and the building of a general atmosphere of insecurity among the masses in general. On the one hand, the share of total labour force in the unorganized segment has been steadily increasing, on the other hand, that of net domestic product in the same segment is moving towards opposite direction. The first generation of economic reforms did not show any substantial signs of progress. Rather a contradictory growth is observed. During the post-1991 period, India has witnessed a mix of political stability and instability, affecting the reforms one way or the other. This may be one of the reasons that did not allow globalization to live up to its promise. It has benefited only limited part of business and industry of India.

Notwithstanding certain benefits resulting from the percolating effects of globalization, some of the adverse consequences of globalization on India can be highlighted as follows:

- Gradual shrinkage in employment opportunities in various sectors of the economy.
- Inflationary trend without any corresponding rise in real income of the people in general.
- Decline in investment in agriculture leading to the further marginalization of marginal cultivators.
- Extermination of many cottage and small scale industries due to uneven competition.

- Disinvestment and privatization of even profit-making public sector undertakings.
- Retrenchment of workers without providing suitable alterantive avenues.
- Problems arising from price dumping, patenting, WTO regulations, and the compliance of conditions laid down by World Bank/International Monetary Fund.

In theory, globalization provides an opportunity to raise incomes through increased specialization and trade. But this opportunity is conditioned by the size of the markets in question, which in turn depends on geography, transportation costs, communication networks, and the institutions that support markets. There is a general consensus among opponents of globalization that completely free unregulated capitalist growth is not likely to address poverty, unemployment etc. and that some deliberate measures are to be adopted by governments. The state intervention is absolutely necessary in the developmental strategies of LDCs like India.

What is ideally and presently needed is a fundamental approach to define development and a new development strategy, which puts redistribution of gains of globalization and human needs at the pinnacle of its agenda. The achievement of rapid increase in wealth without a corresponding increase of the welfare of the masses cannot and should not be the ultimate goal of the global economy.

Human beings have closer relationship with the natural resources. Entire human sustenance is derived directly or indirectly from natural resources which are limited in quantity. Production of food and extraction of minerals out of land come under same principle of nature niggardliness as Ricardo pointed out. As such over exploitation of natural resources raises cost and also endangers environment. The limit of sustainability of forest and mineral resources is set by the cost benefit assessment in terms of individual and society.

However, the neo-classical growth model has visualized as the dynamic process of growth with the adoption of technology as Schumpeter explained in the importance of innovation. Therefore, limit to growth is set not so much by expansion of natural resources (renewable and non-renewable) but by low level of technical efficiency and productivity (Banarjee, 2004).

Resource Abundance as Constraint to Growth

The greater the natural resource endowment, the smaller is the allocation of labour and capital to the manufacturing sector. Therefore, when natural resources are abundant, tradeable production is concentrated in natural resources rather than manufacturing, and capital and labour that otherwise might be employed in manufacturing are pulled into the non-traded goods sector. As a corollary, when a economy experiences a resource boom, the manufacturing sector tends to shrink and the non-traded goods sector tends to expand. The shrinkage of the manufacturing sector is dubbed the "Dutch Disease" and a source of chronic slow growth. If manufacturing is characterized by externalities in production, the shrinkage of manufacturing sector caused by resource abundance can lead to socially insufficient decline in growth. Manufacturing has larger positive externalities than other forms of economic activity. The empirical support for this is based on the observations that countries with more diversified exports seem to do better and that growth tends to be positively correlated with growth in manufacturing production and manufacturing exports.

We refer to the regression analysis that designed in Matsuyama's model mainly to demonstrate that the inverse association between natural resource use and economic growth. In the first regression, GDP (divided by the economically active population between 1970 and 1990, denoted by GEA 7090) on the log of initial GDP (per economically active population denoted by LGDPEA 70) and the share of primary exports in GDP in 1970 (SXP). A higher share of primary exports in 1970 is associated with lower growth in the next two decades with an estimated co-efficient of –9.43 and t statistic of –4.45.

It is possible that this negative association between natural resource intensity and growth is spurious, reflecting an association between resource wealth and growth. Some common arguments are that resource rich countries are more likely to adopt import substitution, and state-led development strategies are less likely to accumulate capital at home because they can live off natural resource rents and are less likely to develop market supporting legal institutions. In addition, a long standing view in the development literature is that countries that specialize in natural resource, exports are more likely to suffer from unpredictable and disruptive shocks in global commodity prices.

It is interesting to note that even with the small set of fast growing Asian Tigers there is an adverse effects of natural resource abundance, since resource poor Singapore, Hong Kong and Korea have grown faster than resource rich Malaysia and Thailand.

Table 10.1: Association between Natural Resource Abundance and Other Explanatory Variables

	National Savings % GDP 70-89 (2.1)	*Investment % GDP 70-89 (2.2)*	*Human Capital Acumulation Change 70-90 (2.3)*	*Relative Prices of Investment Goods 70-89 (2.4)*
LGDPEA70	6.38 (7.69)	—	0.05 (0.45)	–0.16 (–2.71)
SXP	0.19 (0.03)	0.40 (1.19)	–0.95 (–1.05)	0.80 (0.26)
SOPEN	—	0.14 (1.19)	—	—
Adjusted R^2	0.36	0.67	–0.01	0.31
Sample Size	104	80	90	102
Standard Error	7.64	0.31	0.89	0.43

Source: Matsuyama's Model.

We find evidence that natural resource abundance may affect growth indirectly through extent of trade openness. First, we postulate, and find supporting evidence, for a u-shaped relation between openness (measured SOPEN, on the Y-axis) and resource intensity (measured as SXP, on the X-axis). Resource abundance squeezes the manufacturing sector, as in Dutch Disease. In almost all countries, the squeeze of manufactures provokes some protectionist response that aims to promote industrialization despite the Dutch Disease effects. For most highly resource endowed economies (such as Middle East), the natural resource base is so vast that there is no strong pressure to develop an extensive industrial sector. Thus for most extreme resource-based cases, openness to trade (SOPEN) would tend to be high. The overall effect would, therefore, be a u-shaped relationship between SXP and SOPEN.

The foregoing analysis resembles with the Ricardian-Malthusian premise that non-renewable resources are fated to diminish over time (since as gift of nature they can't be replenished). The impression has been prevalent for atleast two centuries that economic progress entailed moving away natural resources into sectors based on knowledge, skills, capital and technology. Recent studies in development economics add quantitative rigor to this impression summarizing extensive econometric research. Richart M. Auty writes, "resource rich developing countries have under performed compared with the resource deficient economies". Other supporters of the view are Sachs and Warner. This concern is especially acute in those studies for which resource-based sectors are taken to include crop-growing agriculture. This inverse relationships between resources and economic performance seem stronger for agriculture than for minerals and forest products.

Application in North-Eastern Economy

The concept of regional development is appropriate in case of North Eastern Region of India comprising eight states. There are striking similarities in topography, vegetation, livelihood pattern as well as social customs among the North Eastern states. This region is endowed with oil, natural gas and huge mineral resources, such as coal, limestone, gypsum, sillimanite, fireclay, kaoline, pyrites, uranium and gold.

The North Eastern region has been pioneer in India in exploration and production of petroleum. Asia's first successful mechanically drilled oil was in Makum (Assam) way back in 1867. This was followed by the first commercial discovery of crude oil at Digboi (Assam) in 1889 making the beginning of Oil Industry in India. In the year 1959, the Oil India Limited (OIL) and Oil and Natural Gas Commission (ONGC) were set up in India for exploration and production of hydrocarbons (Maiti *et al.*, 2004). The following tables shows the natural resource position of North East India.

Table 10.2: SDP Growth Rate in 8th and 9th Plan in NE States

States	*8th Plan*	*9th Plan*	*10th Plan*
Arunachal Pradesh	5.1	4.4	8.0
Assam	2.8	2.1	6.2
Manipur	4.6	6.4	6.5
Meghalaya	3.8	6.2	6.3
Mizoram	—	—	5.3
Nagaland	8.9	2.6	5.6
Sikkim	5.3	8.3	7.9
Tripura	6.6	7.4	7.3

Table 10.3: Estimated Reserves of Geo-Energy Resources in North East India

Geo Energy Resurces	*Estimated Figures*
Coal	893,000,000 tonnes
Natural Oil	876,000,000 tonnes
Natural Gas	114 cubic metres

Source: Tenth Plan.

Table 10.4: Regional Distribution of Primary Commercial Energy Sources in India

Region	*Coal (bt)*	*Lignite (bt)*	*Crude Oil (mt)*	*Natural Gas (BCM)*	*Hydel Power (TWH)*
Northern	1.06	2.61	0.03	0.0	225.00
Western	56.90	1.67	519.47	516.42	31.40
Southern	15.46	30.38	45.84	80.94	61.80
Eastern	146.67	0.0	2.19	0.29	42.50
North-Eastern	0.89	0.0	166.17	—	239.30
Total	220.98	34.76	733.70	749.65	600.00

bt—Billion Tonnes, BCM—Billion Cubic Metres, TWH—Trillion Watt Hours, mt—Million Tonnes.

Source: Tenth Plan.

Table 10.5: Ninth Plan Actuals and Tength Plan Outlays for Energy, Industry and Minerals

(Rs. in crores)

States	*Ninth Plan Expentiture*	*Tenth Plan Projected Outlay*
Assam	7211.44	8315.24
Manipur	1787.01	2804.00
Meghalaya	1827.15	3009.00
Mizoram	1758.77	2300.01
Nagaland	1513.64	2227.65
Tripura	2291.47	4500.00

Source: Tenth Plan.

Table 10.5 shows the Ninth Plan expenditure and Tenth Plan allocation of outlay in the North Eastern states. It is clear that allocation is very low.

Mineral Resources of North East India reveal that coal deposits in Assam were assessed at 371.00 million tonnes, Meghalaya 564.00 million tonnes, occurring in Khasi, Jaintia and Garo Hills. Petroleum is the largest mineral resource in Assam and Tripura. Crude oil is available at Naharkatiya, Moran, Hugrijan, Rudra Sagar Lake in Assam. Oil Refineries are established at Digboi, Noonmati, Bongaigaon and Numaligarh, which provide large employment. Total reserves are estimated at 158 million tonnes.

Table 10.7: Coal Reserves in North East India

(in tonnes)

State	*Coal Reserves*
Assam	371.0
Meghalaya	584.91
Arunachal	91.000
Nagaland	17.200

Source: NEDFi Data Bank.

Empirical Results

We have two hypotheses to the relationship of resource endowment and growth, one considers resource endowment as impediment to growth while the other account for resource endowment as stimulant to growth. Thus we are faced with the obvious question as to which approach is applicable in case of North Eastern Region since intensity of resource endowment in North East is high.

To analyse the relationship, both correlation and regression analysis were applied as tools of analysis. First, we assume the relationship of economic growth and resource endowment as hypothesised by development theories. A moderate correlation of 0.578 was found between economic growth and resource endowment.

Next, to determine the weightage of resource endowment that determine growth, we have applied regression model. It is assumed that economic growth is dependent variable and expenditure on resources as independent variable. State Domestic Product (SDP) represents economic growth, while expenditure on resurces is a better explanatory variable on growth, than resource endowment. Moreover, resource endowment is a crude measure to evaluate its direct effect on SDP. Allocation in resources better explains the growth prospect. So the function which specifies the relationship is—

$$SDP = a + b\ Exp.$$

Where SDP = State Domestic Product
and Exp. = Plan Expenditure on Natural Resources
The results of the regression test is
$SDP = 6.635 - 0.579\ Exp.\ R2 = 0.335$
$t = (3.872)\ (-1.229)\ F = 1.510$

Since R2 value is low and t values of the co-efficient of independent variable is also statistically insignificnat, we decline the hypothesis that there is positive relationship of resource endowment and economic growth. So the hypothesis which considered resource endowment as hindrance to economic growth is true in case of North East and our analysis conform to that of Matsuyama's model.

Conclusion

Development of North Eastern Region in general and industrialization in particular suffers from various reasons. In spite of the vast natural resources, government policy failed to take any bold step for extraction of the renewable and non-renewable resources for rapid industrialization and eradication of poverty. Such industrialization programmes are explicitly weak and lack any dynamic and robust attitude. (i) The well-known constraint of lack of infrastructure is further burdened with low investment, both public and private; (ii) Exploitation of renewable resources for rapid industrialization is not properly programmed. The forest and water resources are completely devoid of any coordinated plan; and (iii) The extraction of untapped mineral resources has been very slow. Only eco-friendly investment projects for use of natural resources can expand the industrial base in these states (Banerjee, 2004).

In North Eastern Region, where rate of savings is very low and the development of the region is dependent on central doles, foreign capital can play a very dominant role in the development of the region. The Foreign Direct Investment (FDI) and Foreign Institutional Investment (FII) are highly required in North Eastern Region of India. The prospect of globalization for the region is not very promising. North Eastern economy is unable to attract and successfully negotiate a deal with global capital embodied in powerful MNC and TNC structures. Government is also lacking on its part to provide physical and institutional infrastructure that is conducive to growth. In the global economy North East must strive for better infrastructural support to attract foreign capital and technology to be utilized in its natural resource sector. In North Eastern Region the nature of the learning process must be improved through which the economic potential of the resources are to be achieved. Collective learning on resources, large scale investment in exploration, transportation, geological knowledge and technological knowledge of mineral extraction, refining and utilization must be applied in North East.

REFERENCES

Agnoli, J. (2002): "Emancipation: Paths and Goals", in Bonefeld, W. and S. Tischler (eds.).

Akira, Kudo: "A Note on Globalisation and Regional Integration".

Amin, Samir (1997): *Capitalism in the Age of Globalisation,* London, Zed Books.

Aqueil Ahmad (2001): "Globalization and the Developing Countries, With Especial Reference to Cuba", a ahmad@uncg.edu

Baker, Dean, Gerald Epstein and Robin Polin (1998): *Globalization and Progressive Economic Policy,* New York, Cambridge University Press.

Bhalla, A.S. (1995): *Uneven Development in the Third World: A Study of China and India,* New York, St. Martin's Press.

Chanda, N. (2002): "Coming Together: Globalization means Reconnecting the Human Community", Yale Global Online.

Chandra, P., Ghosh, A., Kumar, Ravi (eds.) (2004): *The Politics of Imperialism and Counterstrategies.*

Chomsky, Noam (1998): "Power in the Global Arena", *New Left Review.*

Dhani, Rodrik, (2001): "Globalisation, Growth and Poverty: Is the World Bank Beginning to Get it"?

Dutta, Dillip (2002): "Effects of Globalisation on Employment and Poverty in Dualistic Economies: The Case of India", dilipd@econ.usyd.edu.au.

Dutt, R. and Sundaram, K.P.M. (2004): *Indian Economy,* S. Chand and Company Ltd., New Delhi.

Foster, J.B. (2002): "Monopoly Capital and the New Globalization", *Monthly Review,* January.

Ishiyama, J. (2005): "Globalization and the Development of Left Parties in Post Communist Politics", jishiyam@truman.edu

Jefferv Round and John Whalley (2003): *Globalisation and Poverty: Implications of South Asian Experience for the Wider Debate.*

Kellner, D. (2004): "Theorizing Globalization", http://www.Kellner.html

Lekhi, R.K. and Choudhury, R.K. (2004): *Economy of India-including Assam and North East,* Kalyani Publishers, New Delhi.

Marfleet, Phil (1998): "Globalisation and the Third World", *International Socialism Journal.*

Martin Wolf, (2002): "Globalisation, poverty and growth", *Financial Times,* November, 11.

Mazumdar, A. (1998): "Globalisation and Reginal Imbalance: Prospects of North East India in a Super Colonial World Order?" in G. Das and R.K. Purkayastha (eds.), *Liberalisation and India's North East,* New Delhi: Common Wealth Publishers, 40-67.

Mazumdar, A. (2004): "Globalisation of Capital, LDC Labourers and the Prospects of North East India", *Souvenir,* North East India Political Science Association, Thirteenth annual conference, Silchar, 19-24.

McGrew, Anthony G. and Paul G. Lewis eds. (1995): *Global Politics,* Cambridge, MA: Blackwell.

Michael, V.P. (2000): *Business Policy and Environment,* S. Chand and Company Ltd., New Delhi.

Moyo, A. and Amin, H. (1992): "The Development Experience of Post Colonial Sub-Saharan Africa", in W.L.M. Adriansen and J.G. Waardenburg (eds.), *A Dual World Economy: Forty Years of Development Experience,* Oxford Univesity Press, Bombay.

Paul, M. Sweezy (1997): "More (or Less) on Globalization", *Monthly Review,* September.

Round, Jeffery and Whalley, John (2003): "Globalisation and Poverty: Implications of South Asian Experience for the Wider Debate".

Roy, A.N. (1999): *The Third World in the Age of Globalisation: Requiem or New Agenda?* Zed Books, New York.

Sen, A. (2002): "How to Judge Globalism", *The American Prospect,* Volume 13, Issue 1, January 1, 2002.

Wood, A. (1997): "Openness and Wage Inequalities in Developing Countries: The Latin American Challenge to East Asian Conventional Wisdom", *The World Bank Economic Review,* Vol. 11, No. 1, January.

World Bank (1995): *World Development Report 1995: Workers in an Integrating World,* Washington, D.C., World Bank.

World Bank (2000): *Poverty in an Age of Globalisation,* Washington, D.C., World Bank.

11

Reform and Inclusive Growth of North East Economy

Amalesh Banerjee

I. Indroduction

Economic reform was started in India since 1991 when the economic growth was slow and the balance of payment crisis had developed. The objectives of the reform package were to attain rapid economic growth through liberalization of government controls, privatization of public enterprises and globalization of Indian economy (LPG). Consequently, (a) new industrial policy, (b) foreign trade policy, (c) fiscal and monetary policies were announced in different phases. By the close of the century industrial sector has been mostly opened and the public sector enterprises were largely deregulated. Industrial growth under private sector began to expand. On the fiscal sector tax reform and government fiscal management became effective which aimed at reducing budgetary deficit. On the external sector imports and exports have been liberalized. Indian tariffs have been reduced under the pressure of WTO dictum. Indian exports have also increased and balance of payment has improved. Our foreign exchange reserve has increased to historic level. India's financial reform has also proceeded step by step. The stabilisation policy has become largely succeessful. Given this broad spectrum of economic reform what are the macro economic impacts of these reforms and the associated regional patterns?

From the sectoral and regional point of view the economic reform has cast a dismal picture. While the manufacturing and the service sectors have pushed ahead the growth rates, the agricultural and social sectors have posed a serious drag.

The states which have picked up the trails of these growth potentials, have recorded high rates of growth. The states which, on the other hand, are saddled with stagnant agriculture and lower level of human development are lagging behind. Most of the North Eastern states, along with a few other states (BIMARU states), are at the lower rung of the ladder of growth. Low per capita income and low NSD of these states are due to their over dependence on the primary sector, and lack of growth of secondary and tertiary sectors. These factors coupled with high rates of growth of population have kept most of the North-Eastern states in the vicious cycle of poverty and stagnation.

In this paper we examine the impact of reform in the north-eastern states and then explain what ought to be done by the government in the NE states in order to catch up with the rising growth momentum of the economy. In section II the pattern of growth of Indian economy and that of N.E. region is stated. stated. Section III deals with the agenda for rapid growth. Section IV explains the policy and the new industrial policy look east. Section V discusses issues of governance. Section VI offers the conclusion.

II. Economic Growth and NE

The LPG Programme has brought about a significant transformation of Indian economy. The emphasis has been shifted from the direct govenment intervention to the mixed programme of the private and public sector for the development of the economy. This transition from a planned economy to the market economy has induced competitiveness and efficiency as the principal criterion of investment. Public and private investments are considered on the principles of efficiency, social welfare and optimal allocation.

This has yielded some good results in respect of economic growth. Even with some limitations and risk of imbalances of different sorts, the economy has attained a 9.2 percent rate of growth in the last quarter of 2006-07. As it appears from the current trend, Indian economy is poised for a sustained growth of 9-10 per cent rate over the Eleventh Five Year Plan.The current resurgence of the economy is presented in the following reports of the Economic Survey 2006-07.

Table 11.1: Indicators of Progress

Year	*GDP per cent (1999-2000 Prin.)*	*Import*	*Export*	*Index of Industrial Production*	*Rate of Invest-ment*	*Rate of Savings*
1	*2*	*3*	*4*	*5*	*6*	*7*
2003-04	8.5	27.3	21.1	7.8	24.7	29.7
2004-05	7.5	42.7	30.8	9.5	25.9	31.1
2005-06	9.0	33.8	23.4	9.5	30.1	32.4
2006-07	9.2	36.3	36.3	10.0	33.8	35.1

Source: RBI Bulletin, March 2007.

Table 11.2: Sectoral Pattern of Growth: (a) Average Growth Rate, (b) Weighted Contributor (Per Cent)

Year	*Agriculture*		*Industry*		*Services*		*Overall*	
	(a)	*(b)*	*(a)*	*(b)*	*(a)*	*(b)*	*(a)*	*(b)*
1970s	0.6	39.7	4.7	21.5	4.1	38.8	2.9	100
1980s	4.4	19.5	7.4	27.0	6.4	53.5	5.8	100
1990s	3.0	10.7	5.9	18.1	7.4	71.1	5.8	100
2000-2005	1.4	0.1	6.0	21.5	7.8	78.3	5.9	100
2005-2006	6.0	13.5	8.0	17.5	10.3	69.0	9.0	100
2006-2007	2.7	5.8	10.2	21.4	11.0	72.7	9.2	100

Source: RBI Bulletin, March 2007.

Against this record of progress of Indian Economy during the Tenth Plan, the Elevanth Five Year Plan Approach holds the scenario of sustained growth.

In absolute sense India's growth strategy has assumed a sustained position. The region has strengthened the private sector

Table 11.3: Alternative Scenarios for 11th Plan (2007-2012)

(in per cent)

Target for GDP growth rate	7.0	8.8	9.9
Average Investment rate	29.1	32.0	35.1
Average CAD as PC of GDP	2.0	2.4	2.8
Domestic Saving Rate	27.1	29.6	32.3
(a) Household	20.1	20.5	21.0
(b) Corporate	5.0	5.5	6.1
(c) PSE	3.1	3.1	2.8
(d) Government	–1.1	0.5	2.4

Source: Approach Paper quoted in *Yojana* April 2007, p. 33.

which is now capable of leading the economic expansion. Including railways, seven major infrastructure industries have led a sustained rapid growth. Railways has attained 10 per cent growth and electricity, coal, steel, crude oil, refinary products and cement have attained 11 per cent growth in 2006-07. Thus the growth prescription has been brought about by manufacturing and infrastructre growth, in spite of low growth of agriculture. Growth composition shows that in total GDP agriculture is 18.5. per cent, industry 26.4. per cent and services 55 per cent.

This has given a new dimention to the economic growth achieved recently. Depending on this high-tech capital industries the country's growth trajectory is proceeding from take-off stage, to self-sustained growth. We shall see the implications of this macro strategy in the next section. Let us now see the impact of economic reform at the state level in general and the N.E. states in particular (Table 11.4).

Economic reform has brought about an upsurge in over-all economic growth of Indian economy. The performance of a number of states is equally good. However, a number of states are languishing at a low-level equilibrium.

In the N.E. states Tripura, Manipur and Mizoram stepped ahead of Nagaland and Assam, Arunachal Pradesh and Meghalaya. Net per capita state domestic products of NE states (Tables 11.3 and 11.4) show poor records. A major state, Assam lags behind many major states as well as some smaller states in NE region.

Table 11.4: Per Capita Net State Domestic Products (State Income) 1993-94 to 1999-2000 at 1993-1994 prices

Arranged in Rank Order of Growth Rate in Descending order

States	*1993-1994*	*1994-1995*	*1995-1996*	*1996-1997*	*1997-1998*	*1998-1999*	*1999-2000*	*Exponential growth rate*
Pondicherry	9781	9644	9841	13468	17390	19300	19895	15.7
Chandigarh	19699	19653	21962	24055	24614	27717	29661	7.5
Karnataka	7835	8095	8363	8997	9228	10282	10928	5.8
West Bengal	6781	7121	7514	7903	8438	8900	9425	5.7
Sikkim	7550	7113	7633	8236	9125	9440	9816	5.6
Rajasthan	6192	7158	7209	7851	8641	8735	8272	5.3
Tamil Nadu	8952	9944	10191	10583	11240	11775	12504	5.3
Delhi	18023	19454	18996	20189	22326	22977	24032	5.0
Manipur	5833	5565	5612	6331	6773	7014	2744	4.8
Goa	15602	15655	16180	18320	18122	NA	NA	4.7
Gujarat	9796	11535	11649	13206	12937	13493	13022	4.6
Tripura	5350	5107	5339	5724	6115	6556	6604	4.5
Maharashtra	12290	12299	13406	13784	14114	14312	15410	3.8
Andhra Pradesh	7447	7739	8083	8531	8214	9018	9318	3.6
Kerala	7938	8516	8748	8987	9079	9542	10107	3.6
Himachal Pradesh	7364	7934	7966	8326	8583	8905	9177	3.5
Haryana	11090	11617	11570	12664	12544	13003	13709	3.4
Uttar Pradesh	5358	5411	5498	5965	5848	6117	6373	3.2
Meghalaya	6705	6679	7150	7161	7331	7727	2826	2.8
Madhya Pradesh	6537	6441	6686	6962	7022	7407	7564	2.8
Bihar	3810	4086	3723	4093	4203	4397	4475	2.7
Punjab	12714	12778	12989	13687	13705	14007	14678	2.4
Jammu & Kashmir	6443	6619	6732	6978	7128	7296	7435	2.3
Orissa	4797	4913	5053	4852	5272	5264	5411	2.0
Mizoram	15192	16191	15354	15896	16357	NA	NA	1.3
Nagaland	9129	9410	9646	9880	10287	9118	NA	0.8
Arunachal	8579	8407	9424	8635	8693	8401	9170	0.4
Assam	5715	5737	5760	5793	5796	5664	5978	0.4

Source: Vol. III, p. 74, Tenth Plan.

The low growth of the NE states may be ascribed various reasons. However one important reason is the low growth of agriculture. Along with most of major states of the country the NE states, particularly their industrial sectors are in a poor state.

Impact of economic reform in the social sector is equally dismal particularly in the states which are lagging in general rate of growth. Although the NE states have high rate of literacy, in March 2006 number of out-of-school children is 3,75,820 in Assam and 1,09,636 in Meghalaya. Intensity of poverty has come down in many states as a result of intervention programme of the government. Table 11.5 presents the head count ratio of poverty of the major states as revealed in NSS 61st round. Here the index of Assam in used for all NES. 20 per cent head count poverty ratio of Assam in 2004-05 is certainly not any big problem compared to BIMARU states. Social expenditure of the NE states (Table 11.6) indicates that only Tripura spends 37.6 per cent of total expenditure in the social sector, and other NEs spend a lower percentage. Nagaland spends 27.6 per cent and Sikkim only 22.2 per cent of total expenditure in the social sector.

The North-Eastern states with 7 per cent of area of the country, is the home of around 4 per cent of total population of the country. All the NE states are special category states. However compared to position that prevailed two decades ago the present position of the states, barring one or two, are for the better. Economic reform has therefore yielded some good results.

But the area has great potentiality of industrial production, power generation and exports that remain unexplored. What is the agenda or new vision of the N.E.? This includes physical and financial infrastructure, eduction, skill and knowledge formation, credit delivery and extension of small enterprises. The agenda in further detail is explained here.

The NE states can be classified in two categories better performing and poor performing states. While Mizoram and Tripura are better performing states, the rest of the NE states are poor performers. According to 2001 census, Nagaland and Arunachal Pradesh have a high rate of growth of population. In fact, the determinants of present high rate of growth of Indian economy are largely absent in NE states. Neither did the earlier push factor of green revolution take place in this region nor were

Table 11.5: Head Count Ratio of Poor in Major States

States	*Rural*			*Urban*			*All*		
	1993	*1993-94*	*2004-05*	*1993*	*1993-94*	*2004-05*	*1993*	*1993-94*	*2004-05*
Andhra Pradesh	27.31	16.64	10.85	37.49	37.63	25.41	29.75	22.30	14.80
Assam	41.92	44.43	23.05	23.07	10.19	3.83	40.03	40.46	20.46
Bihar	64.89	57.24	43.06	47.49	36.54	31.66	62.71	54.50	41.53
Gujarat	27.92	22.44	19.76	22.38	29.44	11.96	31.11	24.92	16.75
Haryana	21.77	26.62	13.42	25.47	17.54	15.06	22.59	24.26	13.92
Himachal Pradesh	17.77	29.27	12.50	16.01	8.26	3.87	17.83	27.37	11.61
Jammu and Kashmir	25.23	19.73	4.81	17.48	7.38	4.81	23.57	16.75	4.81
Karnataka	37.51	30.24	23.73	42.88	39.67	33.04	39.08	33.25	27.65
Kerala	38.46	26.49	12.27	45.11	25.45	20.86	39.81	26.22	14.48
Madhya Pradesh	48.21	40.43	38.17	53.11	48.29	34.44	49.23	42.30	37.21
Maharashtra	45.04	37.66	30.36	39.69	34.74	29.42	43.13	36.50	29.95
Orissa	67.52	50.11	47.76	49.19	41.02	43.34	65.31	48.35	47.07
Punjab	14.03	13.72	9.55	23.52	11.83	5.57	16.88	13.14	8.12
Rajasthan	37.72	26.80	18.91	38.81	31.55	29.81	37.95	27.96	21.48
Tamil Nadu	56.22	32.99	22.96	47.94	38.92	34.06	53.48	35.20	26.31
Uttar Pradesh	46.38	42.33	34.06	49.47	36.15	30.29	46.94	41.08	33.25
West Bengal	61.56	37.35	28.49	31.05	23.24	18.05	53.60	33.45	25.67
All India	45.76	37.26	29.18	42.27	32.56	26.02	44.93	36.02	28.27

Source: N.S.S. 61st Round, p. 5, Mahedra Dev. C Ravi, Poverty and Inequality, All India and States, 1983-2005, *EPW*, February 10, 2007.

the present market-oriented private investments found in this area.

Table 11.6: Social Sector Expenditure to Total Expenditure

1.	Andhra Pradesh	41.7	38.8	29.3
2.	Arunachal Pradesh	32.1	33.9	31.2
3.	Assam	34.7	37.3	32.4
4.	Bihar	38.3	42.7	30.5
5.	Chhattisgarh	—	—	37.7
6.	Goa	40.9	29.1	31.4
7.	Gujarat	36.4	35.3	29.0
8.	Haryana	32.4	30.8	24.2
9.	Himachal Pradesh	39.7	36.1	29.0
10.	Jammu & Kashmir	29.7	24.3	27.9
11.	Jharkhand	—	—	44.1
12.	Karnataka	37.0	38.2	28.5
13.	Kerala	43.7	42.1	36.2
14.	Madhya Pradesh	41.3	41.3	24.7
15.	Maharashtra	35.2	33.6	28.1
16.	Manipur	33.4	34.0	33.6
17.	Meghalaya	39.3	42.0	35.8
18.	Mizoram	30.6	43.0	35.6
19.	Nagaland	83.0	32.1	27.6
20.	Orissa	36.5	48.3	28.9
21.	Punjab	28.1	22.7	17.8
22.	Rajasthan	39.5	39.2	34.1
23.	Sikkim	33.3	15.1	22.2
24.	Tamil Nadu	45.1	39.2	32.6
25.	Tripura	43.1	43.8	37.6
26.	Uttaranchal	—	—	36.6
27.	Uttar Pradesh	38.5	33.7	28.6
28.	West Bengal	46.9	41.2	29.1
29.	Delhi	—	41.6	33.1

Source: RBI Bulletin, February 2007.

During the planning period public investments were scanty and in the present liberalized regime private investments are thin for various reasons.The NE states thus remain neglected in both the regimes over the last fifty years.

Hill economy is affected by private profiteers and tribals are rendered homeless. On the other hand, import of foreign products is reducing the demand for the traditional products of the tribal economy which provided the source of employment for women. First, let us see the pattern of growth at all-India and state levels.

Table 11.7: Statewise Outstanding Credit of Scheduled Commercial Banks (including RRB), March 2005

State	*A/c per '000 population*		*A/C as per Branch*	
	Rural	*Urban*	*Rural*	*Urban*
Northern Region	55.29	75.26	675.03	770.76
North Eastern Region	35.16	41.04	792.48	780.58
Andhra Pradesh	40.88	—	522.13	—
Assam	30.28	47.72	661.79	777.58
Manipur	15.57	38.85	514.76	963.57
Meghalaya	41.04	51.15	510.54	643.08
Mizoram	56.79	29.89	370.39	1198.36
Nagaland	24.44	—	547.73	—
Tripura	88.42	45.79	1561.01	690.63
Eastern Region	44.70	46.96	887.50	692.80
Central Region	45.26	49.23	858.59	797.14
Western Region	45.61	121.36	662.81	1530.40
Southern Region	136.16	185.97	1576.88	2121.09
All-India	64.16	103.62	999.94	3320.99

Source: RBI Bulletin, March 2007.

Table 11.8: Domestic (a) Saving and (b) Investment Rates in India

(per cent)

Period/ Year	*Household*		*Private Corporate Sector*		*Public Sector*		*Total*	
	(a)	*(b)*	*(a)*	*(b)*	*(a)*	*(b)*	*(a)*	*(b)*
1970s	12.2	7.6	1.6	2.4	3.7	8.2	17.5	17.6
1980s	14.6	7.8	1.8	4.2	3.0	10.0	19.4	21.2
1990s	18.5	8.5	3.7	6.7	1.0	7.8	23.2	24.5
2000-05	22.2	11.6	4.8	6.8	–0.2	6.6	26.8	26.3
Memo.								
2004-05	21.6	11.4	7.1	9.9	2.4	7.1	31.1	31.5
2005-06	22.3	10.7	8.1	12.9	2.0	7.4	32.4	33.8

Source: RBI Bulletin, March 2007.

Table 11.9: Selected Indicators of India's Progress

Year	*Per Capita Income (in 1993-94 prices) (Rs.)*	*Poverty (Per cent)*	*Literacy (Per cent)*	*Life Expectancy (Years)*	*Power Capacity (MW)*
1951	3,687	45	18	32	1,362
1961	4,429	45	28	41	4,653
1971	5,002	52	34	46	14,709
1981	5,352	43	41	50	30,214
1991	7,321	35	52	59	64,000
2001	10,308	26	65	65	102,000
2005	12,414	19	—	—	118,419

Source: RBI Bulletin, December 2006.

Table 11.10: All-India and State-wise Poverty Line and All-India Percentage Distribution of Poor Persons

States	*Rural*						
	1983		*1993-94*		*1999-2000*	*2004-2005*	
Andhra Pradesh	72.66	4.70	163.02	3.49	262.94	292.33	2.81
Assam	98.32	2.89	232.05	3.86	365.43	392.77	2.54
Bihar	97.48	16.82	212.16	19.22	333.07	355.92	20.11
Gujarat	83.29	2.73	202.11	2.65	318.94	355.38	2.97
Haryana	88.57	0.93	233.79	1.45	362.81	413.10	0.96
Himachal Pradesh	88.57	0.30	233.79	0.60	367.45	405.26	0.32
Jammu & Kashmir	88.57	0.51	233.79	0.52	367.45	394.75	0.18
Karnataka	83.31	4.15	186.63	4.04	309.59	335.88	3.85
Kerala	99.35	3.22	243.84	2.43	374.79	419.74	1.34
Madhya Pradesh	83.59	8.49	193.10	9.03	311.34	323.86	11.14
Maharashtra	88.24	7.71	194.94	7.91	318.63	363.70	7.97
Orissa	106.28	6.58	194.03	5.94	323.92	325.46	6.99
Punjab	88.57	0.73	233.79	0.84	362.68	406.67	0.71
Rajasthan	80.24	4.35	215.89	4.08	344.03	375.10	4.03
Tamil Nadu	96.15	7.56	196.53	4.94	307.64	353.23	3.47
Uttar Pradesh	83.85	17.87	213.01	20.95	336.86	373.91	22.80
West Bengal	105.55	10.47	213.01	8.04	350.17	381.18	7.80
All-India	89.45	100.00	205.56	100.00	327.56	359.89	100.00

Note: All-India figures are in percentage and figures in second column are in percentage.

Source: As Table 11.5.

Table 11.10(A): All-India and State-wise Poverty Line and All-India Percentage Distribution of Poor Persons

States	*Urban*							*All-India (per cent)*		
	1983		*1993-94*		*1999-2000*	*2004-2005*		*1983*	*1993-94*	*2004-05*
Andhra Pradesh	106.43	7.54	278.14	9.35	457.40	526.79	6.89	5.31	4.89	3.88
Assam	97.51	0.66	212.42	0.37	343.99	382.06	0.18	2.41	3.03	1.92
Bihar	111.80	6.53	238.49	5.99	379.78	456.35	6.46	14.64	16.07	16.53
Gujarat	123.22	6.40	297.22	6.11	474.41	517.51	3.18	3.51	3.47	3.03
Haryana	103.48	1.16	258.23	1.08	420.20	498.93	1.37	0.98	1.37	1.07
Himachal Pradesh	102.26	0.08	253.61	0.05	420.20	475.21	0.03	0.25	0.47	0.25
Jammu & Kashmir	99.62	0.36	253.61	0.20	420.20	475.71	0.17	0.48	0.45	0.18
Karnataka	120.19	7.25	302.89	7.96	511.44	601.40	8.32	4.81	4.97	5.02
Kerala	122.64	3.56	280.54	2.66	477.06	562.02	2.22	3.29	2.48	1.57
Madhya Pradesh	122.82	9.08	317.16	10.78	481.65	507.29	9.82	8.61	9.45	10.79
Maharashtra	126.47	15.52	328.58	17.08	539.71	626.25	17.08	9.04	9.71	10.36
Orissa	124.81	12.44	298.22	2.51	473.12	536.68	3.32	5.70	5.12	6.03
Punjab	101.03	1.72	253.61	1.05	388.15	462.52	0.66	0.94	0.89	0.70
Rajasthan	113.55	4.48	280.85	4.61	465.92	540.30	5.52	4.38	4.21	4.42
Tamil Nadu	120.30	11.83	296.63	11.08	475.60	652.62	13.48	8.47	6.80	6.10
Uttar Pradesh	110.23	15.75	258.65	14.55	416.29	482.41	15.66	17.42	19.43	20.93
West Bengal	105.91	7.17	247.53	6.13	409.22	474.42	5.62	9.77	7.59	7.23
All-India	117.50	100.00	281.35	100.00	454.11	523.18	100.00	100.00	100.00	100.00

Note: All-India figures are in percentage and figures in second column are in percentage.
Source: As in Table 11.5.

III. The Agenda

How can the NE states make the best use of reform programme in order to break the stagnation and ignite the forces of growth?

(a) The first important task is to regenerate the rural economy of NE states. This includes agriculture and non-farm activites. If the area has missed the opportunity of the first green revolution, time has now come for application of the second green revolution with diversification of agriculture and raising the productivity of land. Alternative strategy has to be applied for transfoming agriculture from the subsistence level to a profitable and commercially viable venture. High varieties of seeds, fertilizer, water management, new technology and credit are important ingredients of the alternative package of second green revolution. High value production and linkage with agro-manufacturing activites are the core components of the package. Water management is a serious issue for the NE states. Flood water discharge and excess water management of Brahmaputra is the most important part of agricultural development strategy.

(b) Infrastructure is the first channel of transmission of globalisation. Lack of road connectivity, rail linkage and marketing structure are the serious deterrents to the flow of market force. Within the region interstate movement and outside the region connectivity with rest of India has to be vigorously taken as a first priority. Greater interstate movement of men and material will break the stagnation and stimulate prosperity.

(c) Application of skill and modern technology is the prime mover of economic reform and growth. The North Eastern states have to upgrade the skill and technical knowledge so that new area of production and exploration of innovation is possible in this area of abundant resources. Since the knowledge-based innovation is the basis of modern manufacturing industry, the NE states have to catch up with this trend by upgrading education and skill formation.

(d) Economic reform will take root in the rural and urban sector if sufficient capital is available. Sufficient flow of rural credit and venture capital in the urban sector will be an important condition for effective reform. Financial institutions will have to extend their network more extensively in different productive channels. The current microfinance strategy of SHG programme has to be extensively implemented. The flow of institutional credit to the rural sector has to be increased. The banking sector has to be more aggressive and committed for credit flow to the rural sector. The present trend (Table 11.7) of limited credit flow has to be altered and the credit-deposit ratio to the NES has to be raised.

(e) Economic reform has brought about rapid growth in those states where human resource development has attained high level. In the NE states human resource development is at a low level. Hence rapid economic growth in the NE states must be preceded by human resource development.

(f) Massive public investment in infrastructure and setting up of modern industries will encourage private investors. Liberalization will pay only when extensive private investment can be applied without subversion. Public investment in road and transport is the urgent task. Market oriented reform agenda will be effective when the market connection is strong.

IV. Look East Policy

The Look East policy consists of two components: (a) the link with the ASEAN and other countries, (b) the New Industrial policy for the Eastern Region.

One aspect of economic reform is the opening of the external sector. Liberalization of foreign trade with South-Eastern Asian countries and Bangladesh is an important channel of economic growth of the NE states. Current Look East policy of Government of India is yet to be effective. Even the SAFTA is yet to take force. Globalisation will pay high dividend only when the otherwise closed economy of NE becomes an open economy and the products of NE states will find an extended market in other parts of Asia. NE require extensive push force of development. While the extensive public investment in infrastructure will encourage domestic entrepreneur, the trade relation with ASEAN countries will equally strengthen the capital inflow and increase employment.

Currently the Central Government has declared package of new Industrial policy. The two components of policy are (a) subsidies to the private investors, and (b) massive public investment in infrastructure development. Rail, Road and air connectivity of each with other north-eastern states is a significant step. Along with that, the development of mineral, water and forest resouces of the region also has become an important part of the industrial policy.

Small and medium enterprises (SME) have been specially emphasized. Since the NE states have some specialised skill in textile, craft and traditional goods, those can be exported by standardization of their quality. Globalization opens an opportunity.

V. Governance

Economic reform has come to stay in our country and over the decade the reform process has set a new direction of growth. The task particularly in the NE, has now to reap the benefits of reform and reduce the negative aspects of that process. The NE states have to first attain high rate of growth permitted within their factor endowments and scientific adaptation. Correspondingly equity and social justice have to be established with efficient governance and distributive mechanism. Growth, poverty elimination and employment are the three components of reform agenda. When the NE states can attain higher growth, poverty will be reduced through host of special poverty elimanating programmes and employment generating activities. Given the admirable skill and dexterity of tribal people in the NE states reform agenda will have a better impact on the society when those earnestly adopted.

Governance comprises efficiency in management of resources, maintenance of peace, effective administration for containing corruption in delivery of inputs and welfare materials. Specifically governance must ensure inclusive measures through (a) decentralisation, (b) dissemination of information, (c) ensuring people's participation, (d) mobilisation of resources and (e) establishment of sound revenue system.

State finances in the NE states are in coldrum. Although these are all special category states, the state finance gives the wrong signal of weak financial management. The matter is worse due to widespread leakages of public fund to the under-ground activities.

VI. Conclusion

Inclusive growth of the NE states through the implementation of reform programme is based upon a number of conditions. Over the last fifteen years of economic reform the rates of economic growth of most of the NE states are unsatisfactory. In order to catch up with the fast growthing states, the north east region has to take up certain steps along the following lines.

(a) In many states like West Bengal agriculture is the growth propelling force. In the NE states diversification and improvement of agriculture is most important. (b) Human resource development and improvement of high skill and knowledge is also a priority area. (c) Improvement of physical infrastructre and greater connectivity, more inclusive financial delivery system are also important agenda. (d) More extensive interaction with East Asian countries through effective application of Look East Policy is an additional opportunity of this region. (e) Improvement of the quality of governance, effective implementation of decentralization and improvement of law and order are certain important issues which have to be taken into consideration in order to reap the benefits of LPG programme.

REFERENCES

Banerjee, Amalesh (2007): *Economic Reform and Vision of North-East,* Kanishka Publishers, New Delhi.

Banerjee, Amalesh (2002): *Planning and Development of North-Eastern States.* Kanishka Publishers, New Delhi.

Banerjee, Amalesh (2006): *India's Economic Reform and Response of States.* Kanishka Publishers, New Delhi.

Government of West Bengal (2004): West Bengal Human Development Report.

Government of India (2005): Econmic Survey.

Himangshu (2007): Recent Trends in Poverty and Inequality, *E.P.W.* Feburary 10.

Passap, P.M. (2006): *In Defence of Regional Economic Development in India,* Akanksha Publishing House, New Delhi.

Planning Commission: Tenth Five Year Plan.

Vijay Sankar, P.S. (2007): Rural Credit in 20th Century. India, "Overview of History and Perspective", *E.P.W.,* April 14-20.

12

Globalization and FDI in North East India

G.P. Prasain and *E. Nixon Singh*

Introduction

Globalization is an inevitable and irreversible process of economic, technological, social and political integration of the world wherein an economy should capitalize on its positive aspect, mutilating the negative ones as the most important challenge perhaps for the new millennium. In this process a single but large free market economy called global market is emerging in the world with a lot of opportunity for people to tap into. Albeit, the bottom line for success in such a market is competition. The degree of success in the competition will determine the extent of the opportunities that one can avail of. In fact, no country can afford to remain isolated from globalization process. One should make oneself compatible to share the benefits arising out of increased efficiency of integrated economic activities of the world. It is, therefore, necessary to understand the current status of globalization for setting course for future to reap the full benefits of globalization.

In fact, new international economic order began after the Second World War in which four major trends emerged in the world including the expansion of international trade, financial flows, movement of people and spread of knowledge. In the beginning, many underdeveloped countries including India stayed away from this trend considering it as a peril rather than an opportunity. However, in recent time, most of the countries in the world have liberalized their economy, realizing the benefits of increased efficiency of new economic order. In the case of India, the government faced severe foreign exchange crisis by 1990 and its foreign exchange reserve had reached an unsustainable level. The requirement of such reserve in sufficient volume that arose mainly due to the domestic pressure to meet the imports of essential commodities and the external pressure to liberalize Indian market forced the Government of India to accelerate the liberalization process in India.

The integrated new global market does not ensure equal benefit to all. Likewise, liberalized economy of India and its rapid growth does not provide equal benefit to all regions of the country. The North East which is the poorest and remotest part of the country, is yet to enjoy significant share of the benefits of liberalization process due to one or other factors. Though India becomes one of the powerful magnets of FDI in Asia, the inflow of FDI in the NE Region is quite meagre. This underlines a need to find a suitable strategy for stepping ahead in this regard.

The present paper will focus on the line of above arguments and its broad objectives will address: (i) FDI atmosphere in India particularly in the post-liberalization period; (ii) the degree of 'absorption capacity' of FDI in the NE Region; and (iii) the strategy required in the region for its attractiveness to FDI.

FDI in India

Indian economy has been entering into progressive liberalization since the beginning of 90s. Its reform has been realized in the form of industrial delicensing, liberal FDI regime, freedom to invest and expand, simplification of investment procedures, tax rationalization, current account convertibility and WTO compatibility etc. It is popularly known as the first generation reforms. Recently as the second generation reform started, there has been progressive reforms in the form of public sector disinvestments, cutting fiscal deficit, amendments to crucial economic legislations, further tax reforms, financial sector reforms, labour reforms and corporate governance etc. Government of India replaced FERA, 1973 that regulated all foreign exchange transactions with Foreign Exchange Management Act (FEMA), 1999. Many of the FDI approval process have been simplified to smoothen the approval process with the enactment of this act. Progressive liberalization of FDI policy in India can be justified with Table 12.1 below:

Table 12.1: Progressive Liberalization of FDI Policy in India

Parameter	*1991*	*2002*
FDI Policy	FDI in 35 high priority industries on automatic route upto 51 per cent; 100 per cent under very special circumstances; Foreign Technology Collaboration (FTC) opened up.	FDI in all activities except for a small negative under automatic route; ownership restrictions only in 14 industries based on strategic/Security concerns; FTC by and large under automatic route.
Institutional Framework	Three-tier (FIPB-EPCI-CCFI) FIPC	Two-tier (FIPB-CCEA); Transparent and time-bound approval mechanism; FIPC; FIIA for investment facilitation.
Approvals	US $ 0.22 billion	US $ 2.3 billion (most sectors under automatic route) US $ 76 billion (cumulative)
FDI as per cent of GDP	0.03%	0.5%
Inward FDI flows as per cent of GFCF	0.6%	2.4%
Inward FDI stock as per cent of GDP	0.7%	3.6%

Source: Government of India Policy, UNCTAD World Investment Report 2001 and the World Bank, World Development Report, 2000-01.

A major feature of economic reforms in India since 1991 has been a progressive liberalization of external capital flows especially non-debt creating one like FDI and Foreign Institutional Investment (FII)[1]. With the progressive liberalization of FDI policy, the perception of the foreign investors in India has also been changing. It was argued that compared with FIIs and NRI deposits, the FDI inflow tend to have a large impact on domestic capital formation, effect a smaller fall in domestic saving and create less problems for monetary and fiscal authorities.[2] FDIs are also usually preferred over other forms of external finance because they are non-debt creating and non-volatile. India appears on course to attract a record $ 12 billion of FDI this fiscal year, going by inflows in the first four months which have almost doubled from a year ago at $ 2.9 billion.

"FDI inflows in April–July 2006-07 increased by 92 per cent to $ 2.9 billion from $ 1.5 billion during the previous corresponding period. India is set to receive $ 12 billion in the current year against $ 8.3 billion in 2005-2006".[3]

India has received $ 50.1 billion of FDI since 1991. Of this, $ 16 billion has come in since April, 2004. While investment into India is increasing Indian companies too are making investments abroad. According to figures compiled by CRISIL for Confederation of Indian Industry, the total investment by Indian companies abroad in April–August 2006 is $ 2.8 billion.[4]

Investment Opportunity in India

The following factors had made investment opportunities favourable in India:

- Easily accessible to the vast domestic and South Asian market.
- A large developing economy.
- Sufficient skilled man-power available at competitive price.
- Low cost of infrastructures and operation.
- English is widely spoken and undestood.
- Rupee is convertible on current account at market-determined rate.
- Sophisticated financial sector.
- Sophisticated legal and accounting system.
- Rich base of mineral and agricultural resources.
- No restriction of using foreign brand name.
- Liberal government policy environment, i.e. freedom of entry on investment and choice of technology.
- Corporate tax holidays for 5 years for 100 per cent export oriented units in Export Processing Zones.

In short, investment climate in India is favourable. Nevertheless, when a foreign investor considers making any new investment decision, it goes through four stages in the decision making process and action cycle, namely, (a) Screening, (b) Planning, (c) Implementing, and (iv) Operating and expanding. The biggest barrier for India is at the first screening stage itself in the action cycle.[5] So the problem at the screening stage needs to be seriously addressed through improving the image of India and conveying a positive approach towards foreign investment.

Benefits of FDI in the Globalized Economy of India

The different categories of FDI are commonly grouped into two, such as (a) 'Greenfield' investments, i.e. those to build new capacity; and (b) 'mergers and acquisitions (M&A)', i.e. the acquisition of assets of existing local firms. The benefits of these two groups of FDI, as of all other capital flows, to developing countries are expected to arise through two major mechanisms (i) by increasing total domestic investment, and (ii) by increasing productivity. Ultimately, both effects are expected to result in higher growth rates. Further, the benefits of FDI can be elaborately discussed on the following points.

FDI can be used in bridging the financial gap between the quantum of funds needed to sustain a level of growth and the domestic availability of funds.

It gives opportunities to Indian industry for technological upgradation, gaining access to global managerial skills and practices, optimizing utilization of human and natural resources, and competing internationally with higher efficiency.

FDI and offshoring activities like IT, contact centres, distribution back office, knowledge management, research and development etc. are also creating jobs, exports and new industries. Indian cities like Bangalore, New Delhi and Mumbai have arisen as popular offshore hubs in Asia. The largest transnational corporation in the world, General Electric has 2,400 employees in India, conducting R&D in a variety of areas ranging from aircraft engines and medical devices to consumer durables.[6] FDI can in fact enhance domestic competition if a global player sets up a

Greenfield project, thus expanding the number of domestic producer of the goods.

FDI Inflows in India : Emerging Trends

FDI can enter India through two possible channels: (i) The automatic route under which companies receiving FDI need to inform the RBI within 30 days of receipt of funds and issuance of shares to the foreign investor, (ii) For sectors that are not covered under the automatic route, prior approval is needed from the Foreign Investment Promotion Board (FIPB). Further, FDI is permitted in India in the forms through financial collaborations, joint ventures and technical collaborations, capital market via euro issues and through private placements. But some sectors are prohibited for FDI to enter like retail trading (except single brand product retailing), atomic energy, lottery business, and gambling

Table 12.2: FDI inflow in India

(Million Dollars)

Year	*FDI Inflows*	*% of increase/decreased*
1991-92	129	—
1992-93	315	144.18
1993-94	586	86.03
1994-95	1,314	124.23
1995-96	2,144	63.16
1996-97	2,821	31.57
1997-98	3,557	26.09
1998-99	2,462	–30.78
1999-2000	2,155	–12.46
2000-01	4,029	86.96
2001-02	6,130	52.14
2002-03	5,035	–17.86
2003-04	4,322	–7.18
2004-05 (P)	5,652	30.77
2005-06 (P)	7,751	37.13

Source: RBI Bulletin (June 2004 and July 2006).

Note: FDI data have been revised since 2000-01 with expanded coverage to approach international best practices. Therefore, these data are not comparable with that of previous years.

and betting.[7] However, it is worth mentioning here that the policy of Foreign Direct Investment has been reviewed on a continuing basis and several measures announced from time to time for rationalization/liberalization of the policy and simplification of procedures.

Acceleration of liberalization process and globalization of FDI prove significant change in the FDI policy of the country. Taking regular review and its appropriate changes in the policy, now, FDI is permitted in most of the sectors of our economy. The FDI inflows since 1991-92 till 2005-06 is gradually increasing from US $ 129 million in 1991-92 to US $ 7,751 million in 2005-06 with some volatility in between the years. Till 1997-98 there has been gradual increase since 1991. Then the fluctuation started from the next financial years, i.e. 1998-99 onwards (Refer Table 12.2).

Country-wise and Sector-wise FDI Inflows in India

The major sources of FDI inflows to India have been UK, USA, Germany and Japan. But Mauritius remained the largest source

Table 12.3: Foreign Direct Investment to India* (Country-wise)

(US $ million)

Countries	*2004-05 (P)*	*2003-04*	*2002-03*
Mauritius	820	381	534
USA	469	297	268
UK	84	157	224
Germany	143	69	103
Netherlands	196	197	94
Japan	122	67	66
France	44	34	53
Singapore	64	15	39
Switzerland	64	5	35
South Korea	14	22	15
Others	300	218	227
Total	2,320	1,462	1,658

* Data in this table excludes FDI inflows by way of acquisition of shares by non-residents under Section 6 of FEMA, 1999.

P Provisional.

Source: RBI, Annual Report, 2004-05.

during 2002-05 followed by USA, UK, Germany etc. which can be seen in Table 12.3.

The largest recipient sector of FDI inflow during August 1991 to December 2005 was Electrical Equipments (including computer software and electronics) followed by Transportation Industry, Services Sector, Telecommunication etc. Sector-wise FDI inflows of 10 important sectors in order of their ranks are shown in Table 12.4.

Table 12.4: Sector-wise FDI Inflows to India from August 1991 to December 2005 (Ten Largest Recipient Sectors)

(US $ million)

Ranks	*Sector*	*Amount of FDI Inflows*	*%age of total Inflows*
1.	Electrical Equipments (including Computer Software and Electronics)	4,885.88	16.50
2.	Transportation Industry	3,143.09	10.24
3.	Services Sector	2,971.66	9.64
4.	Telecommunications	2,890.12	9.58
5.	Fuels (Power and Oil Refinery)	2,521.49	8.41
6.	Chemicals (Other than Fertilizers)	1,889.51	5.86
7.	Food Processing Industries	1,173.51	3.67
8.	Drugs and Pharmaceuticals	948.54	3.18
9.	Cement and Gypsum Products	746.79	2.54
10.	Metallurgical Industries	627.32	2.12

Source: India Investment Centre.

State-wise Scenario of FDI Inflows

Though the FDI inflow has been increasing in the country with its liberalization process, there is a lot of difference in the volume of FDI received in different states within the country. States like Delhi, Maharashtra, Karnataka, Tamil Nadu, Andhra Pradesh, Gujarat etc. are getting major share of FDI inflow in the country. The volume of FDI received in all seven states of NER together share only 0.04 per cent of the total inflow during January 2000 to March 2006 (Refer Annexure-2). Indeed, when we compare these states mentioned above with that of NER, they have advantages in getting benefits of liberalized India in the way of better infrastructure, availability of capable manpower in competitive prices, growth of IT hubs, better industrial regulations, provision of large incentives and of course, better care by the Central Government. In short, these states have better investment climate. In a major step ahead, these states have already played important role themselves and took many initiatives, like forming FDI policy of their own. Whereas, the NE India is yet to answer questions like—what role state can play?; How to design the incentives? etc. Moreover, mindset of Government of India needs valuable change from simply categorizing of the NER only as a strategic area that needed concentration of military strength towards the idea of taking initiatives so that the region be covered by the growth process of liberalized India.

Socio-economic Profile of NER

This region consists of eight states, viz. Assam, Arunachal Pradesh, Manipur, Meghalaya, Mizoram, Nagaland, Tripura and Sikkim. It covers as area of 2.62 lakh sq. km. and account for 7.9 per cent of total geographical area of the country. With a total population of 39 million (2001), it accounts for 3.8 per cent of total population of India (NER-Databank). The western side of the region is connected to the eastern part of the Indian subcontinent by a narrow land corridor, sometimes referred to as the 'Siliguri Neck' or 'Chicken's Neck'. The region is one of the most biodiverse regions in the world. The NER as a whole is placed amongst the poorest regions in the country. The per capita income at Rs. 12407 is less than the national average of Rs. 17978 (2001-02). In spite of covering 7.9 per cent of the country's total geographical area, NER produces only 1.5 per cent of the country's total food grain production (NER-DB). However, agriculture provides livelihood support to about 70 per cent of the population in the region. The region has considerable unexploited and untapped natural resource potential. Industrially, the region continues to be the most backward and main factors are poor governance, lack of infrastructure development, inadequate supply of electricity, violence and extortion etc. In terms of the Index of Social and Economic Infrastructure for 1999, computed by the Eleventh Finance

Commission, the North East scores the lowest at 76 as against 104 for the Western states, 119 for the Northern states and 147 for the Southern states.[8]

Regarding investment, the main problem faced by the region is the lack of capacity to absorb the huge quantity of funds in the absence of training and expertise to successfully come up with implementable location specific projects. Many central aid packages are being left out largely unimplemented in this region and consequently, neutralize the intended impact of the packages. The main factors behind this problem may be of poor monitoring, lack of an accountability and non-adherence to the set time frame for project execution. Thus, the government's development strategy for the NER during the Tenth Plan, strongly emphasizes capacity building for the effective use of aid, policy and institutional reforms and sustainability of the development efforts with the involvement of the people of the region. While such packages/aids are necessary, it is not sufficient by itself to ensure that development actually takes place. Therefore, State Government concerned should carefully implement such package so as to make it effective, as effectiveness is as important as the volume of aid to achieve growth in the region.

Investment Climate of NER

In spite of the fact that the region is better known to the outside world as a land of rugged beauty and constant turmoil, its abundant natural resource endowment is certainly a matter of important concern for investment. Therefore, the region's enormous investment potential needs proper exposure to the outside world. The investment potential in NER can be looked in the following areas, activities and opportunities.

- Easily accessible to the large South Asian market as the region share a length of about 4,600 kms. border with China, Myanmar, Bhutan and Bangladesh.
- *Tourism*—The region has its definite identity due to its peculiar physical, economic and socio-cultural characteristics. It is a virtual paradise for travellers

searching for continuous joy in pilgrimage, adventure, culture, nature, heritage, wildlife, golf, polo and many more. Indeed, there is investment potential in Eco-Tourism including Hotel and Restaurant, Spa, Resort, Amusement Parks, etc.

- *Handicrafts and Handlooms*—The area enjoys a pride of place in India with its rich heritage of artistic craftsmanship. Moreover, handloom forms an essential part of everyday life of the people in the NE of India. There is sufficient demand in the outside world for these products because of their uniqueness in design, quality and material-in-use.
- *Hydroelectric Power*—The region has a large hydroelectric power potential. It has 34,920 MW accounting for 41.50 per cent of all-India potential (NER—Databank).
- *Horticulture and Floriculture*—NER has vast potential for commercial plantation of fruits and vegetables. The region is suitable for plantation of citrus fruits like lemon, lime, orange, etc. A new thrust area is cultivation of mushroom. Many rare herbs are also available in the region which can be used in producing pharmaceutical products. Such plants can also be grown for commercialization.
- *Mineral-based Industry*—Due to abundant mineral endowment in the region, there is investment potential in this sector too. There exists India's oldest and major petroleum and natural gas source, with shares of 16 per cent and 8 per cent respectively of total production of the country. Other major mineral resources available in the region includes coal, limestone and dolomite etc. (NER—DB).
- *Forest-based Industry*—The Region accounts for 26 per cent of the forest cover of India. It is the largest producer of bamboo in the country (NER—DB). Much more than this fact, trees of heterogeneous types are available in the thick forest of the region. Scope for establishment of rubber industries may be worth mentioning in this context.

- *Tea*—The NER is the largest producer, sharing about 55 per cent of the total production of tea in India. Moreover, the region is the world's single largest tea growing region, sharing about 16 per cent of the total tea growing area of the world (NER—DB).
- *Jute and Silk*—The region is suitable for plantation of jute and mulbery. In fact, it produces premium quality of jute and silk. It indicates investment scope in this sector.
- *Agro-based Food Processing Unit*—There is enough scope for establishing such industries in the NER, as well as preservation and packaging business of fruits and vegetables.

Besides, investors can also look for electronic industries including computer hardware and software, and IT related industries, with the growth of skilled labour that induced demand for such industries in the region. Biotechnology becomes another thrust area in the region because of new well-organized farming including organic farming for commercialization which is in demand increasingly now-a-days.

Absorption Capacity of FDI in NER

The present paper will deal with only subjective concepts and make no attempt to get absolute volume of absorptive capacity. Indeed, the absorption capacity of a region generally depends upon:

- *Human Capital*—There is less opportunity to produce skilled labour and expertise of various fields in large quantity in the region. The number of Technical and Industrial School in most of the states except Assam till the year 2000 are very few, e.g. only one in Mizoram. Also the number of universities that provide higher stream of study is only 11 (eleven) altogether in the seven states (excluding Sikkim) till the year 2000. [Basic Statistics of NER (2002)] Under these circumstances, effective utilization of huge investment becomes a challengeable task in the region.

- *Infrastructure*—Investment like FDI can be absorbed only when there exist efficient infrastructures like electric power, well developed networks of roads, railways, airports, riverines etc. However, in the NER, actual position of power supply during 2001-02 was 1043 MW which had a shortfall of 42 MW than the total requirement of 1085 MW. Also road per 100 sq. km. as on 31-03-1997 in the region was 54.8 km. only against 74.9 km. of all India average. Moreover, Broad Gauge railhead touches only Assam and Nagaland; any heads of railways is yet to touch Meghalaya [BS of NER (2002)]. Condition is more worse regarding Airports and River routes in the region.
- *Financial Market Structure*—Credit sanction/Deposit Ratio (%) of Scheduled Commercial banks in 1998 (March end) was only 29.9 against 55.5 of all India average. Investment plus credit deposit ratio (%) of Scheduled Commercial banks in 2001 (March end) as per utilization in NER was 49.3 against 64.3 of all India [BS of NER (2002)].
- *Political Stability*—Political condition in these states of NER changes largely in the tune of political environment of the centre. One fact that needs to be taken into account is that the continuity of the programmes gets snapped with the change in government at the centre and in the state concerned of NER. It creates a situation of investment uncertainty in the region.
- *Government Service*—These services in the NER is unsatisfactory. Delayed service, corruption, lack of coordination among various departments, low degree of responsibility etc. are some of the main characteristics associated with these services in the region. All these make a real hindrance in the implementation of any development project.
- *Incentives*—Some incentives as a part of new industrial policy of NER 1997, are provided by the Centre in the form of tax concession, tax holidays, investment subsidies, etc. as a step to boost growth of industry in the region.

However, State-specific incentives are not properly designed in NER, may be due to lack of capital resource, expertise or some other reasons.

In the light of above background, it is certain that NER has low absorptive capacity of FDI. Albeit, the story should not end here but can continue somewhere beyond it. By closely integrating the NE States with the rest of India and its neighbours, such regionally focused projects will help re-position the region as a strategic base for foreign and domestic investors for tapping the vast contiguous markets of SAARC countries, South East Asia and the People's Republic of China. With the adoption of 'look east policy', the Govt. of India is already active to improve relations with the South Asian neighbours through the BIMSTEC, SAFTA, SASEC, ASEAN, APEC, etc. The NER can now be used as gateway to these countries. The benefits of market integration with these countries can be derived through NER as a mouth and further spread to other part of the country through the 'chicken neck'. The Government of India need to take more responsibility as the State Governments concerned have limited capacity to improve the absorption capacity of FDI in the region.

Strategies Required in NER to Attract FDI Inflow

Under globalization, heaven is defined as an American salary, a Chinese cook, an English house, and a Japanese wife. Similarly a hell is defined as a Chinese salary, an English cook, a Japanese house, and an American wife.[9] All good things of all sides of the globe are amalgamated for heaven and from bad to worse things for hell. We have to devise our strategies accordingly to make our nation India in general and North East in particular a heaven. Further, old skepticism about FDI disappeared from the mind of policy-makers and scholars, and now they tend to take the beneficial effects of FDI for granted, turning to the question of how to attract FDI. In this junction, in order to develop a concrete strategy for attracting FDI inflows in NER, we have to look into diversified areas of the followings:

- To change the mindset of Government of India which still consider the NER as its far eastern periphery rather than as gateway to South-East Asia. As well as mindset among local people needs to change suitably with globalization to preserve tradition and culture in dynamic sense.
- Great emphasis has to be given on development of transport infrastructure including airports and riverine, since such a thing is a cause for concern amongst the investor community.
- Extensive and regular exposure of local experts of various trades to modern and up-to-date technology of the world is highly needed.
- Governance in the region needs strengthening for capacity building.
- Incentives by the government, both Central and States should be widely advertised to popularize possible opportunities.
- A special marketing effort is needed for export oriented FDI—inflow in the region.
- Security and terrorism concerns weigh heavily on the mind of foreign investors. So, security provision to investors must be a part of the strategy to attract FDI.
- Investment promotion agencies of the region like Industrial Development Corporation of each state should incorporate special incentive provision in their policy to attract FDI.

In fact, as it happens anywhere, the important factors that we can consider for attracting FDI in NE Region of India are political stability, sound macro-economic policies, availability of infrastructure and suitable government incentives, rules and regulations regarding entry and operations etc. In this context, facilitating private sector-led growth is desirable in the region since across the world, disinvestments have acted as a magnet for FDI across the world.

Recently Government of India had reviewed the FDI policy and decided to allow FDI upto 100 per cent under the automatic route in many sectors. Out of these sectors, NER can seriously look for FDI inflows in the few sectors, shown in Annexure-1.

So far only a small volume of FDI has been attracted towards NER of India. The amount of FDI approved in NER during August 1991 to December 2004 was only Rs. 769.90 million sharing only 0.03 per cent of total of all India. (Refer Table 12.5). The actual inflow in this region during January 2000 to March 2006 was Rs. 41.74 crores, sharing only 0.04 per cent of total of all India (Refer Annexure-2).

Table 12.5: FDI and FTC Approved in NER (August 1991 to December 2004)

States	*No. of Approvals*			*Amt. of FDI Approved*	
	Total	*Tech.*	*Financial*	*Absolute Value (Rs. Million)*	*% to Total of All India*
Arunachal Pradesh	2	0	2	110.60	0.004
Assam	19	15	4	14.95	—
Manipur	2	0	2	31.85	—
Meghalaya	5	0	5	529.60	0.021
Mizoram	1	0	1	15.22	—
Nagaland	2	1	1	36.80	—
Tripura	4	1	3	30.88	—
Sikkim	N.A.	N.A.	N.A.	N.A	—
Total of NER	35	17	18	769.00	0.030
Total of All India	26,466	7,644	18,802	25,04,196.00	100.00

Source: Ministry of Commerce and Industry, Department of Industrial Policy and Promotion.

Government Policy *vis-à-vis* FDI Inflows in NER

Indeed, an absolute FDI policy for NER as a whole is required to improve investment climate of the region which at present is very unfavourable, considering its low absorption capacity and absence of specific incentives for attractiveness of FDI. With the hardening of globalization process in the world, incentives also become a very important determinant of international investment decisions besides the traditional factors discussed above. This situation creates an issue—How should FDI incentives for NER specific be designed?

Designing an efficient incentive programme in such a region where unfavourable investment atmosphere prevails, is a complex task. Rather, it is a challenge under globalized and liberalized structure of Indian economy because competition between host government within as well as outside that are trying to attract FDI, tends to shift profit to foreign multinationals. But, such an incentive under global competition is often proved justified on the ground that it supports local firms to strengthen their capacity to absorb foreign technology and skills, including training, R & D activities, linkage between foreign and local firms.

Incentive programmes can be designed under two tiers such as central incentives through the regional nodal agencies like NEC, DoNER, NEDFi etc. for the NER as a whole and state incentives for specific FDI inflow. Such Central incentives can be provided under the schemes like Special Economic Zone (SEZ), Export Promotion Zone (EPZ) and Industrial Promotion packages that can be announced from time to time.

Central incentives may include fiscal incentives such as tax holidays and lower taxes for foreign investors, financial incentives such as grants and preferential loans to MNCs. States in NER may have limited capacity to provide financial help to foreign investors but measures like market preferences, infrastructure choice and sometimes even monopoly rights to foreign investors can be taken up in the core area of development of the state. Such steps, sometimes, may be useful to highlight the intention of the concerned state to MNCs and Central Government as well, embodying the eagerness of the state to develop the specific sector. However, effectiveness of such incentives needs scientific calculation and it has to be implemented suitably.

Conclusion

In these days of globalization, transforming NER of India under its prevailing social and economic atmosphere into an attractive destination for FDI is a daunting challenge. The region, at present, has low absorption capacity of FDI. The situation suggests a necessity for a vibrant FDI policy for the region specific, incorporating some concrete strategies for attracting FDI. The attitude and mindset of the people in the centre and states as well need remarkable change. Along with this, all opportunities which crop up in the region from time to time need proper and widespread exposure to outside world. In short, a strong publicity mechanism needs to be put in place in the context of advanced IT-scenario of the world.

Nevertheless, FDI is clearly not a panacea for the growth; it may provide a private benefit at a public cost. We, therefore, should not rely for investment only on FDI but should do all needful to stimulate domestic investment in many new activities for the sustainable growth. NER sought for special attention of the Central Government because of its social uniqueness and economic backwardness. The issue is a matter of serious consideration of the NE States by the centre as India's gateway to South-East Asia under its "Look East Policy" and not as states on its far eastern periphery.

NOTES

1. Rakshit, M. (2006): *On Liberalizing FIIs.*
2. *Ibid.*
3. Kamal Nath, Union Commerce Minister, *The Times of India,* October 7, 2007, p. 9.
4. RBI Report 2005-06.
5. Government of India (2002): 'Report of the Steering Group on FDI', p. 21.
6. Laudicina, P. and White, J.M. (2005): *India and China: Asia's FDI Magnets.*
7. Government of India (2006): 'Rationalisation of the FDI Policy', p. 3.
8. Jonghe, L.D. (2004): 'Address presented in the Second NE: India Business Summit'.
9. Reddy, A.R. (2005): *Impact of Globalisation of Indian Economy,* p. 1.

REFERENCES

Government of India (2006): "Rationalization of the FDI Policy" Press Note No. 4 (2006 Series). Ministry of Commerce and Industry, Department of Industrial Policy and Promotion (FC-Section).

Government of India (2002): "Report of the Steering Group on Foreign Direct Investment", Planning Commission, New Delhi, August.

Government of Manipur, Department of Comm. and Industries (2002): "Investment Potentials in Manipur", NE India Business Summit, Mumbai.

Hussain, W. (2004): "India's North East: The problem", Interaction on the North East Observer Research Foundation, New Delhi, November 28.

Jonghe, Louisde (2004) Country Director, ADB: Address made on Second NE Business summit 20 and 21 January, New Delhi organized by DoNER and Indian Chamber of Commerce.

Laudicina, P. and White, J.M. (2005): "India and China: Asia's FDI Magnets"—*Far Eastern Economic Review:* Vol. 168, No. 9, October.

Penalver, M. (2002): "Globalization, FDI and Growth: A Regional and Country Perspective" (Paper prepared for the Capacity Development Workshop on the State, the Private Sector and Civil Society: Partnership for Development and Democracy). United Nations Department of Economic and Social Affairs. Marrakesh, Morocco. December 10-13.

Rakshit, M. (2006): "On Liberalising Foreign Institutional Investments"—*EPW,* March 18, Vol. XLI, No. 11.

Reddy, A.R. (2005): "Impact of Globalization on Indian Economy"—*Journal of Global Economy,* Vol. I, No. 2, April–June.

Reserve Bank of India, (2002): "Report of the Committee on Compilation of Foreign Direct Investment in India", Mumbai, October.

Singh, Bhupal (2005) RBI, Mumbai: "Methodology, Compilation and Reporting of FDI Statistics: The Indian Experience." Expert Meeting on Capacity Building in the area of FDI: Data compilation and Policy formulation in Developing Countries, UN Conference on Trade and Development, 12-14 December.

ANNEXURE-1

Sectors in Which FDI is Allowed upto 100 per cent under the Automatic Route and where NER can look for attracting FDI

Sector/Activity	*Conditions*	*Relevant Press Note (PN) issued by D/o IPP*
1	*2*	*3*
Airport-Greenfield Project	Subject to Sectoral regulations notified by Ministry of Civil Aviation	PN 4/2006
Alcohol Distillation and Brewing	Subject to licence by appropriate authority	PN 4/2006
Rubber Processing and Warehousing		PN 4/2006
Cigar and Cigarettes Manufacture*	Subject to industrial licence under the Industries (Development and Regulation) Act, 1951	PN 4/2006
Coal and Lignite mining for Captive Consumption by Power Projects, and iron and steel, cement production and other eligible activities permitted under the Coal Mines (Nationalisation) Act, 1973.	Subject to provision of Coal Mines (Nationalisation) Act, 1973	PN 4/2006
Construction Development Projects, including housing, commercial premises, resorts, educational institutions, recreational facilities, city and regional level infrastructure, townships.	Subject to conditions notified *vide* PN 2/2005	PN 2/2005 and PN 2/2006
Floriculture, horticulture, development of seeds, animal husbandry, pisciculture, aqua-culture, cultivation of vegetables, mushrooms, under controlled conditions and services related to agro and allied sectors.		PN 4/2006

(contd.)

(contd.)

Sector/Activity	*Conditions*	*Relevant Press Note (PN) issued by D/o IPP*
1	*2*	*3*
Power including generation (except Atomic energy), transmission, distribution and Power Trading.	Subject to provision of the Electricity Act, 2003	PN 2/1998 PN 7/2000 and PN 4/2006
Tea Sector, including tea plantation	Subject to divestment of 26 per cent equity in favour of Indian Partners/ Indian public within 5 years and prior approval of State Government for change in land use	PN 6/2002
—Trading for export —Trading of items sourced from small scale sector*	Subject to guidelines for FDI in trading issued by Department of Industrial Policy and Promotion *vide* PN 3/2006	PN 4/2006
Special Economic Zones and Free Trade Warehousing Zones covering setting up of these zones and setting up units in the zones.	Subject to special Economics Zones Act, 2005 and the Foreign Trade Policy	PN 9/2000 PN 2/2006 and PN 4/2006

* Entry route is FIPB (not automatic).

Source: Press Note No. 4 (2006 series) [PN 4/2006], Department of Industrial Policy and Promotion, Government of India.

ANNEXURE-2

FDI Inflows[1] Received (as per reported to Regional Offices of RBI) (from January 2000 to March 2006)

Ranks	*RBI's Regional Office*[2]	*State covered*	*Amount of FDI Inflows*		*Percentage with FDI*
			Rupees in crore	*US$ in million*	*inflows (in rupee terms)*
1.	New Delhi	Delhi, Part of UP and Haryana	23,074.29	5,116.9	24.58
2.	Mumbai	Maharashtra, Dadar and Nagar Haveli, Daman and Diu	20,535.68	4,533.5	20.90
3.	Bangalore	Karnataka	6,984.17	1,546.3	7.44
4.	Chennai	Tamil Nadu and Pondicherry	5,432.52	1,193.2	5.79
5.	Hyderabad	Andhra Pradesh	3,083.46	681.1	3.28
6.	Ahmedabad	Gujarat	2,883.90	631.9	3.07
7.	Chandigarh	Chandigarh, Punjab, Haryana, Himachal Pradesh	1,481.41	320.3	1.58
8.	Kolkata	West Bengal, Sikkim, Andaman and Nicobar Islands	1,277.24	280.7	1.36
9.	Panaji	Goa	494.42	107.6	0.53
10.	Kochi	Kerala, Lakshadweep	333.45	73.6	0.54
11.	Bhubaneshwar	Orissa	315.88	70.6	0.34
12.	Bhopal	Madhya Pradesh, Chhattisgarh	168.84	37.3	0.18
13.	Guwahati	Assam, Arunachal Pradesh, Manipur, Meghalaya, Mizoram, Nagaland, Tripura	41.74	9.0	0.04
14.	Jaipur	Rajasthan	18.76	4.2	0.02
15.	Patna	Bihar, Jharkhand	2.74	0.6	0.00
16.	Kanpur	Uttar Pradesh, Uttaranchal	0.03	0.0	0.00
17.	Not indicated[3]		27,764.24	6,118.8	29.57
	Total		93,892.76	20,726.3	100.00
18.	Advance of Inflows (from 2000 to 2004)		8,962.22	1,962.8	—
19.	Stock Swapped		284.87	61.2	—
20.	RBI's Schemes		589.15	134.4	—
	Total		103;729.00	22,884.7	—

Notes 1. Includes 'equity capital components'only.

2. The Region-wise FDI inflows are classified as per RBI's—Region-wise inflows, furnished by RBI, Mumbai.

3. Represents inflows through acquisition of existing shares by transfer from residents. For this, region-wise informationis not provided by the RBI.

Source: India Investment Centre.

13

Globalization and its Impact on Society
Some Reflections

Surojit Sen Gupta

Globalization has become the overarching fact to be reckoned with in the contemporary world. It is one of the challenges that all the countries have to meet and wrestle with. Globalization in its generic and broadest sense is viewed as a "movement of history itself", and it seems as "capital's final of the rest of the world" (Tandon, 1997). Globalization has been defined in two inter-related contexts. One is the economic context and the other is non-economic which broadly includes social-cultural, historical and political dimensions of globalization. In the economic context, the European Commission defined globalization as the process by which markets and production in different countries are becoming increasingly interdependent due to the dynamics of trade in goods and services and flows of capital and technology. The non-economic domain of globalization is more complex than its economic counterpart as it includes all aspects of human life of which economy is only a part. In this sense globalization has been defined as the intensification of worldwide social relations which link distant localities in such a way that local happenings are shaped by the events many miles away and *vice versa.*

The main objective of the process of globalization is to achieve competitive efficiency for optimization of resource use at the global level. This depends on the withdrawal of trade barriers or at least lowering of tariff walls and loosening of restrictions on flow of resources across national frontiers. The process of globalization is not the panacea for the developing countries to quicken the pace of achieving growth and development for eradication of poverty. The process of globalization, as pointed out by the UNDP, has not ensured the distribution of benefits evenly amongst nations and within nations. The process of globalization does not only affect economic performances of people but also their social, political and cultural institutions and traditions (Shroff, 1999).

The phenomenon of globalization is in itself global and hence an all-encompassing and global response to this phenomenon is an obvious imperative. Globalization has led to the interdependence of economies, internationalisation of capital markets and integration of telecommunications. Globalisation leads to interconnections and interdependence in the economic sphere and cultural homogenisation of the social arena. It has a 'differential reach' (King, 1995) with its consequences not uniformly experienced across the globe. Globalization is also perceived as a process of capital accumulation that has gone on for centuries and intensified and heightened by modern technological innovations. The consequences of globalization relate to denationalisation of nation-states, erosion of state sovereignty, centralisation of corporate power and concentration of the global structure of power, increased poverty and dependency among developing countries, transnationalisation of production and standardisation of consumer wants and cultures.

Globalization has enhanced interconnectedness among states mediated by new communication technology transcending the existing organisational administrative and legal boundaries. The States have little choice but to actively cooperate and collaborate with one another, resulting in what is known as crises. Global interconnectedness has reduced border controls which earlier served to restrict transactions in goods and services, production factors and technology, ideas and cultural interchange.

Globalization creates, through export led expansion, the potential of rapid overall output growth, increasing national wealth and contributing to improve living standards, in developing countries. Globalization is the access to a wide variety of consumption goods, new technologies and knowlege. Globalization allows the access to ideas and international best practices in different fields and realms: a new production technology, a new managerial practice; it can even be a certain set of institutions that has proved successful in other places, and, eventually, a model of society. The tension of globalization lies in its social effects. As globalization is often associated with increased instability of output and employment, this affects, among other things, job security. Globalization gives a premium to people with sophisticated skills, high levels of education, and entrepreneurial traits. These are people better equipped to survive and succeed in the more competitive world brought about by globalization. The mirror image of this is that unskilled labour, uneducated workers and marginalised population are likely to benefit less in a more competitive world economy.

Globalization has both positive and negative potentials as well as dangerous consequences. Positively, it avails the scientific, medical and other innovations. The negative consequences of globalization are growing unemployment due to inability of smaller industries to compete with the international industrial firms, loss of livelihood for traditional artisans and craftsmen, and migration of people for jobs and livelihood. As globalisation takes the whole world as a single market, labour is loosing its voice, national governments are losing their powers, and due to privatization, there is loss of guaranteed employment, which are the common features all over the world. Globalization currently is viewed from multiple perspective—functional, critical, post-modernist and ethical. Variety of views and options prevail and one has to grapple with niceties and angularities in each of them.

Globalization, thus, refers primarily to integration of various nations of the world at the economic level through free competition in the world market, technology transfer and sharing of information with the help of the expanding electronic media and satellite communication. However, the primary thrust of globalization is economic integration, it also includes as a significant component of cultural exchange and emergence of a cosmopolitan culture through creation of new habits of thoughts and feeling, new behaviour patterns and attitudes which are supposed to be in broad consonance with the operation of the logic of world market.

Globalization—The Concept

Globalization broadly referred to the condition of complex conectivity evident in the world today, seen in terms of both the compression of the world and the intensification of global consciousness. Some theorists held that globalization had been occurring throughout history, only its form had changed over the different historical periods.

Globalization could be called the concept of the 1990s. It had began to replace terms like 'internationalization' and 'trans-nationalization' as a more suitable concept for describing the ever intensifying networks of cross-border human interaction (Hoogvelt, 1997). Globalization referred to an empirical condition of the complex connectivity evident everywhere in the world in recent times. Complex connectivity involved overcoming cultural distances through penetrating experiences provided through education, employment, consumer culture and the mass media and had been described as being more significant than technological advances and physical mobility (Tomlinson, 1999).

Giddens defined globalization as "the intensification of world-wide social relations which links distant localities in such a way that local happenings are shaped by events occurring many miles away and *vice versa*" (Giddens, 1990). Robertson observed that globalisation as a concept that referred, both to the compression of the world and the intensification of consciousness of the world as a whole (Robertson, 1998). In McLuhan's terms, globalization means, the world was reduced to a 'global village' (McLuhan, 1989). McGrew also spoke of globalization as "simply the intensification of global interconnectedness" and stressed the multiplicity of linkages it implied—goods, capital, social-institutional relationship, technological developments, ideas all readily followed across territorial boundaries. In its peculiar 20th century manifestation of a holistic consciousness, globalization involved the relativization of individual and national reference points of general and supranational ones. It involved cultural, social and phenomenological linkages between the indivdiual self, national society, international system of societies and humanity in general (Waters, 1995). Martin Albrow, accepted globalization on its own terms and spoke of "The Global Age" which is replaced by the "Modern Age". The Modern Age had been supplanted and superseded by a new Global Age, with its own axial principles and specific cultural imaginary.

R.G. Harris, defines globalization as an economic process, that is, 'the increasing internationalisation of production, distribution and marketing of goods and services' (cited in Streeten, 2001). To Thomas Friedman globalization is 'that loose combination of free trade agreements, the internet and the integration of financial markets that is erasing borders and uniting the world into a single, lucrative, but brutally competitive market place' (Streeten, 2001). Another aspect of this overwhelming economic view is that globalization is nothing but liberalisation. Liberalisation refers to a process of removing government imposed restrictions on movements between countries in order to create an open borderless world economy. The evidence for such globalization in recent decades can be found in the widespread reduction or even abolition of regulatory trade barriers, foreign exchange restrictions, capital controls, etc. Streeten states, 'Globalization is transforming trade, finance, employment, migration, technology, communications, the environment, social systems, ways of living, cultures, and patterns of governance' (Streeten, 2001). A World Bank publication defines globalization as 'the growing integration of economies and societies around the world'. This is a complex process that affects many aspects of our lives (World Bank, 2002).

Castells looks at the present global age as essentially a net-worked society. The Sociologist Manuel Castells has distinguished a network of society in which a new space of flows exists alongside the old space of places (Castells, 1989). Many scholars look at globalization as a process emanating from the West and therefore another form of Westernization. They equate globalization with westernization or modernization. This view propounds that globalization is a dynamic process whereby the social structures of modernity are spread the world-over, normally destroying pre-existent cultures and local self-determination in the process (Spybey, 1996; Taylor, 2000). Globalization in this sense is sometimes described as an imperialism of McDonald's Hollywood, Cocacolanisation, MTV generation and CNN (Schiller, 1991). A leading thinker belonging to the hyper-globalization, Kenchi Ohame believes that globalization is leading us to a "borderless society", a world in which market forces are more powerful than national governments (Ohame, 2002). Thus, in all spheres of life, issues could no longer be looked at independently from a local perspective. Globalization had connected the whole world, which is clear from the above definitions.

Aspects of Globalization

Globalization has many aspects which can be understood from the different historical processes and the philosophical angle that developed in global civilization. Globalization in the history of mankind is seen as a continuous process of changing societies beyond frontiers in one or the other way. The tools may differ, the techniques may change and the extent and expanse may vary but the items to be changed have largely remained the same—political power structure, economy, people and culture. It is true that 'total globalization' is not possible and it is also true that the process of globalization of any age and any kind has not been uniform in all societies; it does not create the same kind of effects in different and/or the same society for a variety of reasons. Historically, globalization may be divided into: Pre-historic; Pre-industrial revolution; Post-industrial revolution; and after the electronic, informatic and ultra-economic revolution. The factors responsible for man's global thrust may be enumerated as (1) satisfaction of basic needs; (2) development of science and technology; (3) industrial revolution; (4) communication—electronic and information revolution; (5) republican/democratic revolution; and (6) growth and development revolution. These factors are psychological, sociological, political and economic in nature but it is difficult to place anyone of these in any specific category because they have related effects and cannot be isolated.

The economic theory relates globalization to the model of a free world market without restrictions of competition and mobility, a global mass culture and a world-encompassing infromation society. The economic aspects of globalization refers to an increasing interconnectedness and interdependence of enterprises through the world market. This interdependence results from world trade, foreign and joint venture investments, worldwide consumer markets, process of concentration, international financial speculation, international labour migration, computer networks etc.

The technological aspect of globalization is seen in the field of information technology and telecommunication. Large parts of production in a global age concerns information, and a flexible network of temporary contracts and cooperative relations that functions via computer net and mobile phone, often on a world scale. Information technological paradigm have fundamentally changed society with regard to its material basis. The new technological paradigm engenders an increased flexibility of organization in production, consumption and management and thus minimises the distance between economy and society.

Political aspect of globalization is closely connected to the discipline's historical points of reference-society and nation-state in early modernity. Scholars agree that governance has become much more dependent on international organizations, bilateral and multilateral contract, so that sovereignty decreased. According to Bamyeh (1993), in spite of globalization process, governance is still represented and expressed in the inter-state system, while transnational forms of political organization have been comparatively less successful. The reason is that international organizations such as the UN are made up by nation-state representatives and quota, while non-state organisations and associations are excluded from participation. A nation-state is very often more important from the international than the domestic perspective. The internationalization of this inter-state system was related to the spread of standard rules of representation according to the nation-state model.

The ideological aspect of globalization is what has been called triumph of liberalism/capitalism. Lack of an alternative to liberalism gives rise to the view that capitalism is an inevitable world-wide phenomenon. With the collapse of socialism as a serious alternative to capitalism, the opportunity of the non-western world took the advantages. International organizations like World Bank and IMF force national governance into structural adjustment and deregulation, opening up these countries for western products and capitals.

Cultural aspects of globalization are tied up with modernity. Most commonly it is assumed that it is spreading from the west and produces uniformity and standardization through technological, commercial and cultural synchronization. Naderveen Pieterse (1994) holds against this simplistic view that globalization of culture is not the same as Americanization or Westernization. Cultural communication exposes the communicators to foreign influences. Not only non-western societies were infiltered by an American way of life being supposed to cause a loss of cultural values, customs and manners, also America and Europe adapted elements of foreign civilizations: like eastern philosophies, food, music, dress styles and others. The two-sided permeation of cultural influences engenders a new global hybrid culture.

The environmental aspect of globalization refers to the world being a highly fragile ecological system. An imbalance causes effects on both local and global levels. People have realised that technical progress and production of risks for the environment are closely related to each other. According to Ulrich Beck (1986), who calls the contemporary western societies 'risk societies', global risks are quite different. Western people and educated people in non-western societies are aware of these risks due to reflexivity of modernity, spread of information by news, scientific warning, ecological movements and first visible effects on the globe like changing weather conditions such as global warming and green house effect. The severe problem of global risks is that they cause enormous cumulative effects on the entire world.

Sociological aspects of globalization have much deeper implications for individuals and community as well as their institutions and traditions. Sociologists of the classical period had identified globalizing solvents in terms of capitalist commodification (Marx), differentiation (Durkheim) and rationalization (Weber). Of all the classical theorists, the one most explicitly committed to a globalizing theory of modernization was Karl Marx. Globalization caused an enormous increase in the power of the capitalist class because it opened up new markets for it. Emile Durkheim's legacy to globalization was his theories of differentiation and culture. The state and the collective consciousness had progressively become more weak and abstract in order to encompass intra-society diversity. All this implied that industrialization tended to weaken collective commitments and open the ways for dismantling the boundaries between societies. Max Weber identified rationalization as the globalizing agent. To him the success of rationalization and with its spread from the seedbed origins of Calvinistic Protestantism to infect all western culture implied a homogenization of cultures as well as reduced commitment to such values as patriotism and duty. But even this globalizing effect was restricted to Western Europe. Weber saw no prospect of the spread of rationalised culture preferences to say India or China that he regarded as inevitable mired in religious traditionalism. In the contemporary period Roland Robertson has specifically defined the term globalization sociologically. According to him globalization needed to be understood as involving a dialectic of opposed principles and tendencies—local and global, particular and universal, integration and differentiation.

Social scientists like Adam Smith, Emile Durkheim, Max Weber and Karl Marx had envisaged this process and urged at length on merits and demerits of cataclysmic changes being introduced by modern science and technology. The pursuit of science and technology laid the first foundation of social change, slowly transforming agricultural societies and their institutional practices, first in the Great Britain, and then in other countries. Colonial conquest marked one distinct method of expanding frontiers for promotion of trade and economic hegemony, with visible effects on the human and natural resources of the colonised or subject countries—be that of India and others.

It can be seen that all the aspects of globalization are closely connected to each other. Globalization is not entirely a new phenomenon. It has been slowly maturing and has a history of over 300 years. Industrial revolution marked the beginning of this process, and it steadily penetrated other areas of social activity and institutions with varying consequences.

Impact of Globalization on Society and North East Situation

The North Eastern region of India comprises the eight states of Assam, Arunachal Pradesh, Manipur, Meghalaya, Mizoram, Nagaland, Sikkim and Tripura. Often described as a microcosm of the Indian subcontinent, the North East is represented by all three physiographic divisions of the country, though on much smaller scale, the northern mountains, the central plain and the southern plateau. The global perspective in different spheres of life is not an unknown phenomenon in North East. Through the access to the phenomenal development of information technology the people of this region are already aware of the global dimension of various developments and issues that affect their social, cultural, economic and political life styles and activities.

Globalization as a process signifies a unique development in human history. Globalization leads to homogenization of culture in some significant aspects throughout the world. Unlike the colonial cultural contact that several developing countries had with the West, and which was largely characterised by a relationship of domination rather than reciprocity, globalization involves interdependency, reciprocity, and exchange of mutual skills and resources in a large measure. It does not, however, imply that the nature of reciprocity in global relationships is entirely equilateral, the inequalities based on capital, technological powers and human resources remain. The process of globalization which involves tremendous exposure of local, sub-regional and regional social entities to the forces of market and finance on the one hand, and on the other access to revolutionary means of communication and media influence and energise latest aspirations in the society.

Expansion of the telecommunication networks, people's additional exposure to entertainment and information through mass media, particularly television and cinema, have brought about changes in north east in people's taste and have also increased the incidence of acceptability of inter-regional and international items in areas of food, beverages, dress patterns and many other cultural traits in the style of living. For instance, low waist jeans is now a popular dress among young women in North East. The use of modern cosmetics, generally of western origin has become very fashionable these days and it also commands a big market. North East is also not lacking behind in the homogenisation of consumption patterns and life styles. The prominent popular western cultural symbols, such as coca cola, blue jeans, rock music, cheese, pizza and burgers are spread all over the region. The cultural threats globalization poses to society are noted as displacement of the traditional norms of society due to exposure to de-humanising and retrogressive cultural products in the form of fashion, entertainment, consumerism, exposure to new styles of life etc., leading to high incidence of crime and moral deviance such as prostitution, cult of money and loss of traditional humanistic values, disintegration of family life and age-old family values like care of the elderly and emotional bond among the members of the family.

The anxiety about the preservation of cultural identity in the process of globalization seems to vary in terms of quality and urgency depending upon the initial social and cultural structues of the society as well as their economic resilience. The reaction also varies on account of the degree of social, structural and cultural differentiation and pluralities in the society. Ethnically more homogeneous a society is, greater is the ease with which the leadership and people of that society get ready to cope up with the challenges of globaiization. But in societies where ethnic and social structural pluralities and differentiation are strong, cultural and social anxieties on account of globalization remain very acute. The impact of globalization in North East shows uneven results across inter-ethnic, inter-religious and inter-class boundaries. The lack of access to the fruits of globalization on acount of the educational, economic and social deprivation among the people enlarge their anxiety and hostility towards globalisation.

The process of globalization sets into motion several predictable as well as unanticipated problems in societies and cultures that encounter it in course of their social and economic developments. The recent economic turmoil in the society and the kind of social, economic, political and ethnic crises have created the flight of international capital and financial collapse of the economy, and has made both the public and the intelligentsia extremely sceptical about the bounties of the reform paradigm of globalization. Globalization also did not contribute to the cultural, social and economic integration of the people in North East through equitable access to the fruits of developments available through its process. Cultural conflcits and contradictions sharpen in the society due to the unlimited exposure of the people to foreign cultural and entertainment packages beamed from television and other mass media.

The scope of trade market which accelerates the processes of globalization poses formidable cultural problems in the society. The new changes have been noticed in the life style, consumption pattern, production of cultural objects and their marketing and usages. These changes have altered the traditional modes of cultural expressions, usage of language and communication media at the local and regional levels. These have also created many sub-cultures of an entirely new kind in the urban areas.

The changes in consumption and life style have been accelerated by the market forces and their changing structure. Today, markets in North East are not only extensive in their network, they also perform qualitatively new functions. With an extensive network of markets and with changing style of living, the challenges of globalization to local culture assume deeper significance. Now-a-days, there no longer exists a link between community and the hereditary occupations. The changes in the life style and increased use of consumer durables such as motor-cycle, cars, electronic devices like television, computer, music system, washing machine, etc. is also visible. Globalization of markets has led to conversion of traditional objects of art and aesthetics having mostly ritual uses in the local communities into marketable communities. This has not only rapidly disrupted the autonomy of folk cultures, but also destabilised the life of the artisans by creating new networks of competition.

In the educational field globalization did not escape from its trap in North East. Privatization and commercialization of education can be seen to be happening in the form of private tuitions, coaching classes and vocational training. It also exists in the form of expensive boarding schools. The competitive ethos that globalization created has made entire private business in tuition and coaching classes a concurrent reality along with formal education. The enrolment in the traditional programmes of degree (Arts/Science/Commerce) is continuously declining and the rush is seen in the job oriented and professional courses like Management. The increasing involvement of information and communication technology in education poses serious challenges to most of the existing institutions, while it also offers them enormous opportunities. The collapse of the barriers of time and space is one of the severest challenges in the post-modern era in education. At the same time, new sources of dissemination of information and knowledge are emerging at a rapid pace, ushering in not just globalization, but more importantly, an era of fierce competition in education in the North Eastern states.

To sum up, globalization as it functions today has compelled many to think beyond the conventional paradigm, and come up with new and more radical ways of addressing the onslaught on their fundamental rights to survival and development. The era of globalization has thrown up several avenues to states and regions to obtain the advantages of the worldwide economic boom and concomitant industrial, technical and market oriented linkages available to all the participants. The process of globalization does usher in many technological, economic, ecological and social changes in society which affect the traditional cultural styles, forms and ideologies and North East is no exception from this. The extent to which it may constitute a threat to local and regional cultural identities depends largely on the manner in which globalization is perceived by the concerned people in the society.

REFERENCES

Arjun, Appadurai, (1996): *Modernity at Large: Cultural Dimensions of Globalizations,* University of Minnesota Press, Minneapolis.

Bamyeh, M.A., (1993): Transnationalism, *Current Sociology* 41(3) (Special Issue).

Behera, M.C., (2004): *Globalization and Development Dilemma: Reflection from North East India,* Mittal Publication, New Delhi.

Castells, Manuel, (1989): *The Informational City: Information Technology, Economic Restructuring and the Urban Regional Process,* Oxford, Blackwell.

D'Souza, Leela, (2005): *The Sociology of Religion: A Historical Review,* Rawat Publications, New Delhi.

Das, Gurudas (eds), (1998): *Liberalization and India's North East,* Common Wealth Publications, New Delhi.

Giddens, A., (1990): *The Consequences of Modernity,* Stanford University Press, Stanford.

George, Sudhir Jacob, (2004): India's Federal Experience in the North-Eastern States and Globalization: An Overview, In Harshe, Rajen, *Interpreting Globalization: Perspective in International Relation,* Rawat Publication, New Delhi.

Ganguly, J.B., (2002): 'Globalization and North East India: Opportunities and Challenges for the Twenty-first Century', In Deb, Bimal J., *Development Priorities in North East India,* Concept Publishing Company, New Delhi.

Harshe, Rajen, (2004): *Interpreting Globalization: Perspectives in International Relation,* Rawat Publications, New Delhi.

Hoogvelt, A., (1997): *Globalization and the Post-colonial World,* MacMillan Press, London.

Jogdand, P.G. and Michael, S.M., (2003): *Globalization and Social Movements: Struggle for a Human Society,* Rawat Publication, New Delhi.

King, A., (1995): 'Representing World Cities' in Knox Paul L. and Taylor Peter, (eds), *World Cities in the World System,* Cambridge University Press, Cambridge.

Kothari, Rajni, (1995): Globalization and Revival of Tradition: Dual Attack on Model of Democratic Nation-Building, *Economic and Political Weekly,* March 25.

Lodge, C. George, (1995): *Managing Globalization in the Age of Independence,* Pfeiffer and Co.

Mohan, Sudha, (2004): *Civil Society Activism in the Age of Globalization, Ibid.*

McLuhan, M. and B. Powers, (1989): *The Global Village,* Oxford University Press, New York.

Nederveen, Pieterse J., (1994): Globalization as Hybridisation, *International Sociology* 9(2).

Ohmae, Kenichi, (2002): *The Borderless World: Power and Strategy in the Global Market Place,* London, Profile Books Ltd.

Punalekar, S.P., (2003): *Other Side of Globalization, Ibid.*

Prasad, Rajeshwar, (1999): 'Globalization, Culture and Women's Development', In: Sethi, Rajmohini, *Globalization, Culture and Women's Development,* Rawat Publications, New Delhi.

Robertson, R., (1998): *Globalization—Social Theory and Global Culture,* Sage Publication, New Delhi.

Schrader, Heiko, (2003): *Globalization, Fragmentation and Modernity, Ibid.*

Singh, Yogendra, (2002): *Cultural Change in India,* Rawat Publications, New Delhi.

Singh, Yogendra, (1973): *Modernization of Indian Tradition,* Thompson Press, New Delhi.

Singer, Hans (eds), (2001): *Globalization, Technology and Trade in the 21st Century* (Part-1), B.R. Publishing Corporation, Delhi.

Sarangi, Prakash, (2004): *Role of the State in an Era of Globalization, Ibid.*

Sethi, Rajmohini, (1999): *Globalization, Culture and Women's Development,* Rawat Publications, New Delhi.

Spybey, T., (1996): *Globalization and World Society,* Cambridge, Polity Press.

Streeten, Paul, (2001): *Globalization—Threat or Opportunity.* H. Forlag, Copenhagen, Copenhagen Business School Press, Denmark.

Tandon, Y., (1997): The Emergence of Global Society, *The Electronic Journal,* 8(12).

Tomlinson, J., (1999): *Globalization and Culture,* U.K., Polity Press, Cambridge.

Teltumbde, Anand, (2003): *Globalization and Education for the Dalits: A Perspective for the Future, Ibid.*

Waters, M., (1995): *Globalization,* Routledge, London.

World Bank, (2002): *Globalization, Growth and Poverty-Building and Inclusive World Economy.* (A World Bank Policy Research Report), Co-publication of the World Bank, Washington and Oxford University Press, New York.

14

Economic Policy and the North East
Looking Beyond Neo-Classical Praxis

Gorky Chakraborty

Introduction

The term 'reform' may broadly imply two contrasting scenarios. Firstly, it might deal with a situation, where the 'present reality' is to be 'reformed' in a way so that it might lead to a pre-established 'standard-ideal' position (from which the present reality has deviated) or secondly, it might refer to a scenario, where the 'present reality' has to be 'reformed' in accordance with the 'emerging reality' of new 'standard-ideal' paradigm (emanating from a changed world order). India's economic reforms, in more than one-way, seem to be an attempt related to the latter proposition. Here the aspect of 'reform' has been related with the economic system, where changes were attempted through various policy interventions and restructuring of the economic order.

This paper attempts to analyse the pre-reform economic situation in India, the policies through which the reforms were attempted during 1991, the process of reforms *vis-à-vis* the North Eastern region and along with it tries to ascertain various causes associated with the less than desired performance of reforms in the peripheral states of North East India. In this particular exercise, the paper tries to understand these issues from the standpoint of 'institutional' economics rather than using the much-hyped neo-classical praxis of analyzing development or lack of it, in terms of resource endowment and technological changes.

Pre-reform Scenario[1]

India's *'tryst with destiny'* sought to achieve a relatively autonomous model of economic growth, where 'freedom' not only meant freedom from hunger, illiteracy and impoverishment but also from the domination of 'metropolitan' capital. The Nehru-Mahalanobis model bestowed this responsibility to the Indian state, which due to its newly acquired 'legitimacy' (largely due to a long drawn freedom struggle as well as, the importance that was ascribed to 'it' by various development plans[2] proposed by planners of different ideological standpoints during that period) and was supposed to occupy a pre-emptive position and provide the required stimulus for growth. The state attempted to achieve growth through its policies of expenditure, trade restriction and creation of protective environment for the domestic producers against the commodities and 'reach' of 'metropolitan' capital. In this particular model, the public sector was assigned the dominant role and the 'might' of the Indian state was evident through its presence in each and every 'sphere' of the Indian nation.

But there seemed to be an inherent contradiction in this model of growth as the state attempted to fulfil two conflicting propositions simultaneously. On the one hand, due to its pre-emptive position, it had to maintain a growing rate of expenditure in general and investment expenditure in particular, to create employment opportunities, augment sources of income and expand the domestic market; on the other, due to the feudal-bourgeoisie character of the state, it was unwilling to collect requisite public revenue through direct means (as that would have meant hitting hard those groups and classes, who provided the ideological sustenance to the state) to sustain its ever increasing patterns of expenditure. This basic contradiction of the Indian state, emanating from its class-character remained all throughout the pre-reform period and got reflected in its balance sheet also.

Due to the contradiction mentioned above, deficits started to loom large in various accounts of the Indian economy. The state on its part chose to minimize these deficits by curtailing investment expenditures instead of forcing the 'haves' to contribute resources necessary for maintaining higher investment patterns. This thereby had a negative impact upon the economy in the long run. In fact, during 1951-65, when the state was the biggest investor, the manufacturing sector grew at an annual average rate of 7.8 per cent, while during the subsequent period of expenditure curtailment; it fell to 3.3 and 4 per cent respectively (in the 1970s). On the other hand, despite increasing dose of indirect taxation and hike in administered prices, the surplus in the revenue account turned into deficits by the end of 1970s. Thus restriction of investment expenditure to manage the deficits on the part of the state meant contraction of economic growth (as the state was the only major investor during those days), which the Indian state sought to manage through various short-term and shortsighted measures during the next phase.

Curtailment of investment expenditure was the route to control deficits up to late 1970s while resorting to public debts both external and internal, seemed to be the way out of finance growth during the 1980s. But the deficits could not be curtailed, largely due to the utilization pattern of these debts. On the one hand, the first major domestic fall out of this fiscal stimulus has been an increase in the total fiscal deficit as a share of national income. The gross fiscal deficit, of Central and State Governments together averaged 9.5 per cent of GDP during 1980s and further rose to 10.1 per cent during 1991. This deficit it should be noted, arose not due to an increase in public investment, but mainly due to decline in share of public savings reflected in ever increasing revenue deficits.

On the other, there were certain 'external' fall-outs related with the pattern of utilization of these public debts. Imports of capital goods that were undertaken during the 1980s were used mainly for producing luxury items that catered to the needs of upper income groups. It is estimated that 40 per cent of the increase in import value between 1984-85 to 1988-89 was on account of those capital goods which enhanced the production of variety of consumer goods for upper income groups. This pattern of debt utilization did not add significantly either to the process of income or employment generation and there by could not enhance the size of the domestic market in India.

The external debts quadrupled in dollar terms during 1980s from around $20 billion in 1980 to $82 billion during 1990. It led to a situation where there was a high balance of payment deficits as well as a high current account deficit. To add further to this high deficit situation, the international lenders were unwilling to advance soft international loans to India. Above all, the remittance inflow also stagnated during the period, which gave rise to a stituation, where foreign exchange reserves fell abruptly but no other option emerged, which could tide India out of this acute problem. On the other hand, although during the 1980s, a comparatively higher rate of growth was achieved compared to the 1970s, yet the total factor productivity did not show any sign of improvement. Over the economy, it was (-) 0.0035 during the 70s and (-) 0.0039 in the 80s[3]. Above all, the growth rate differential between employment and net value added in Industry was (-) 6.4 in 1981-80 compared to (-) 2.3 between 1971-80[4]. So growth rates of employment in most of the sectors and the economy as a whole, slowed down in the 80s, which had a severe repercussion for the society as a whole.

Under such a situation[5], planning got reduced to bureaucratic regulation and a crisis-driven reform process was initiated by the Indian state not by accepting the crisis as a challenge to turn the tide in its favour but by acting as a comprador to metropolitan capital, which it attempted to 'restrict' during the launch of its *tryst with destiny.*

Policy Reforms and Its Advocates

The Indian state attempted to introduce economic reforms with the collaboration of the Fund-Bank finances and conditionality. There were essentially two aspects to this reform process, namely stabilization and structural adjustment. While stabilization was to be a temporary phase, meaning deflating the economy, devaluating the rupee and curbing imports to reduce balance of payments deficit, structural adjustment was a long drawn process, which required a complete restructuring of the Indian economy. It is difficult to analyze all policies of economic reforms in its totality in a section of this paper, yet an attempt has been made to identify the broader parameters of reforms initiated during its initial phase.

- The introduction of reforms meant curbing of state expenditures and allowing the private sector to play the most important role in ushering an era of sustained growth and development. This essentially meant redefining the role of the Indian state.
- Liberalization and structural adjustment meant reduction of the role of the state in the economic sphere and bringing in the 'market' to the centre of economic activities. Tariffs, controls and barriers to entry that restricted the free flow of capital, both finance and investments, were to be withdrawn and a level playing field without any restrictions was to be implemented where the rationale of the market and 'competition' would be the guiding principles.
- Industrial policy was sought to be overhauled in such a way so that there is 'dereserving' and 'delicensing' as well as abolition of the licence-permit-*raj*. Moreover the monopolies and restrictive policy for industrial diversification and expansion were to be withdrawn and foreign investment regulation were also to be withdrawn accordingly.
- Trade liberalization was another important feature during this period of reform. Reduction of peak tariff rates, liberalization of import of capital items, placing number of items in the OGL category and phase-wise import liberalization of consumer goods was to be allowed.
- Financial liberalization during this phase meant greater autonomy for the public sector nationalized banks to determine their asset portfolios, increase in credit rating capacities through reduction of CRR and SLR and on the other hand allowing global and domestic private sector

financial players to play a major role in the Indian financial sector.

- In terms of the exchange rate policy an attempt was made to shift from a situation of administered exchange rate policy to a market determined exchange rate system, where rupee was made fully convertible in the current account (with an intent to make it fully convertible in the capital account at a later date). Inflow of portfolio capital was also permitted and domestic companies were allowed to raise capital in the international market.

This certainly is not an exhaustive list of policy measures introduced during the reforms in 1991 but it highlights the major macro-policy initiatives launched by the Indian state in order to 'reform' itself in order to ally with the changed standard-ideal global paradigm, commonly referred as neo-liberal globalization. But the question remains as to why Indian 'capital', which was the major beneficiary of the 'restrictive' pre-reform regime, stood for liberalization. Again, we will not attempt to deal with this aspect in its comprehensive details but will try to analyze the broader contours of this less than often debated issue among the academicians.

It is evident from the pre-reform section of this paper that the 'state' provided the major stimulus to growth during the post-colonial period. On the one hand, it protected the domestic capitalists from the 'reach' of 'metropolitan' capital through a restrictive regime (which provided them with 'zero-competition' in the domestic market, as there were no competitor worth its name in the market) and on the other, the Indian state favoured them with its current and capital expenditures, infrastructure projects and mobilization of adequate resources through the industrial development banks. But despite of these incentives, the Indian state failed to *discipline*[6] the capitalist class in general and the industrialists in particular, in a way, which could make them competitive to intervene in the global market. India here seems to have lost a golden opportunity, which was utilized efficiently by the Koreans, the Chinese and the Japanese state along with other South East Asian countries.

Under such a situation, the capitalist class in India was faced with a dilemma, due to the absence of land reforms and restrictive investment policies of the state (to curtail deficits). The size of the Indian market was limited and it was already reaching a level of stagnation. On the other hand, they did not possess either a sustainable level of 'innovation' nor the cutting-edge technology or the requisite capital by dint of which they could make their presence felt at the global scale. So, opening up of the economy through liberalization and globalization provided Indian capital the much-required opportunity to enter the international market albeit as an appendage of the 'metropolitan' capital, which possessed all the prerequisite ingredients for manufacturing commodities and 'brands' for the global consumers.

Secondly, 'withdrawal of the state' provided Indian 'capital' to move into 'space', which was earlier occupied by the public sector. Deregulation and delicensing gave them the opportunity to take over these apparently loss-making but custodians of huge stock and reserve of capital and assets including real estate. In other words, they could now own the same institutions, which provided them the adequate stimulus for building their private empires during the era of protection.

Thirdly, liberalization provided Indian 'capital' the opportunity to venture into new areas and diversify into new sectors, which was not possible under the restrictive regimes of MRTP and FERA. The Ambanis which were initially in the synthetic fibre trade found this opportunity rewarding to diversify into new areas ranging from petro-chemicals to setting up of agro-marketing chains. So, in this case also, liberalization provided the Indian capital the adequate 'breathing space' to augment their fortunes.

Again, a substantial section of the agrarian rich, who were the product of state patronization (largely due to non-implementation of land reforms) during the pre-reform era found liberalization providing them the opportunity to venture into the industrial sector. Interestingly, it provided them with a dualistic scenario. On one hand, they held huge protests against the withdrawal of agricultural subsidies as well as, subsidized credit; on the other, they favoured the option of exporting agricultural produce, which could fetch them higher prices in the international market. So liberalization promised to be a bag of mixed boon for the rural rich, landed gentry, *kulaks,* beneficiaries of green revolution and other rural power brokers, who otherwise had a strong clout among the political class in India.

Above all, to provide a degree of legitimacy to reforms, a section of the upward mobile urban middle class, section of top bureaucracy and a politically assertive intelligentsia argued for liberalization, which promised to provide them the opportunity to ally themselves with the global elites with whom they were familiar with during their overseas business trips and through the fast emerging global media. They provided the much-needed rationale for reforms, which was much sought after by Indian monopoly 'capital' for a while. Therefore, the Indian state initiated the crisis-driven reform process in collaboration with Fund-Bank conditionality, of course, with few face-savers.

Economic Policies and the North East: Need for Soul Searching

In the midst of *India shining* and much trumpeted higher statistical figures of GDP growth during the period of reforms for the nation as a whole, it is worthwhile to look into the basic macro-economic indicators of the constituents of the North East during the same period. India's compound annual rate of growth of gross state domestic products during 1993-94 to 2001-02 (at 1993-94 prices) has been 6.20 per cent. If we compare this figure with the North-Eastern states, it is observed that other than Tripura (9.20 per cent) and marginally in case of Manipur (6.60 per cent) and Meghalaya (6.50 per cent), all other states of the region has a growth rate which is far from encouraging. Assam with a rate of 2.30 per cent has been the worst performer. Similarly, in terms of the compound annual growth rate of the net state domestic product, it is observed that other than Tripura (8.00 per cent) and marginally in case of Meghalaya (4.10 per cent) and Manipur (4.00 per cent)

North-Eastern states have a dismal record. Again, the worst performer has been Assam. Moreover, the individual state's share to India's GDP portray that majority of the states showed no positive growth pattern during the era of economic reforms. In case of Assam it has shown a declining trend from 1.9 per cent to 1.4 per cent respectively.

Other scholars[8], comparing these figures with different methodologies have also arrived at similar conclusions. They have observed that the GDP per capita of the region has remained below India's per capita income and the gap has widened further during the post-reform period. Similarly, the shares of North-Eastern states in India's national income reveal the same story. For the region as a whole, not only the share of these states declined gradually but also the decline has been much worse during the post-1991 phase.

It is, therefore, important to understand (other than the depressing statistical figures) what are the broader issues associated with the North East, which retard growth in this region? Do our policy-makers fall short of understanding the region, which is thereby depressing the growth scenario despite its potentials? Are the nation builders trying to mitigate various problems of this peripheral region of India utilizing 'yardsticks' of the mainland? Again, one may question the very rationale of neo-classical paradigm, which assumes that economic activities will automatically be generated in those areas that are endowed with resources. Are we somewhere failing to reorient the ethno-historical and ethno-economic linkages of the past with the emerging future? Or, is there an absence of proper institutional set up which can deliver growth? The answer to the question regarding lack of growth perhaps lies in more than one cause mentioned above and in this section we try to locate some of them in the overall context of the economic reforms.

The first and the foremost problem lies with the language of reforms, which is based on the neo-classical praxis that explain the differing rates of development in different societies focusing primarily on resource endowments and technologies while ignoring the institutional aspects of a society, in its past, present and the emerging future. Economic reforms of any sort can only succeed in a milieu where individuals, communities and socities are able to bring in this aspect of economic advancement at the centre-stage of their existence and forge right type of institutions which sustains the growth process. In the North-Eastern states, which are still in their tribal-feudal continuum, there are large pockets, inhabited by various population groups, who are yet to ascribe the needed 'economic' point of view the much-required centre-stage status, for the success of economic reforms. Under such a condition, it is our sincere view that prior to framing economic policies for the North East, it is necessary to understand and reinterpret the social customs, shared beliefs, market and non-market exchange systems, structures of property rights, customary laws etc. of the various population groups and then frame policies so that they do not seem to be alien imposition in terms of their ethno-economic foundations[9].

Development of distinct skills and competences are in many ways related to the historical patterns of occupational specializations. When the economic paradigm changes, it requires communities to diversify into alternative or new occupations. The time and effort required for such transition is not only under estimated but more than often misinterpreted by our planners. The example of shifting cultivation is one such example, where the planners and their pen pushers have discouraged this practice using their mainland 'yardsticks' of production, yet *jhuming* as a 'way of life' and livelihood has continued unabated all throughout the region. This has been a typical case of prescribing the 'economic' rationale of neo-classicism to the population groups, who are more attuned to the paradigm of institutional economics. This hiatus often results in societal dislocations, which further hampers the process of growth in these areas.

Again, historically North East is an area that is land-locked, which had very little trade linkages with the outside world. Under such a situation, land happened to be there only 'capital' worth its name. Now, when there is an attempt of transition from tradition to modernity, in these circumstances, there will certainly be replacement of authority-based transactions to contract-based exchange relations. In this respect, allocation of property rights over land and other productive resources will be a matter of great concern. Although it is true that the process of replacement of authority-based exchange relations started during the colonial period yet the present era of globalization will exert a qualitatively different and more ruthless pressure of exploitation and appropriation of resources in these region than any other period in its memorable history. Lack of proper stock taking of the situation and inability to frame a proper institutional mechanism concerning the utilization of resources might generate further instability in the region.

During the colonial era, the 'strategic' interest of the empire and the 'commercial' interest of the mercantile lobby became synonymous and so there was no conflict regarding the issue of exploitation of resources in these areas in general and the hills in particular. Whenever the people raised their voices of protest against colonial exploitation of resources, the colonial historians referred it as *resistance of the savages to the civilizing mission of the whites.* Things changed during the post-colonial era, where there was a confrontation between the state control/management of resources *vis-à-vis* community control/management of the same. In the contemporary era of globalization, it seems that the state-community confrontation will be less but will be accompanied with a clash of 'interest' of metropolitan capital and its local collaborators on the one hand and the people's movement for preservation of resources and environment, on the other. Prof. Roy Burman[10] states that a situation seems destined to emerge, where crafty individuals belonging to the community itself, with the backing of the neo-colonial money power will occupy the position and promote green capitalism in these areas. This process of usurpation of resources by the elites of the traditional societies, at the behest of 'metropolitan' capital, will surely add newer dimensions to the already flaming frontiers called the North East.

In Lieu of Conclusion

Importance of maritime trade determined the economic activities during the colonial era. Bombay, Calcutta and Madras grew up as the segments of a dependent colonial economy, which served the colonial interest of the metropolitan economy of the imperial powers. This led to a geographical division of labour not only between the 'metropolitan' core and the 'secluded' segments of its dependent enclaves in various colonies but also fostered another kind of division between these 'colonial' segments and the vast 'hinterland' within the colonies, where the latter regions provided both raw materials and man power for the sustenance of the colonial segments. Post-colonial India attempted to minimize this aspect of 'geographical dualism' by setting up of industries in the backward areas in the name of balanced regional development. This process of development dispersal saw setting up of industries in areas such as Bihar, Orissa and Madhya Pradesh and later on in Assam after the bitter 'Barauni episode'. But these initiatives although had major successes yet they failed to transform into growth engines, in the backward areas, in the long run, due to their capital intensive nature. As a result, these major projects generated another set of 'enclaves', which had little impact upon the hinterlands. Moreover, these industries disrupted the traditional occupational, economic and social life in these areas without creating sustainable options for the emerging future. Thus, this process of growth, like its earlier one, also gave rise to a pattern of 'geographical dualism' albeit at a much dispersed scale.

Now the question remains as to whether the process of globalization will be able to reduce this pattern of 'geographical dualism' already existent in the erstwhile colonies and the backward regions of India? Existential reality suggests that the present pattern of globalization has a strong current of centralization, which draws disparate economies and its various sectors into the vortex of an 'unseen' centre controlled by few decision-makers. Under such a scenario, globalization will enhance the 'geographical' spatial dualism, which was evident in the earlier order. It will increase inequalities of all sorts affecting the masses. However, there would always be a 'dominant minority', who will support integration of their respective economies to the global order, as they tend to benefit maximum from it since they are comparatively better endowed with resources, being the major beneficiaries under the pre-reform order. In terms of the North East, the dominant tribal elites, the emerging tribal and non-tribal middle class, the white collar employees both among the tribal and non-tribal areas, as well as, the votaries of mercantile capital and not to forget, the paid intellectuals, will be the biggest advocates of such an 'open' and 'market oriented' integration. They will be psychologically elated to ally themselves with the global elites and their brands, as it will create new vistas for their increased income and livelihood generation, albeit as compradors of 'metropolitan' capital.

While the elites in the domestic economies of the North East will maximize their attempts of greater appropriation of natural and common property and/or community resources for upgrading themselves as the local agents of 'metropolitan' capital, globalization might appear as means of 'immiserizing' growth for the masses in these areas. Above, all, as the 'state' sheds off its duties from the social sphere and cease to be the major source of development expenditure under the diktats of globalization, it will increase the sense of alienation, heighten societal dislocations and further promote secessionism among the lot of these impoverished masses. Economic deprivation and/or dispossession will create grounds for political assertion for an extended political 'space' and greater 'share' of economic disbursements. Considering the ethnic map of North East, different population groups in this region will further assert themselves for a greater share of the already diminishing 'pie' of state expenditure either by seeking 'reservation', mainly as Scheduled Tribes or agitate for political autonomy or self-rule for determining their course of action (that will be nothing but a mirage without economic autonomy, which seems to be eluding under present pattern of globalization) or resort to extra-constitutional means for safeguarding their identity or organize to secede from the Indian state. For any down to earth observer of the North East affairs, all these tendencies mentioned above, are nothing but the realities of the emerging order.

Under such a situation, how does the new economic order benefit the people in the North-Eastern region? Existential reality suggests that the 'state' has to play an important role in shaping the future of this region[11]. But in order to do so, the state's 'policy from above' approach has to be altered along with its colonial style of functioning and over emphasis upon the 'trickle-down' model of growth. Looking beyond the established praxis is imperative in this direction. 'State' intervention should in no way mean bureaucratic service delivery but new operational style of functioning, which through its activities will try to reinvent the traditional genius of the people of the North-Eastern region. The historical roots of ethno-economic occupational specialization of the diverse population groups should be reinterpreted and researched, in a creative way, so that a proper framework of economic regeneration is identified. In this direction, treating the population groups of the North East in a non-historical matrix has been the biggest casualty of our development model so far.

Another area of utmost importance is related with the aspect of allocation of property rights over land and natural resources in these areas. The state should also play a major role here, not as a custodian of 'monopoly' capital but as the protector of the interest of the people who reside in the region and who are the actual owners of resources existing in this area. Property rights in the North East particularly among the highlanders and the traditional societies are in a state of continuous flux, where traditional local authority structure has eroded and the vacuum so created has not been replaced by new authority structures. This situation is ideally suited for monopoly capital (both domestic and global) to exploit the resources of the region, to suit their design of profit maximization without caring for the people or the environment surrounding them. Forging new type of institutions to manage these resources on an equitable, efficient and sustainable manner is, therefore, of utmost importance. How deftly the society is able to forge right type of institutions will have a decisive impact upon peace and stability in this region.

Thus, identifying the resources of the region and involving the masses in its utilization, understanding the ethno-economic roots of its population groups in terms of historical pattern of occupational specialization and helping the process for evolution of right kind of institutional arrangements are important for a sustainable development pattern of the North East. Left otherwise, the North East with its 'duality' of vast stock of resources but under development, will continue to have the same meaning for the Indian 'state', as has been Latin America for the United States and presently the countries of Eastern Europe hold for the European Union.

NOTES

1. In this section all the statistical figures (other than those indicated separately) has been quoted from Chandrasekhar, C.P., and Ghosh, Jayati, *The Market that Failed: A Decade of Neo-liberal Economic Reforms in India* (New Delhi: Leftword, 2002). I have also extended upon the broader logical framework used in this book to analyze and conclude about certain aspects and interpretation of economic reforms in India.
2. All the plan formulations representing different ideological standpoint namely, The Bombay Plan framed by the capitalists, The Peoples' Plan formulated by M.N. Roy focusing the position of the Left and The 'Gandhi Plan' authored by Shriman Narain emphasized upon 'planning' and the role of the 'Indian state' (although from varied point of view) which also must have provided the justification for its overwhelming presence in every sphere of the Indian nation. For a detailed analysis see, Patnaik, Prabhat, 'Some Indian Debates on Planning', in Byres, Terence J., (ed.), *The Indian Economy: Major Debates Since Independence* (New Delhi: Oxford University Press, 2000).
3. Mohanty, Deepak, *Growth and Productivity in the Indian Economy,* R.B.I. Occasional Papers, Vol. 13, No. 2, 1992.
4. Ajit, D., 'Industry and Employment: An Analysis of Labour Absorbtion in Manufacturing Sector in India' as quoted by Vyasulu, Vinod, 'Public Enterprise in a Restructuring Economy', in *The Administrator,* Vol. XL, No. 1, January-March, 1995.
5. During the 1980s another significant development was occurring at the global scale. As the post-war growth in metropolitan industries slowed down, the power of *capital-as-finance* became all the more significant. It happened at large number of countries around the world, e.g. OPEC countries are estimated to have accumulated surpluses to the tune of $475 billion, out of which, $400 billion was parked in the developed industrial nations; net international bank loans as proportion of world output, rose from 0.7 per cent in 1964 to 8 per cent in 1981 and 16.3 per cent in 1991; relative to world trade, net international bank loans rose from 7.5 per cent in 1964 to 42.6 per cent in 1980 and 104.6 per cent in 1991; the daily volume of foreign exchange transactions in the international financial markets rose to

$1.2 trillion per day by the mid-1990s, which was equal to the value of world trade in every quarter of a full year; volume of transaction of bonds and securities between foreign and domestic residents were as high as 135 per cent in the US, 170 per cent in Germany and 80 per cent in Japan respectively. All these figures prove the importance of the rise of *capital-as-finance vis-à-vis capital-as-production* and its insatiable hunger for very short-term-footloose-windfall profits that played a major role in changing the course of history during the end of the twentieth century.

6. By the term 'discipline' we mean that the 'state' could have urged upon the manufacturers to utilize the domestic availability of cheap labour to produce manufactured mass consumption goods for the international market. In the process, the 'state' could have provided them with soft institutional credit for setting up plants for manufacturing these items. This has been done successfully in various East Asian economies and China for producing manufactured items for the international market. In hindsight, it seems that the Indian capital enjoyed the benefits of cheap labour and easy credit yet it failed to establish itself in the global markets due to the lack of 'discipline', which the Indian 'state' failed to enforce upon them.
7. These statistical figures has been mentioned by Banerjee, Amalesh, 'Economic Growth and Sustainability of North-Eastern States' in Passah, P.M., (ed.), *In Defence of Regional Economic Development in India: A Case for North East* (New Delhi: Akansha, 2006).
8. Bezbaruah, M.P. and Dutta, M.K.: 'Development Experience and Perspective in the North-Eastern Region', in *Assam Economic Journal,* Vol. XVII, 2004.
9. For analysis regarding the neo-classical paradigm and its difference with the stand point of institutional economics, as well as for a proper understanding of the term 'institution' and its various connotations, see Shah, Tushar, 'Institutional Dimensions of Agricultural and Rural Development in India', in *The Administrator,* Vol. XL, No. I, January-March 1995.
10. As narrated in 'Interview with Professor Roy Burman' in Datta, P.S., *North East as I See it* (New Delhi: Omsons Publication, 1994).
11. By arguing for the importance of the 'state', we do not mean a return to the pre-reform era of a 'restrictive' regime or deny the role of private sector but try to highlight upon the fact that considering the socio-political scenario and the reluctance of the Indian capital as well as the international capital to invest in a meaningful way in the region, the state has to play its desired role as an investor in the North East. But while doing so it should stand as the protector of the masses and its resources in the region instead of being their 'colonial' master.

15

New Economic Policy and Development in NER of India

P.C. Dutta and *B.C. Pradhan*

"The population census provides detailed information on demographic characteristics and other variables. It has no information on income, asset, ownership, consumption pattern and other variables. It was felt that a unified survey covering different facets of Human Development, level of living, employment and wages, literacy and education, morbidity, disability and nutrition, effectiveness of public services such as PDS, education and health care etc., and Demographic characteristics would be useful. Such a unified survey would enable researchers to draw interrelationships between these different variables and thereby better understanding". [UN Human Development Report, 2000]

Introduction

Indian economy has witnessed multi-dimensional changes during post-reform period. The government headed by Narasimha Rao introduced structural adjustments during 1990-91 in order to make Indian economy more competitive at the international scenario. At the same time this new economic policy of 1991 opened many new economic issues for discussion. As a result the discussion on economic reforms divided into groups—one which praises the miracle of reforms and opines that the economic reform would bring progress in every field and every sector whereas another group opposed vehemently the new economic reform in our country due to the ill-effects of economic reform in different sectors.

So far as the history of post-independence development is concerned the process of planned development in India was introduced in 1950 with mixed economy approach by the then Prime Minister of India, Pandit Jawaharlal Nehru. Consequently, over centralization and nationalization of socialistic pattern of development led to corruption and economic inefficiency in our country. Protection and subsidy system encouraged permanent dependence rather than growth. When Indian economy was gripped with more serious problem of eighties the earlier mixed economy approach was evaluated and it was realized that Indian economy must acquire improvement in productivity, absorption of modern technology and full utilization of resources. At the same time it was supposed that the private sector will play an important role in shaping the country's economy. As a result in 1991 New Economic Policy (NEP) was introduced by the Government of India involving structural adjustment programmes with basic characteristics of Liberalisation, Privatisation and Globalization (LPG). Under such policy profit motive was the guiding principle for investment. Domination of profit motive policy paved the way for development of those regions where the developed infrastructural facilities are quite high. Therefore the NEP increased the regional inequalities in India. India's North-Eastern Region (NER) is badly affected by the introduction of NEP and Structural Adjustment Programme (SAP).

From 1994 to 1997, Indian national income grew at over 7 per cent per annum and during the entire last decade, the growth rate has been around 6.5 per cent. A study by K.V. Ramaswami has shown that growth in the post-reform period has been significantly higher than in the pre-reform period.

There has been a considrable debate on the contents of the reform package, their sequencing and pace, their implementation and their impact (Kumar, 2000). The debate is highly polarized between two groups of economists. One group claims the achievement of reforms and seeks faster implementation on remaining issues related to reforms. Prominent contributors among them are Bhagwati (1994), Srinivasan (1998), Ahluwalia and Little (1998), Parikh (1998) and Mohan (1999) among others. The other school is more critical of reforms. It focuses on the adverse effects on the society, especially the vulnerable groups, questions the sustainability of growth and reforms themselves. Thus they ask for rethinking on the coverage, sequencing and pace of implementation of reforms. This group includes Nayyar (1996), Ghosh (1998), Nagraj (1997), Patnaik and Chandrasekhar (1997), among many rebels of reforms.

Jha (2000) argued in his Paper "Economic Reformation or Deformation in India" that New Western model of economic growth is not suited to the developing countries and even after 50 years of implementation a meaningful development is far away. The economic reform initiated in India during the nineties with the plethora of privatization, liberalization, structural adjustment, globalization and Dunkel proposals in further whipping the cart in the wrong direction and deforming the economy. Interestingly the, "developing countries could not afford to follow the wisdom of Adam Smith in their initial stage of development". Singer cautioned the underdeveloped countries "not to initiate blindly the modern technologies of the industrialized countries which have been based on altogether different sets of factor endowments". In India and Third World countries there is need to develop soft, non-violent and intermediate/appropriate/middle technology sutied to the local needs and conditions. The so-called economic reform is deforming the growth rates and distribution and causing crisis in the Asian countries.

Dutta and Pradhan (2004) have rightly pointed out that under the backward conditions of the North-Eastern Region special initiative will have to be taken by the governments of the concerned states to improve infrastructure as well as to ensure food and nutritional security to the poor and steps taken by the governments are not sufficient through Public Distribution System. They also suggested that the NGOs should come forward to protect the interest of the North East by starting a revolution to bring a change in the quality of life of the people in the region and no policy can be successful unless and until the people's participation in all respects of development is realized.

Ray (2000) argued that after highlighting general symptoms of poor governance and corruption, governance issues need to be examined within the context of intra and inter-relationships between various components of the State apparatus, including government, and the community. In his case study of India, he considers administrative reform issues in conjunction not only with constitutional, bureaucratic and judicial reform issues, but also with issues related to political pluralism. For good governance Ray reiterates, amongst others, five mantras of the anti-corruption drive, namely monopoly regulation, official transparency and accountability, detection of and penalties for corruption.

Dutta (2003) observed that in the era of globalisation rapid socio-economic transformation has been taking place in Indian economy without addressing the problems of regional disparity, for which the states of NER are suffering from paucity of funds to improve their socio-economic backwardness. The study revealed that the states of NER were far behind from other states of the Indian Union so far as the basic amenities of life such as health, education, safe drinking water, food security, banking facilities, communication etc. are concerned. All these created the seeds of contention amongst the people of NER for which a dangerous feeling of regionalism grew more and more.

Dutta and Pradhan (2006) observed that the agriculture was the key to the development of NER. Although India had emerged as a food surplus State in the world, the NER was still suffering from food deficit. In almost all the states of NER there existed substantial urban-rural and inter-district variation, along with the marked variation between tribal and non-tribal population within the district, for which it was always a difficult task to measure the nutritional standard and quality of life of the population in the region. They suggested that it was necessary to improve all the factors employed in agriculture along with the use of best quality of seeds, application of modern technology, fast communication between research and extension, Agricultural Information Net Working System etc. in the era of globalization.

Saramma (2000) mentioned that the new economic policy had not benefited the agricultural sector duly and it seemed that it has been affecting adversely the agricultural growth and employment generation in the rural sector. In fact, the agricultural sector has been suffering from structural weaknesses and as a result the liberalization of the economy will not help the large number of the rural masses to receive any benefit.

Several studies on Liberalisation, Privatization and Globalization show that the New Economic Reform has success as well as failure stories.

From the above studies it is clear that economic growth and development cannot be defined in absolute terms and it has to be assessed relatively. Development of any society originates from its socio-cultural process. It springs up from the heart of each society and within the ambit of the natural environment, social relations, education, health and nutrition, per capita income, position of women in the society, production, consumption and welfare activities. The primary objective of development is to satisfy essential material needs of the society and not depend upon any outside paradigm. Any development at the cost of local environment and people's culture cannot be welcomed.

Hence there is need to examine the pattern of development in NER in the light of New Economic Policy (NEP) of 1991 adopted by the Government of India.

Under the above circumstances, the main object of this study is to see whether or not the New Economic Reform would suit the people of NER as supporters of the policy had advocated. For the convenience, the study has been designed to discuss:

(i) The socio-economic status of the people in the region according to latest Human Development Index (HDI).
(ii) The post-reform developments in the states of NER.
(iii) The study is concluded with viable suggestions for the policy-makers and planners of the region to adjust the policies of the concerned states of the region coping with New Economic Reform for the real development of the states of NER.

The study has been made with the help of statistical information collected from various secondary sources.

Economic Reforms and NER

After independence, the policy-makers of India introduced measures to bring development in different areas of life such as health, education, social security etc. The measures introduced by the state at the national and regional levels came to be known by the term 'Human Development'. The effects were also made to help the disadvantaged groups by the affirmative action. The disadvantages were identified on the basis of the social and economic backwardness of the communities, and regional imbalances. However, the impact of these measures have not been uniform across the country, with different regions and sectors showing different levels of development. The chief motive of the policy-makers was 'Economic Growth' and they adopted socialism or a mixed economy approach for the realization of the same. In the eighties it was felt that only economic growth will not bring the real development of the nation due to regional disparity, absence of social security, ill effects of industrialization, urbanization, negligence in social sectors like health, education etc. That is why the policy-makers got awakened with a new slogan 'Limits of Growth'. Adequate attention should be given for the promotion of education, health and nutrition, standard of living, gender equality, environmental sustainability etc.

In 1990s India's development strategy shifted its gear from the state monopoly to New Economic Reforms intertwined with the principles of LPG (Liberalization, Privatization and Globalization) at par with world economic system. The then Prime Minister, P.V. Narasimha Rao introduced New Economic Policy in July 1991. The New Economic Policy aims at making the Indian economy competitive and much better integrated with the world economy. Since the New Economic Reforms, the people of India are in a different path with dramatic political, social, economic, cultural and environmental changes. The process of globalization can be viewed as an economic phenomenon with the expansion of markets for goods and services, capital and labour beyond national boundaries. The state intervention in the affairs of development has been replaced to a large extent by market forces. Under such circumstances, the term 'development' receives much more attention of the scholars and they are in a state of confusion whether the New Economic Reform would bring progress in the backward regions of India or not. Experience shows that the New Economic Policy (LPG) is successful in the developed states (Andhra Pradesh, Punjab, Maharashtra etc.) but has adverse effects in the backward states like Bihar, Orissa and the States of North-Eastern Region. Again, development of a society cannot be measured through the yardstick of economic growth. Development of any society stands from its integral socio-cultural process. Since the chief motive of New Economic Reform is 'profit' it will definitely bring regional inequalities in India and the people of North-Eastern society will be affected in many ways. Development of any society must be woven around people and not people around development. Hence development of NER in the context of New Economic Policy can be adjudged through the indicators of latest Human Development Index (HDI).

At the world level, the UNDP (United Nations Development Project) was the apex body to prepare the HDR (Human Development Report) for all the countries. It was a fact that the development cannot be measured through the single criterion, i.e. Gross National Product (GNP). Many scholars looked for a more comprehensive socio-economic measures because they believed that "Human Development is about people and about how development changes their choices. It is about more than GNP growth, more than income and wealth and more than producing commodities and accumulating capital. A person's access to income may be one of the choice, but it is not the sum total of human endeavour."

Thus the study used the following indicators to measure the achievements and failures of New Economic Reforms in the NER.

Population

The UN's latest global population report predicted that India would reach 1.593 billion by 2050, while China will reach 1.392 billion. India will surpass China by 2030. Currently India's population is

16.7 per cent of the global population. It is the second largest in the world and occupies 2.4 per cent of the earth. The growth rate is 1.7 per cent which implies that this burgeoning population has to be catered to, no mean task even for the most booming of economies. We need good governance and population stability to ensure sustanable growth.

Coming to the states of NER, it is observed that the most important problem which creates hindrance to economic development is the problem of population explosion in the region. The total population of the region is about 38.5 million representing about 3.75 per cent of India's total population in 2001. The region's growth rate of population is much higher than the national average. It is striking to note that India's total population increased by 51.80 per cent in the period 1951-71, 54.39 per cent in 1971-91 and 21.35 per cent in the period 1991-2001 whereas for the NER the respective growth rates are 90.86 per cent, 62.11 and 22.02 per cent. At the same time the share of population of NER in India, increased from 2.84 per cent in 1951 to 3.75 per cent in 2001.

Education plays a very important role in promotion of economic, social, political and institutional development. Education promotes development of all the sectors including agriculture, industry and social sector. Higher levels of education may have greater direct impact on economic development but the primary and middle level education are important because they widely distribute the conditions conducive to development. Education promotes development in all the sectors of the economy and yield high social and economic returns. Sustainable development cannot take place without investments being made in people. It is now widely accepted that the improvements in the quality of people as productive agents must be a central objective of development policies.

It is striking to note that except Arunachal Pradesh (42%) and Meghalaya (49%) the literacy level of the region's population is above the national level (52%) according to 1991 census, while in 2001, percentage of literacy rate in the State of Assam (64.28%), Meghalaya (63.31%) and Arunachal Pradesh (54.74%) are below the National level (65.38%).

The female literacy rate is highest in Mizoram (95%) followed by Nagaland (77%) and lowest in Arunachal Pradesh (48%). There is a big gender gap in literacy which is one of the major obstacles in attaining total literacy. Enrolment in various stages of education is growing at a fast rate, but the proportion of girls is low and declines sharply at higher stages of education. The highest gender gap has been found in the states of Manipur (24.03% points), followed by Arunachal Pradesh (21.76%), Tripura (20.93%), and lowest is in Mizoram (7.01%) preceded by Meghalaya (8.27%). However, all the states of NER are below all India (24.84%) level. Almost the same trend has continued in 2001 also. Low female literacy has strong repercussions on other aspects like enrolment of children, population growth, child care and acceptance of family welfare measures (Table 15.1).

Table 15.1: Female Literacy Rate, Total Literacy, Gender Gap in Literacy and Per Capita Expenditure on Education by the Government of different N.E. States

	Female Literacy Rate (in %)			*Total Literacy (in %)*		*PCE (Govt.) on education (in Rs.)*		*Gender Gap in Literacy*	
	1981	*1991*	*2001*	*1991*	*2001*	*1991-92*	*1997-98*	*1991*	*2001*
ANP	30	40	44.24	42	54.74	549	951	21.76	19.83
ASM	43	66	56.03	53	64.28	250	537	18.84	15.90
MNP	48	66	59.70	60	68.87	560	984	24.03	18.17
MGH	45	74	60.41	49	63.31	406	779	8.27	5.73
MZM	79	95	86.13	82	88.49	769	1210	7.01	—
NGN	55	77	61.92	62	67.11	437	762	12.87	9.85
TRP	50	67	65.41	60	73.66	416	836	20.93	16.06
India	**39**	**50**	**54.16**	**52**	**65.38**	—	—	**24.84**	**21.69**

It is striking to note that per capita expenditure on education in 1997-98 is highest for smaller states of Mizoram (Rs. 1210), followed by Manipur (Rs. 984), Arunachal Pradesh (Rs. 951) and Tripura (Rs. 836) while it is lowest in Assam (Rs. 537) among the states of NER.

Economic Disparity

In the 1996, the Food and Agricultural Organisation (FAO) defined food security as a situation which "exists when all people, at all times, have physical and economic access to sufficient, safe and nutritious food to meet their dietary needs and food preferences for an active and healthy life." The *Food Insecurity Atlas of Urban India* adopts a broader definition of the concept and views food security from three different angles—(1) the availability of food, which depends on production and distribution; (2) the access to food, which is determined by an individual's purchasing power, and in turn purchasing power is affected by livelihood access, access to housing, and caste and gender discrimination; and (3) the absorption of food, which is affected by sanitation, clean drinking water and health care. The report identifies 17 key indicators, which fall into six categories (food affordability and availability, livelihood access, access to housing, discrimination in livelihood access, access to sanitation, and health and nutritional outcome) that in turn can be grouped under the classification of availability, access, and absorption of food.

It is interesting to note that so far as the poorest ten per cent of the rural population is concerned the shares of consumption are relatively better in Manipur and Mizoram than other states in NER while for the richest ten per cent, the shares of consumption are relatively better in Assam and Meghalaya (Table 15.2).

Coming to the urban sectors of NER, it is worthwhile to mention that the percentage share of expenditure according to poorest ten per cent groups of consumers were found to be better in the state of Nagaland and worst in Assam while for the richest ten per cent of the consumers, the share is relatively better in Assam among the states of NER.

Table 15.2: Percentage Share of Consumption by Extreme Two Groups (Bottom and Top 10 %) of Population in Rural and Urban Areas in the N.E. States

State	*Rural*	*Rural*	*Urban*	*Urban*
	Bottom 10%	*Top 10%*	*Bottom 10%*	*Top 10%*
ANP	3.43	22.13	3.01	25.04
ASM	3.43	23.28	1.15	37.23
MNP	4.74	19.33	4.01	18.66
MGH	3.02	22.79	2.94	25.61
MZM	4.11	17.46	3.92	18.78
NGN	—	—	5.82	18.52
TRP	3.92	20.52	3.02	21.76
India	**2.65**	**26.16**	**1.83**	**32.02**

Dutta and Choudhury (1996) noted that the pattern of consumption is most uneven in Assam and is one of the highest among the states of NER though it is considerably less than the average for all-India in the rural sector. Thus it may be pointed out that the poorest section of the society in Assam has been badly affected. The results reveal that the extent of degree of inequality in the level of living in the states of NER is much more than what is taken to guide some of the decision-making bodies in connection with resource transfer from centre to these North-Eastern states particularly in Assam.

Poverty

While economic poverty and inequality are nothing new for people in the Third World or for people in India and within India for the people of NER. Population and poverty play hand in hand with each other. Poverty, pollution, and resource depletion are all tied to exploding population growth. However, these are all equally responsible for one another. Statistics tell us that population growth rates are much higher in less developed countries where poverty flourishes. And if a country has a larger population it is going to put a bigger strain on the resources of that country and create pollution.

Monthly Per Capita Expenditure (MPCE) may be accepted as an indicator of standard of living for people, on the basis of minimum calorie intake, suggested by Indian Council of Medical Research (ICMR) which should be 2400 calories for an Indian working person in rural India and 2100 calories in urban India. This exercise yielded the official or Planning Commission's poverty line (per capita expenditure for 30 days) of rural and urban India at 1973-74 prices as Rs. 49.02 and Rs. 56.64 respectively. Thus an estimated people of 46.02 per cent in urban India and 56 per cent in rural India were below the poverty line in the year 1998.[1]

However, economists and statisticians in the year 2000 estimated the monthly income needed for a rural individual to consume 2,400 calories per day was not Rs. 327 ($7.25) but Rs. 567 ($12.60). At this income level, which amounts to Rs. 19 ($0.42) or less per day, nearly 75 per cent of the rural population is poor. Probably over 80 per cent of the rural population (77 million) is below the World Bank's definition using $2 per day. None of these definitions take into account the cost of adequate housing, clothing, education, health care, and entertainment.

Considering the economic condition of NER, it is estimated that the percentage of population below the poverty line is higher in relation all-India level in 1998 which comes out as 56.83 per cent and 42.33 per cent for the rural and urban people of NER respectively (Dutta, 2003). However, as per NSSO's round survey, the poverty ratio has declined in the North East. It has declined to 40.01 per cent in 2000 round survey, as compared to 45.01 per cent in 1993-94.

Employment and Production

In this era of globalization, the interdependence of various sectors is going to increase further. In order to make the products manufactured in these sectors internationally competitive, the use of quality service inputs (whether domestic or imported) is becoming a prerequisite. The New Economic Policy giving primacy to the market forces in national development and integrating Indian into the global economic order was enunciated by the Government of India in July 1991.

In the context of poverty alleviation and employment generation, particularly for low skill labour, the interdependent growth of all the three sectors should be emphasized so that the country can achieve a sustained 8 per cent rate of growth in real GDP, as was envisaged in the Tenth Five-Year Plan (Planning Commission, 2001). Once this happens, there will be a trickle-down effect making growth an instrument of poverty alleviation and employment generation.

A country like India cannot hope to build its future on the services sector alone though it can be and will be a major component of the economy. India cannot afford not to build its strength in agriculture for food and nutritional security. Nor can it afford to ignore manufacturing strength for reasons of economic and national security. Based on the strength of these two sectors, it can build a major economic infrastructure for the services sector and use it to generate great wealth and employment for her people.

During the process of growth over the years 1950-51 to 1999-2000, the Indian economy has experienced a change in the production structure with a shift away from agriculture towards industry and the tertiary sector. The tertiary sector emerged as the major sector of the economy both in terms of growth rates and share in GDP in the 1990s. It is to be noted here that while the agriculture and manufacturing sectors have experienced phases of deceleration, stagnation and growth, the tertiary sector has shown a uniform growth trend during the period 1950-51 to 1999-2000. Table 15.3 shows the share of agricultural sector in real GDP, at 1993-94 prices indicating a decline from 55.53 per cent in the 1950s to 28.66 per cent in 1990s (post-reform period).

The sectoral distribution of the workforce in India during the period 1983 to 2000 reveals that structural changes in terms of employment have been slow in India as the primary sector continued to absorb 60.4 per cent of the total workforce even in 1999-2000, followed by the tertiary and industrial sectors (22.7% and 16.8%) respectively.

Table 15.3: Sectoral Composition of GDP (Average Shares)

(in per cent)

Period	*Primary Sector*	*Secondary Sector*	*Tertiary Sector*
1950-51 to 1959-60	55.53	16.00	28.09
1960-61 to 1969-70	47.37	21.10	31.33
1970-71 to 1979-80	42.68	22.88	34.56
1980-81 to 1989-90 (pre-reform period)	36.06	25.13	38.80
1990-91 to 1999-2000 (post-reform period)	28.66	27.12	44.22

Source: National Accounts Statistics, CSO.

Per Capita Net State Domestic Product (PCNSDP) gives a rough idea about the economic condition of NER with respect to all-India level. It is observed that all the states of NER except Arunachal Pradesh (Rs. 2119—Rs. 3265) and Mizoram (Rs. 2119—Rs. 7743) are below the all-India level (Rs. 1857—Rs. 2553) for the year 1985-86 to 1994-95. In this respect Assam's position is the lowest for ever during the period 1990-91 (Rs. 1544) to 1996-97 (Rs. 1628) and also in the period 1980-81 (Rs. 1254). The picture shows the economic backwardness of the region in general and Assam in particular (Table 15.4).

Table 15.4: Per Capita Net State Domestic Product (At Current Prices 1980-81)

(in Rs.)

State	*1980-81*	*1985-86*	*1990-91*	*1994-95*	*1995-96*	*1996-97*
ANP	1571	2119	2710	3265	3304	3059
ASM	1284	1510	1544	1585	1606	1628
MNP	1419	1598	1739	1986	1993	—
MGH	1361	1412	1733	1673	1808	1837
MZM	1289	2658	4474	7743	—	—
NGN	1448	1653	1916	2270	—	—
TRP	1307	1240	1646	1898	2113	2197
India	**1625**	**1857**	**2267**	**2533**	**2664**	**2814**

In the North-Eastern hill areas food production is subject to wide fluctuations due to shifting cultivation. Hence estimate of production may not give the true picture. However, during the last two decades per capita production has been declining in the states of Assam, Manipur, Meghalaya and Mizoram and are lower than the national average except in the state of Arunachal Pradesh. While the population is rapidly increasing in the states of the region, it is observed, from Table 15.5, that in case of Assam, the per capita food production decreased from 158 kg. in 1972-73 to 154 kg. in 1990-91 which further decreased to 139 kg. in 1997-98. The respective figures for Meghalaya are 120 kg., 87 kg. and 83 kg. only.

Table 15.5: Per Capita Food Grain Production, Consumption of Electricity and Percentage of Households having Electricity, Safe Drinking Water in N.E. States

Item	*1**	*2**		*Per Capita Food Grains Production (in kg.)*				*Water Requirement (in cubic km.)*	
	1996-97	*1991*	*2001*	*1972-73*	*1980-81*	*1990-91*	*1997-98*	*1991*	*2001*
ANP	80.8	40.85	70.02	104	207	253	186	0.024	0.029
ASM	107.6	18.74	45.85	158	150	154	139	0.632	0.883
MNP	127.9	50.92	38.72	159	205	155	152	0.060	0.074
MGH	134.5	29.16	36.16	120	116	87	83	0.053	0.072
MZM	127.8	9.20	16.21	244	70	118	123	0.025	0.035
NGN	88.0	53.42	53.37	107	136	160	150	0.036	0.052
TRP	80.4	36.93	37.18	116	196	187	152	0.080	0.088
India	**338.5**	**42.37**	**62.30**	**172**	**190**	**208**	**198**	**27.111**	**33.521**

1* Per capita consumption of electricity (in kWh).
2* Percentage of households having safe drinking water.

The development of an area is best reflected in the distribution of basic needs. The table confirms the fact of region's backwardness as it is observed that the per capita consumption of electricity is much lower in the states of NER as compared to the country's consumption (338.5 kWh). Among the states of NER, the highest per capita consumption is observed in the state of Meghalaya (134.5 kWh) and lowest in Tripura (80.4 kWh).

The North-Eastern Council (NEC) has contributed to the North-Eastern Region power supply through its power projects.

The country's third hydel power project and the first in the North East, which is located in the heart of Shillong at Mawprem is all set to be revived. The Ministry of Non-Conventional Energy Sources (MNCES) will finance the restoration of the Sonapani Hydel Power Plant, which is expected to light Mawprem and part of Mawlai area. The power plant, which will be "totally unmanned and remote control based" is expected to generate its full capacity of 1.5 Mega Watt for six to seven months especially during the monsoon and 50 per cent to 62 per cent during other seasons. The unique feature of remote controlling is the first of its kind in the North East and will be managed by the Mawlai 132 KV sub-station.

The expansion of irrigation facilities, operation and maintenance of irrigation system and distribution of water have not received due attention. Irrigation sector is today facing twin issues of sub-optimal sector planning and financial management on the one hand and inadequate water management and maintenance on the other. Involving the farmers in the irrigation system is one obvious remedy for addressing the management problems. In comparison to all-India level only 1.4 per cent of area is under irrigation system in the NER and only 1 per cent in the state of Assam (5,39,000 hectares). However, percentage of total irrigated area in Assam is 65 per cent with respect to total irrigated area in NER.

From a look at Table 15.5, it is observed that the maximum amount of water is required in the states of Assam among the states of NER, which is approximately 2.33 per cent as compared to India's requirement in 1991, and the figure (0.833 cubic km.) has risen to 2.63 per cent in 2001. However, there is an increasing trend of water requirement in 2001 over 1991. Drinking water is the most precious commodity in our daily life. Supply of safe drinking water is essential to sustain life. Regarding the safe drinking water facilities, all the states of NER, except Arunachal Pradesh (70.02%) are less than the national average (62.3%). It is striking to note that only 16.21 per cent of total households of Mizoram can drink safe water while water is the life blood of the environment.

It is interesting to note that on a global basis, only 8 per cent increase in foodgrain production in the last 50 years, has been through expansion of cultivable area, the rest 92 per cent coming from improved irrigation techniques and use of high yielding varieties. About 46 per cent of the global foodgrain production comes from irrigated area, which has increased from 80 million hectares in 1950 to 240 million hectares in 1993. It will not be possible to increase the total annual foodgrain productivity in the country beyond 250 million tonnes, with the present agricultural practices, which totally falls short of the requirement to produce a minimum of 400 million tonnes by the year 2050 to provide adequate food security to the projected 1.8 billion population[2].

From a look at Table 15.6, it is observed that regarding availability of cereals, all the states of NER excluding Arunachal Pradesh and Tripura, are below the national average (522.7 gms. per capita per day). In case of per capita per day availability of pulses, it is observed that all the states of NER are below the all-India average over the period 1983-1999.

Table 15.6: Per Capita Availability of Cereals and Pulses (in gms.) Per Day in NER

ITEM	*Cereals*				*Pulses*			
	1983	*1988*	*1994*	*1999*	*1983*	*1988*	*1994*	*1999*
ANP	569.8	675.4	653.9	446.6	—	—	15.3	16.8
ASM	365.8	359.5	410.2	373.9	7.10	7.71	6.72	7.69
MNP	418.5	461.0	492.4	476.4	2.93	—	—	—
MGH	293.8	235.1	208.2	225.9	3.88	4.03	3.54	3.07
MZM	179.1	233.2	398.6	395.8	0.52	4.39	35.2	28.6
NGN	392.6	247.2	432.1	423.6	3.88	9.58	19.82	22.1
TRP	535.6	475.8	457.1	391.9	3.02	4.13	5.91	3.9
India	**448.4**	**443.6**	**520.5**	**522.7**	**45.2**	**37.6**	**40.5**	**41.1**

Table 15.7 gives a picture of per capita per day availability of foodgrains production where the same picture is observed as in case of pulses. It is observed that Arunachal Pradesh, is the only state in NER which tried to maintain its superiority till 1994 but the trend declined thereafter.

Table 15.7: Per Capita Per Day Availability of Food Grains, Growth Rate of Population and Production

State	*Per Capita Per Day Availability of Food Grains (in gms.)*				*Annual Average Growth Rate of Population and Production of Food Grains*			
	1983	*1988*	*1994*	*1999*	*1980-90*		*1991-2000*	
					Population	Production	Population	Production
ANP	569.75	675.42	669.18	463.33	3.1	4.2	3.1	-1.8
ASM	372.88	367.25	416.92	381.58	1.5	1.3	1.2	1.5
MNP	421.44	461.00	492.35	476.35	2.6	-1.7	2.5	2.2
MGH	297.63	239.21	211.78	228.99	2.8	-0.4	2.8	2.0
MZM	179.57	237.55	433.68	424.38	3.4	8.3	3.3	7.4
NGN	396.52	256.81	451.87	445.60	4.3	3.7	4.4	4.5
TRP	538.56	479.93	463.04	395.25	3.4	1.2	2.9	0.2
India	**493.60**	**481.14**	**560.98**	**563.84**	**2.1**	**1.8**	**1.9**	**1.8**

Thus food insecurity is a matter of great concern not only to the people of NER but also to the policy-makers and planners of NER. It is further observed that no proper care has been taken for the development of agriculture to increase production by which the living condition of the society of NER may be a better one. Modern technologies, irrigation facilities, scientific and modern equipments are not being properly used for the real development of agriculture in the age of globalization and liberalization and for which the region is stepping back day by day.

Health is a social goal and is considered as an integral component in over all socio-economic development. The majority of health problems are the products of illiteracy, poverty, ignorance, over crowding, poor environmental conditions and uneven distribution of health manpower and institutions. It is observed that there are only 4.32 per cent of public health centres in the states of NER (958 Nos.) as compared to India's figure (Table 15.8) and only in Assam there are 64 per cent public health centres among the states of NER, while less than 8 per cent are in each of the other states of the region. The same patterns are observed in case of sub-centres and community health centres. Thus, it is high time to make an effort to increase the number of health centres in backward states of NER so that health problems can be minimized to some extent.

Table 15.8: No. of Health Centres (As on 31.3.95) and Annual Requirement of Water for Domestic Purposes (Cubic km.)

	Health Centres			*Coverage of problem villages during*	*2001-02 Number (approx) of*	
	PHC	*SC*	*CHC*	*1990-91*	*Hospitals*	*Bed (in '000)*
ANP	40	203	7	0	15	3
ASM	619	5180	105	356	328	17
MNP	72	420	15	0	19	3
MGH	88	333	10	406	7	3
MZM	43	244	6	68	11	2
NGN	33	244	5	7	17	2
TRP	63	535	10	120	27	2
India	**22156**	**131902**	**2377**	**3031**	**17952**	**915**

Diet survey data from many parts of India show that almost one-third of the children in poor families do not eat enough food needed for normal growth. On top of this, the poor environmental sanitation around them predisposes them to infection. The magnitude of the problem of anaemia is second only to that of protein-energy malnutrition. The problem is less severe in the urban areas than in the rural areas. Anaemia reduces work capacity and productivity, which is particularly important in the context of the agricultural economy of the country. Thus, food insecurity is a matter of great concern not only to the people of NER but also to the policy-makers and planners of NER. The recommended intakes of nutrients of a nation differ from those of international norms set up by FAO and WHO. The term used to describe dietary stand is "Recommended Dietary Allowance (RDA)".

Table 15.9 shows the quantity of items (Recommended Dietary Requirements) that should be consumed by the persons of different sex and age groups. This is the level of intake of essential nutrients, in the judgement of the (national or international) committee on dietary allowances, considered to be adequate to meet the known nutritional needs of practically all healthy persons.

Table 15.9: Recommended Dietary Requirement in Grammes

Food Items	*Adult Male*			*Adult Female*			*Children*		*Boys*	*Girl*
	Seco-ndary Work	Mode-rate Work	Heavy Work	Seco-ndary Work	Mode-rate Work	Heavy Work	1-3 yrs.	4-5 yrs.	10-12 yrs.	10-12 yrs.
Cereals	460	520	670	410	440	575	175	270	420	380
Pulses	40	50	60	40	45	50	35	35	45	45
Leaf Vegetable	40	40	40	100	100	50	40	50	50	50
Other Vegetable	60	70	80	40	40	100	20	30	50	50
Roots and Tubers	50	60	80	50	50	60	10	20	30	30
Milk	150	200	250	100	150	200	300	250	250	250
Oil and Fat	40	45	60	20	25	40	15	25	40	35
Sugar and Jaggery	30	35	55	20	20	40	30	40	45	45

Post-reform Development Scenario in NER

Agriculture in NER has considerable social and political influence. Agriculure has a vital role to play in the economic development in NER, which is a key factor to the economic growth of the region. NER produces a wide array of crops although the food crops preponderate over other crops cultivated in the entire region. Assam is contributing a lot in the fruit and vegetables production as it is not trailing behind as compared to other states of the country. In this sector the state alone covers an area of 5 lakh hectares which produces around 13.24 lakh MT of fruits, 2.05 lakh MT of spices and 36.61 lakh MT of vegetables. In the sphere of industrialization, the industries supporting value addition in agriculture have been given much priority. The agro-based industries have been given much importance in this direction. In Assam as well as in the country, agriculture and allied activities are playing a dominant role to contribute nearly 38.7 per cent of GDP and employment to nearly 67 per cent of total working population. Horticulture sector, which contributes greatly to GDP of agriculture sector in the state is a big unorganized sector, completely owned and managed by the small entrepreneurs and marginal farmers. In the agricultural sector more and more entrepreneurs have opted for processing sector for value addition of horticulture crops mainly spices under Mini-Mission IV. The government has taken initiative to take them outside the state for exposure on special items like spices, tropical and sub-tropical medicinal and aromatic plants, floriculture etc. The entrepreneurs have got much scope for self employment under the horticulture crops and can visualize the future prosperity and profitability in this sector. They have taken much interest in developing the homestead garden to become self-sufficient as regards availability of day to day requirement of seasonal major and minor fruits, vegetables, flowers, spices, condiment and even medicinal plants also.

Under Mini Mission IV, a technology mission, new processing units have been upgraded. Assam Small Farmers Agribusiness Consortium (ASFAC) and State Department of Agriculture sponsored 'Entrepreneurship Development Training Programme' to create awareness among the entrepreneurs. With the declaration of 2002-03 as Spice Year by the Government of Assam, a number of processing units have been set up to give a boost to this sector and the entrepreneurs are playing a tremendous role to develop these units.

In 2002-03, 900 women were trained for entrepreneurship in horticulture sector through the formation of SHG. Setting up of Integrated Mushroom units is also a major development in this direction. The agro-based and food industry in the state has offered job opportunities to 55,000 entrepreneurs who have contributed production to the value of Rs. 19.78 crore during 2001-02. Cottage industries are normally associated with agriculture and provide a subsidiary employment in rural areas.

There is no doubt that the resources pumped down for poverty alleviation and provision of subsidies in the name of poor have not been much effective in Assam. Considering the large number of persons still living below poverty line, the Central Government announced a holistic programme called 'Swarnajayanti Gram Swarojgar Yojana' (SGSY) for the implementation of the erstwhile self-employment programme called 'Integrated Rural Development Programme' (IRDP). This programme was based on a group (community) approach to rural development where the rural poor were organized into Self-Help Groups (SHGs) and provided micro credit to take up viable economic activities on their own. The very striking feature of the scheme is that it is quite different from earlier programme in objectives, strategy, methodology and sustainability. The scheme aims at establishing a large number of micro enterprises specially for poor people in rural areas[3]. The objective is to help every assisted family below poverty line for 3 years by providing them income generating assets through credit and government subsidy. In several districts and development blocks of Assam, this group is participating actively for the uplift of the rural poor. Within a short span of time, the members of the SHGs have been able to generate income and savings and solve the problem on rural employment. This shows the positive impact of SHG members in resisting the social evils in the respective areas. The Government of Assam has taken up the theme of empowerment of the rural poor as one of the main items on its agenda to tackle the rural poverty and socio-economic issues. The self-help members through thrift and credit haye been taken up mass movement in Assam and the State has given primary importance to uplift of the poor through SHGs. If the poor are properly motivated and sensitized through education and training then the conditions of economic reforms will be fulfilled by the people in the state in shaping their own destiny. Then LPG will not be a problem for the region as self reliance is the slogan of the New Economic Policy.

The decision of the Assam Government to request the Centre to increase its stake in the Gas Cracker Project is a welcome move as the state should have a bigger say in the project which is emotionally attached to the people of the State. Till now, the state did not have a major say in industries established with the natural resources available in Assam and if the centre accepts the demand of the State Government, the state would also earn a major share of the profits. Under the present arrangement, the Gas Authority of India Limited (GAIL) with 70 per cent stake in the project is the major shareholder while the Assam Industrial Development Corporation (AIDC), Numaligarh Refinery Limited (NRL) and Oil India Limited (OIL) each will have 10 per cent stake. The Industries and Commerce Department of Government of Assam prepared a proposal in this regard for approval of the cabinet and only then a formal proposal will be sent to the Centre. If the project is realized, the down stream and allied industries will provide employment to at least one lakh persons, which will definitely ease the problem of unemployment. The AIDC has already started the process of engaging a consultant to study the feasibility of setting up of down stream industries and market potentials to prepare an action plan for the same. In this regard, the Central Institute of Plastic Technology (CIPT) can play a greater role by starting the training programme for the unemployed youth of the region. The Gas Cracker would be designed to produce 2.80 lakh tonnes of polymers, which include 2.02 lakh tonnes of linear Low Density of Polyethylene (LDPE) and 60,000 tonnes of High Density of Polyethylene (HDPE) per annum. The opportunities ahead are unlimited with great challenges.

It is needless to say that economic growth of a region cannot be achieved without the growth of large or small industries and for which uninterrupted power supply is badly necessary. There cannot be a second opinion on the fact that industries open avenues for appointment directly and indirectly, whereby the problem of unemployment can be solved considerably. In this regard NER excluding Assam was far lagging behind as the present generation capacity of electricity in the North East is around 1472 MW of which 374 MW is from thermal sources and 994 MW from hydro sources. In the Tenth Plan period the capacity addition is projected to be 239 MW from hydro and gas based projects like KLHEP 100 MW, Bhairabi HEP 80 MW, Lakwa Waste Heat 38 MW and Baramura GTP 21 MW. Further, the Government of India has initiated to set up hydel and thermal projects which are expected to be commissioned by the year 2020 from Subansiri River at different stages 4,600 MW, Kameng HE Project 600 MW,

Tipaimukh HEP 1500 MW and 280 MW for Tripura Gas Project, (through CPSUs) and in all 6980 MW.

Looking at the power scenario of Assam, as of today, the installed capacity has been reduced to 253.5 MW from 574.4 MW owing to suspension of BTPS (240 MW), CTPS (60 MW), Mobile Gas Turbine (19 MW) and Bordikharu HE (mini) project (2 MW) and as a matter of fact, the generation came down to 120-150 MW. As such ASEB has to draw power from CPSUs to the tune of around 500-600 MW to meet up the peak load demands nearing to 750 MW.

In this context, during the 11th Plan period the target is to achieve from Namrup and Amguri together 300 MW (gas based), from Borgolai TPS 60 MW (coal based) and from Lower Kopili and Mintriang hydel projects together 165 MW, in all 525 MW. Further, under NTPC another 500 MW at BTPS (coal based) may be added to this capacity as delcared. From these figures it can be expected that installed capacity in Assam by the year 2012 will stand at about 1416 MW. Considering 60 per cent probable achievement the power generation will be around 900 MW, if not more, against the projected demand of 1423 MW. Though it may appear to be a shortfall, commissioning of the projects will certainly contribute to the stable power position, considering the NER as a whole. To be more certain, there will not be any scarcity of power when Subansiri (Lower) HE Project (1000 MW) which is likely to be commissioned by the year 2011 is put into the grid. Also it will contribute to meet the demands in Assam in particular and NER in general. By the year 2020, if not earlier, there is further scope to increase the generation capacity in Assam by commissioning another 250 unit (coal based) at BTPs, 60 MW at Borgolai Project (coal), 60 MW Upper Barapani HE Project and reviving CTPS (60 MW), altogether 430 MW apart from other projects as may be planned during this time. The proposed natural gas import to the country from Myanmar to Goya through North East, as per proposed route, through Aizwal, Silchar, Guwahati, Siliguri and Goya, if materialized, there is no doubt that this region will be amply benefited by using this gas as feed stock or fuel or both[4].

It is a welcome sign that the Government of Assam has entered into the Oil Sector and the tie up with OIL will create a great synergic force. Such a road map could be a starting point, and let this be a signal that the government in right earnest wants to create an important landmark in oil business.

In the era of globalization, electricity is one of the basic inputs for achieving socio-economic development of a nation. The present per capita consumption of electricity in India is little over 400 kWh, which is much lower than that of the developed countries. To avoid this backdrop Government of India formed an exclusive Ministry for Non-Conventional Energy Sources for implementing the programmes on renewable energy like bio-gas, small hydro projects, wind energy, geo-thermal energy, solar energy etc. Although there is immense potentiality for the development of non-conventional and renewable energy sector in Assam, there is a regular feature of the shortage of power in the state. About 87 per cent of the state's population live in rural areas in 26,247 villages. Of these, as on March 31, 2006, only 21,586 villages have been electrified of which only 16.54 per cent of the total households in these electrified villages have electricity connection. The remaining 4661 villages are still to see light of electricity. Again, 2145 unelectrified villages have been identified as remote and thus unable to provide 'Electricity To All' by 2012 which is a far cry. There is no alternative but to go for non-conventional and renewable energy sources applying modern technologies. It is encouraging to note that the Assam Energy Development Agency, the State Nodal Agency of the Ministry of the Non-conventional Energy Sources identified the potentiality of three renewable sources of energy like small hydro, biomass gasification and solar photovoltaic for electrification of remote villages. Thus the priority of harnessing non-conventional renewable sources of energy will continue for the years to come so as to carryout all the economic activities in rural areas as part of infrastructural development of the policy of globalization.

The Centre's larger attention to tea industry of the country has brightened its prospects of production and exports. The 11th Plan outlay on tea industry stands at Rs. 800 crore. During 10th

Plan period, the industry received funds worth Rs. 350 crore by way of plan funds and around Rs. 30 crore from the proceeds accumulated under the additional excise duty. Besides this, the unspent amount accruing out of the non-lapsable additional excise duty fund would be carried forward. This is in addition to resources from special purpose tea fund that would be made available to tea industry. It may be recalled that following Planning Commission's approval for setting up a special purpose tea fund and the budget announcement of the same by the Union Finance Minister, the Minister of State for Commerce revealed, at a press conference in Guwahati in May 2006, that the Indian tea industry would utilize Rs. 4,700 crore under which Assam alone would get a share of 60 per cent or Rs. 2820 crore. It was also announced that the government would start disbursing the fund from December 2006 when it would provide Rs. 100 crore as the initial components. The minister also revealed that the Centre planned to achieve a proper price structure and build up an encouraging sales strategy starting through the auction route. The objective is to create an environment where more producers and buyers opted for the auction system of marketing. The Union Commerce Minister had earlier promised that he would unveil a 15-year programme for massive replantation and rejuvenation of the country's tea sector.

It is important to note that there is a marketing strategy and quality improvement design structure in the revival package to give the industry edge over its competitors in the global market. The tea package is also designed to create a more transparent mechanism with the setting up of two new auction centres in Assam where an electronic system would be developed and a target of replantation of more than 1.7 lakh hectares over a period of 15 years has been fixed. This is certainly a happy change in sight. What is, however, the latest addition to the package and what will certainly bring cheer to Assam's 70,000 small tea growers in addition to almost another equal number in the rest of the country, is the announcement that five factories in the state, to start with, will be set up for the manufacture of tea from green leaves of the small tea gardens. Since this will help eliminating middlemen's appropriation, the grower's tea is expected to fetch an additional profit of at least Rs. 15 a kg. This would be no mean achievement[5].

Good roads and transport system are the key indicators and facilitators of progress and the part of the scheme of New Economic Reform. Assam will soon be riding the highway to prosperity if the dream projects of the National Highway Authority of India are realized without running into too many hurdles. Thousands of kilometre of roads and highways in the state are to be improved and the carriageways broadened to make way for increased volume of traffic ensuring that the road and transport system are smooth and fast in the region. The most prestigious project, East West Corridor Project—a 678 km. long express way between Silchar and Srirampore (Assam-West Bengal border) will pass through Guwahati besides several other important towns and is expected to be completed by 2008. It promises to provide a hindrance free and fast transport network that will benefit the people of three districts of Barak Valley of Assam who are frequently cut off from the rest of the country due to frequent landslides and other reasons. There are several other projects in the pipeline, including 4-laning of the 315 km. highway between Nagaon and Dibrugarh of Assam. Access to good roads brings all round development by making access to health care, agricultural marketing, education and administration easier. It would increase income, employment opportunities, tourism, indusrial development in many ways. If North East will improve then trade relation with neighbouring border countries should be established. In a bid to explore the ASEAN market, the centre has decided to improve the road connectivity in the North East. At a Conference of Indian Industry (CII) held at Shillong, the Joint Secretary of Investment and Technology Promotion, the Ministry of External Affairs has pointed out that the ministry is now having close look with the North East Council (NEC) to implement some new plans since this region has very close links with Myanmar and Bangladesh. In 2005, the volume of trade between India and ASEAN had touched $15 million and considering the upspring market, we have set a target of $35 billion trade by 2015.

Conclusion and Suggestions

From the foregoing discussion, it is clear that the scene of development in NER was far from satisfactory in pre-Economic Reform period and in the post-Reform period, marks of development can be found in the region in general and the state of Assam in particular. So far as the latest Human Development Index is concerned one thing is certain that the society of NER is lagging behind as compared to other regions of the country due to many reasons such as rise of terrorism, repeated social unrest along with government's apathy towards primary sectors and misappropriation of government fund and non-utilization of sanctioned money etc. After the process of globalization started, the slogan 'enrich thyself' is going to be implemented in right earnest in different states of NER by the respective governments. As a result, initiatives have been taken by the State Governments of NER to cope with the Central Government's NEP. It is a matter of fact that the forces of LPG in economic, social, cultural and political spheres of life have been subjected to both negative and positive aspects. At the outset of this economic reform in India some scholars perceived it as elite-driven and incapable of bringing qualitative change in people's lives. The fear psychosis was that the advanced countries would capture a lion's share in the global market by neglecting the service sector in different regions of the country. However, the present scenario is altogether different and economic reform has come to stay and the region cannot do away with it. Again the present study reveals the fact that globalization has paved the way for rapid technological advancements in the region with developed information technological services, research and development etc. Many young skilled persons have got their employment in MNCs of other parts of India as well as in the world. That reforms has brought new opportunities of trade, business, services and employment in the region cannot be denied. At the same time the region should update the younger generation through research and training to cope with the changing situation. The North-Eastern economy is suffering from inadequate infrastructure. Transportation facilities are poor and inadequate. Communication facilities are not so developed.

There is no encouraging sign for Science and Technology and other sub-sectors. Agriculture, the primary sector, is misguided by the primordial social custom and traditions. Road, water and air transport facilities in the region are far below the requirement. There is no remarkable GDP growth and the region is still miles away from a virtual global village. There is mass unemployment causing constant unrest in the region. Hence following suggestions may be outlined to keep pace with the policies of NEP.

Due to reverse trend of monsoon in 2006-07 in the state, severe draught like situation prevailed which stood in the way of agricultural development. Though the annual average of rainfall in the state of Assam is 2580 mm, it is found to be gradually deceasing to the range of 2118 mm to 2262 mm during the last 5 years. The state witnessed extreme weather aberration during the current kharif season. The monsoon rain considered to be highly beneficial for initiating sowing or transplantation of kharif crop is found to be missing mostly in this year. In most of the districts of the state 45-70 per cent deficit rainfall has been experienced. The agricultural sector in our country remaned susceptible to fluctuating behaviour of monsoon whereas the over all global agricultural scenario remained dynamic with noticeable change in production, stock and trade in this year. The fate of Sali rice or winter rice, the major crop of the state which covers 67 per cent of total area under rice is quite uncertain. At this backdrop, the productivity of Sali rice is likely to come down to 1400 kg. per hectare in 2005-06 from 1595 kg. per hectare in 2004-05. To avoid this critical situation 3.28 lakh litres of diesel were distributed among the farmers to activate the shallow tubewells which has benefited nearly 90,000 farm families. The state of Assam having potentiality of enormous natural resources could occupy a prominent place in the world with pre-dominance in agriculture sector provided it could be free from perennial natural calamities. Through proper research and planning from multi-level authorities like flood control department, irrigation department and agricultural department the state can be saved. Soil erosion, deforestation and preservation of bio-diversity are a crying need of the hour. The water resources of NER accounting for about 33 per cent of the country's water wealth need to be harnessed judiciously to bridge the gap in water requirement for agricultural purposes. With a view to increasing the per capita income of the state from Rs. 14,523 at current prices in 2005-06 which is 43.7 per cent less than the all India average, much emphasis need to be laid on effective water management plan like other agriculturally developed regions of the country.

The issue of inequality and poverty is an important one for global policy. This study reveals that despite abundant natural resources, the region is poorest of the poor and repeatedly neglected by the policy-makers of New Delhi since independence. Although the Union Minister of Heavy Industries from Assam along with few members of Parliament urged on the floor of Parliament for declaring Assam a Special Economic Zone (SEZ), the Central Government is reluctant to allot the same. In the era of globalization, Central Government's SEZ Policy should be extended to Assam not only to boost economic production but also fulfil the need of infrastructural development to attract the Multi-National Corporations and industrialists for removing the malady of regional disparity.

The NER which is known for its rich but unharnessed resources was thought to be heading for a spectacular change in its resource use pattern. The North East Industrial Policy was announced on December 24, 1997 for attracting investment in the areas of industry and infrastructure and removal of regional disparity through sustainable economic development for raising per capita income of people and better standard of living. The region has long been suffering from low level of income with its share of 2.7 per cent of India's total national income having to shelter 3.8 per cent of its population. The short fall of region's per capita income below all-India level at constant prices was Rs. 1950 in 1993-94 and today the difference has climbed up to more than Rs. 5700. Thus if the region wants to eliminate this difference in 20 years from now, it has to aim at an economic growth rate of 9 per cent per annum. This requires the development of both industry and agriculture along with infrastructure. The North East Industrial Policy has failed to attract large investments in the areas of industry and infrastructure. The policy took almost 4 years to take off, and could somehow garner investment of only Rs. 1200 crore, in the last 5 years, but what is much more surprising is that the Centre has extended similar benefits to states of Uttaranchal, Himachal Pradesh and Jammu & Kashmir which are infrastructurally far ahead of this region and closer to mainland market. The government has decided to invest Rs. 4000 crore in Uttaranchal, Rs. 18000 crore in Himachal Pradesh and Rs. 2000 crore in Jammu & Kashmir. Thus step-motherly attitude of the Centre towards the North East is still visible. This policy is scheduled to expire after March 2007 and hence the extension of the period of the policy is necessary to save the region from further deterioration.

One of the most remarkable developments of New Economic Reform is the increasing role of Multi-National Corporations (MNCs), which functions cutting across national boundaries and ignoring the State System. Although the UN recognizes the State System as primary and most important actor in International System, the New Economic Reform would develop a new kind of State and growth of new relationship with traditional power apparatus. Further, with the advent of globalization, the supranational bodies like UN, EU, NAFTA, ASEA, APEC, IMF, World Bank and WTO will formulate policies and lay conditions like reduction of expenditure in social sectors, cut down in employment, government subsidies etc. not necessarily acceptable to the state and NER of India, which is poverty-striken and will be victim of the situation. Under the circumstances it can be suggested that the region wants reform but not at the cost of its people. Hence, the slogan of the region should be "Economic Reform in the Region within the Limits".

NER is famous for its natural scenery and pilgrimages. It attracts tourists from all the countries in the world. Earlier the governments of North-Eastern States earned foreign exchange from the sector of Tourism. But, in the last few decades, due to rise of terrorism and government's apathy towards this industry, Tourism is in a bad shape. As a result the people of North East could not earn from this industry. In the circumstances it may be suggested that the government of the region should take initiative for the modernization of Tourism and creation of proper environment which will attract the tourists. Efffective implementation of e-governance can take information technology to the common man, helping national and State Governments to align their services with the changing needs of both citizens and stakeholders. Versatile Information System for Tourist Attraction (VISTA) is an integrated system that uses the power of Information Technology to promote Tourism and facilitate Tourist operations. An Electronic Tourism Platform (ETP) Core System may be designed corresponding to documentation and generic guides. The ETP will enable small and medium sized enterprises to respond to new demands for Tourist products and allow access to new markets that were not previously reachable.

Local population should be associated with Tourism activities and share with others in the economic, social and cultural benefits they generate and particularly in the creation of direct and indirect jobs resulting from them. Tourism policies and activities should be conducted with respect to artistic, archaeological and cultural heritage. The government should take care for preserving and upgrading historical monuments, shrines and privately owned cultural property and monuments.

The population explosion has hindered the country's growth. The loopholes in the population control need to be identified and action taken to strengthen the programme. The target is to effectively bring down the birth rate and form a policy in accordance with the social, political and economic set up of the state. It is important to improve the status of women in the society. Family planning camps have adopted a holistic approach where complete health care facility is being provided to the rural residents. It was decided to form local societies for effective implementation of routine immunisation and mother and child health care programmes. Issues like female foeticide and male sterilisation need to be discussed, as both are contradictory and yet important for population control programme. Economic and educational progress is the foundation on which we can have effective progress in regard to family planning. The pressure on the limited resources of the country has brought to the forefront the urgency of population control. It is apparent that this can be achieved only by the reduction of the birth rate to the extent necessary to stabilise the population at a level consistent with the requirements of the national economy. The study invites the attention of the policy-makers of the region to check the immigration from neighbouring countries to the region for controlling the population explosion.

The State of the World, 1999 Report from the World Watch Institute suggests that the global economy could be seriously affected by environmental problems, such as the lack of access to enough resources to meet growing population demands. Environmental degradation can contribute to social and political instability, which can lead to security issues. Human Rights can be upheld by ensuring women's empowerment, and realizing that women play a crucial role in the development of society, many underlying issues which lead to conflict and problems can be tackled more effectively. Hence preservation and protection of environment will provide sustainable growth and development in the region.

The rush of the big players to get a berth in the NER will lead to exploitation to the people in general and small and medium industries in the state in particular. The conversion of agrarian society into industrial one has a cascading effect on the society. Before establishing industries in the region by the MNCs certain code of conduct should be framed by the respective State Government of the region for the operation of the same and they must abide by the rules framed by the governments.

No endeavour in this respect will be successful unless and until the people of the region are well conscious and aware of it. To get something, one must pay something. Thus old and traditional structures, social bonds, customs etc. must be sacrificed a little in order to improve. At the same time the governments should implement the reform policies with extreme caution so that it would not arouse the people's emotion and sentiments by interfering in the social laws, customs, traditions etc. Hence the slogan should be *'Globalization within limits or reform in a controlled manner'*.

NOTES

1. N. Bhattacharya, (1998): On Level of Living Surveys in India, Presidential Address, 85th Indian Science Congress, Section of Statistics.
2. V.R. Rao, (1996): General Presidential Address in 83rd Indian Science Congress, Patiala.
3. Namita Devi, (2006): A Success Story of Self-Help Group in *The Assam Tribune,* November 27.
4. J.N. Goswami, (2006): Power Generation Prospects in North East in *The Assam Tribune,* September 14.
5. Indian's Tea Prospects in *The Assam Tribune,* September 27, 2006.

REFERENCES

Ahluwalia, Isher Judge and Little, I.M.D. (ed.) (1998): *India's Economic Reforms and Development—Essays for Monmohan Singh,* Oxford University Press, New Delhi.

Bhagawati, Jagadish (1994): *India in Transition: Freeing the Economy,* Oxford University Press, New Delhi.

Dutta, P.C. (2003): Regional Disparity and its Consequences in North-Eastern Region of India in *Economic Liberalization and Regional Disparities in India—Special Focus on the North-Eastern Region* (ed.) A.C. Mohapatra and C.R. Pathak, Star Publishing House, Shillong.

Dutta, P.C. and B.C. Pradhan (2004): Agricultural Development and Security of Life in *Food Security and Public Distribution System Today—Failures and Success* (ed.) Amalesh Banerjee, Kanishka Publishers, Distributors, New Delhi.

Dutta, P.C. and B.C. Pradhan (2006): Changing Agricultural Scenario in North East India in *Changing Agricultural Scenario in North East India* (ed.) Bimal J. Deb and B. Dutta Ray, Concept Publishing Company, New Delhi.

Dutta P.C. and H. Choudhury (1996): A Note on Inter State Variation in Per Capita Non-Food Household Items of Consumption in the North East India, *IJRS,* Vol. 28, No. 2.

Ghosh, Jayati (1998): *Liberalisation Debates* in Terence Byres (ed), The Indian Economy: Major Debate Since Independence, Delhi, 329.

Jha Prabodh Kumar (2000): Economic Reformation or Deformation in India in *Post-reform Leading Issues of Indian Economy,* Vol. I (ed.) A.D.N. Bajpai *et al.,* pp. 8-18, Atlantic Publishers and Distributors, New Delhi.

Kumar, Nagesh in Raj Kapila and Uma Kapila (ed.) *A Decade of Economic Reforms in India: The Past, The Present, The Future...* (2002), Academic Foundations, New Delhi.

Mohan, Rakesh (1999): *Economic Reforms: The Next Wave,* Lalit Doshi Memorial Lecture, Mumbai, 13th October, 1999.

Nagraj, R. (1997): What has Happened Since 1991 : Assessment of India's Economic Reforms, *Economic and Political Weekly,* p. 2871, 8th November.

Nayyar, Deepak (1993): Indian Economy at the Cross Roads: Illusions and Realities, *Economic and Political Weekly,* p. 639, 10th April, 1993.

Nayyar, Deepak (1996): *Economic Liberalization in India: Analytics, Experience and Lesson,* R.C. Dutta Lectures, Orient Longman, New Delhi, Centre for Studies in Social Sciences.

Parikh, Kirti (1997): India's Economy: Raised for Take off, *Economic and Political Weekly,* pp. 124-130, 1151, May 17-23.

Patnaik, Prabhat and Chandrasekhar, C.P. (1995): Indian Economy under Structural Reforms, *Economic and Political Weekly,* November 25.

Ray, Binayak (2000): Good Governance and Administrative Reforms: Priorities for India in Economic Liberalisation and Institutional Reforms *in South Asia—Recent Experiences and Future Prospects,* (ed.) Dilip Dutta, pp. 369-396, Atlantic Publishers and Distributors, New Delhi-27.

Saramma, A.D. (2000): New Economic Policy of 1991 and the Problem of Rural Unemployment: Some Options in *Post-reform Leading Issues of Indian Economy,* Vol. I (ed.) A.D.N. Bajpai *et al.*, pp. 307-316, Atlantic Publishers and Distributors, New Delhi.

Singh Manminder and Sandeep Singh Saluja (2005): New Economic Reforms and Economic Growth in *Liberalisation and Globalisation of Indian Economy,* Vol. VI (ed.) K.R. Gupta, pp. 1-26, Atlantic Publishers and Distributors, New Delhi.

Srinivasan, T.N. (1998): *India's Export Performance: A Comparative Analysis,* in I.J. Ahluwalia and I.M.D. Little (ed.) *op. cit.*

16

The Micro Finance Experience
Accomplishments and Challenges

Sakiya Khan

Finance is one of the most crucial inputs for economic activity, growth and development. In this regard, financial institutions play an important role by channelizing funds from surplus sector (savers) to deficit sectors (investors). However, these institutions do not show much enthusiasm to put their resources in rural and backward areas for the benefit of poorer people as these are commercial organizations and are basically interested in profitability and sustainability.

Till the 1990s the rural financial system in India was predominantly supply driven with the state playing a major role in improving the access to financial services by the poor. While state intervention considerably improved the outreach of the banking system and expanded rural credit, it also allowed rent seeking tendencies and credit indiscipline to grow (Nanda, 2000). By the late 1980s the rural financial system had virtually collapsed amid heavy regulations, distraught market conditions, dual lines of control, and mounting arrears. In 1991, liberalization of the Indian economy had an important bearing on the financial sectors; banks which have turned weak, were confronted with the challenge of making themselves profitable while maintaining their prudential requirements and competing with private and foreign banks in a new liberalized milieu.

Around this time, Asian countries like Bangladesh, Indonesia, Sri Lanka, Combodia and Thailand and Latin American countries like Bolivia, and Chile were effectively adopting the new micro finance approach. The extraordinary repayment rates (95%) of the micro finance institutions provided the required "leverage" for transforming poverty alleviation exercises into business opportunities.

In India, the adoption of the new micro finance approach by rural financial institutions assumed the form of the "Self-Help Group-Bank Linkage Programme". Considered to be unique among various micro finance interventions, the Programme being implemented since 1992 under the aegis of National Bank for Agriculture and Rural Development (NABARD) stands today at a very crucial juncture.

Based on the rationale identified for micro finance intervention, NABARD's aim is to develop the SHG-Bank linkage model as the core strategy, which could be used by the banking system for reaching out to the poor households (NABARD, 2002 C). The Programme is perceived as a new paradigm capable of changing totally the current banking scenario, which is not really inclined towards dealing with the poor. Incidentally, the SHG-Bank linkage programme being implemented has coincided with the financial sector reforms. There is evidence that the banks under the on-going reforms have been compelled to scale down their rural and priority sector business (Shylendra, 2001). The major question that emerges is, in what way NABARD's aim to make SHG-Bank linkage a core strategy for banking with the poor is consistent with the current predicament of banks owing to reforms. Because of reforms focusing on reduction in NPAs and profitability, bankers are reluctant to evince interest in rural lending. Through SHG-Bank linkage programmes, bankers are advised to increase their outreach of the poor and disadvantaged sections.

Through the SHG-Bank linkage programme the RBI and NABARD have tried to promote relationship between the poor and bankers with the social intermediation of NGOs. The model is predominantly a "Linkage Model", which draws upon the strengths of various partners: NGOs, who are best in mobilizing the poor and building their capacities, and bankers, whose financial strength is financing.

Taking its effective credit delivery potential Reserve Bank of India had, in 1996, advised all banks to treat the SHG lending as a normal business activity under priority sector. The progress of SHG-bank linkage programme in the country is very encouraging. As on 31 March 2005, a cumulative number of 1,618,456 SHGs were credit linked with 573 banks (47 commercial banks, 196 RRB, 330 cooperative banks) covering 24.3 million rural poor families. About 90 per cent of the SHGs linked are exclusive women groups. The programme is implemented in all the states and Union Territories. As many as 4323 NGOs/SHPIs are involved in the promotion and linkage of SHGs with banks. A total amount of more than Rs. 68 billion was provided as bank loan to the SHGs against which NABARD has provided refinance assistance of Rs. 30920 million to banks. The goal of NABARD is to credit link 10 (ten) lakhs SHGs with bank covering 10 crores rural body by 2008. In the light of practical effectiveness of SHG-Bank Linkage Programme, the present paper makes an attempt to review the performance of the programme in the North-Eastern states of India and across three major institutions—commercial banks, cooperatives, and the regional rural banks.

The analytical section of this paper is divided in three parts. The first section reviews the spread of SHG-linkage to banks across three different models that have been adopted by the NABARD to route credit to SHGs. The second section assesses the coverage of SHG linkages since inception of the programme till March 2005 and reviews their spread across North-Eastern states. The third section studies the state-by-state participation of commercial banks, regional rural banks, and cooperatives. The study is based on secondary data published by the NABARD. Statistics are drawn from NABARD's publication: *Progress of SHG-Bank Linkage in India 2004-05.*

SHG-Bank Linkage Programme in North East India: Review of Models

Broadly, three models of linkage have emerged under the Programme. Under Model I, the financial institutions both promote and finance SHGs directly; under Model II, NGOs promote and finance SHGs while the banks provide the credit support and; under Model III, NGOs both promote and finance SHGs using funds borrowed from outside agencies.

The figures in Table 16.1 indicate that across the country Model II, where SHGs were formed and nurtured by the NGOs, was more popular among the bankers. Banks opened savings accounts and then provided credit directly to the SHGs, while NGOs acted as facilitators. This approach has been widely accepted by the practitioners partly because of the large scale participation of State Government through development agencies like the District Rural Development Agency (DRDA), District Women Development Agency (DWDA), and some of the centrally sponsored social section missions, and also because of special initiatives of NABARD (Appendix A).

Table 16.1: SHG-Bank Linkage Model-wise

(Percentage share)

	Regions	*Model I*	*Model II*	*Model III*
1.	Northern Region	11	89	0
2.	North-Eastern Region	78	15	7
3.	Eastern Region	43	45	12
4.	Central Region	23	74	3
5.	Western Region	35	59	6
6.	Southern Region	12	80	8

In North East India there are wide variations in the spread of the Programme across the states. Figures in Table 16.2 indicate the Model I is more popular among the bankers in Assam, Manipur and Tripura. In Meghalaya and Sikkim Model II is widely accepted by the practitioners because of the large scale participation of State Government through development agencies like DRDA/DWDA and some of the centrally sponsored social sector missions. Arunachal Pradesh, where SHG linkage programme is relatively weak, Model II is the only model in operation. This is because NGOs are found to be the sole promoter and financiers. In States like Mizoram, Nagaland Model II is more popular because of the presence of large number of NGOs.

Table 16.2: SHG-Bank Linkage Model: State-wise

(Percentage share)

	States	*Model I*	*Model II*	*Model III*
1.	Assam	81	12	7
2.	Arunachal Pradesh	—	100	—
3.	Manipur	68	42	—
4.	Meghalaya	1	73	26
5.	Sikkim	24	76	—
6.	Nagaland	30	70	—
7.	Tripura	54	46	—
8.	Mizoram	21	79	—

Seven per cent of the SHGs were credit linked under Model III where NGOs acted as facilitators as well as micro finance intermediaries. This Model is only popular in Meghalaya and to a certain extent in Assam. In the rest of the states this Model is totally absent. However, this model is expected to gain wider recognition with smaller banks venturing into large scale financing of SHGs.

SHG-Bank Linkage Programme: Review by State

The SHG-Bank linkage programme has been operating in India since 1992-93 but has gained momentum only since 1997-98. The SHG linkage programme seems to have picked up since the Global Micro Credit Summit held in Washington D.C. in 1997.

Right from the inception, the programme has been a major success in South India (Appendix B). Its share in the SHG coverage is 58 per cent. In the North-Eastern region, the linkage programme had not gained much acceptability.

The programme since its initiation has shown severe spatial preferences. Figures in Table 16.3 indicate that it has been predominant in certain states, namely Assam, Tripura and Manipur. These three states accounted for more than 97 per cent of the SHG credit linkage, with Assam alone accounting for 91 per cent. Some of the factors identified for the outstanding performance of Assam in the SHG-Bank linkage programme were the following: (a) NABARD had taken the initiative of spreading the SHG-Bank linkage programme in the Sonitpur district in Assam on a massive scale. There was as appreciable progress in the number of SHGs promoted and also in credit linkage. It accounts for 21 per cent of the SHG that were credit by bank loan. (b) The RRBs had maximum linkages here. It accounts for 91 per cent of the RRBs operating in the North East. (c) Pragjyotish Gaonalia Bank (5,172 SHGs) which is one of the top three RRBs in the country is in Assam. (d) Presently 10 commercial banks and DCCB, 51 SHPIs including 240 NGOs and 14 Vikas Volunteer Vahini clubs are involved in promotion and linkage of the SHGs in Assam.

Table 16.3: Share of Credit Linked SHG State-wise

	States	*% Share of SHGs*
1.	Assam	91
2.	Arunachal Pradesh	1
3.	Manipur	2.3
4.	Meghalaya	0.7
5.	Sikkim	0.2
6.	Nagaland	0.3
7.	Tripura	4.4
8.	Mizoram	0.1

Tripura and Manipur, next to Assam, are progressing in the implementation of these programmes. Extensive social mobilization at the grassroots levels is being carried out to form SHG and promoting them in credit linkage with banks. Likewise Arunachal Pradesh and Meghalaya are also beginning to catch up the concept of SHG-Bank linkage, though still a long way to go in comparison to Assam, not to speak of other parts of the country. Mizoram, Sikkim and Nagaland are the poorest in the implementation of these development programmes. These programmes are not properly implemented by the Government officials in the state-district-block levels. In addition, the people are ignorant about these programmes.

Some of the states including Meghalaya have been identified by NABARD for having higher potential of increasing SHG outreach. Bosco Reach Out (NGO) works with the government for implementation of the SGSY in Meghalaya and also imparts training for management and organization of SHG in Meghalaya (Appendix C). The Women's Voluntary Organization in Manipur, the National Union of Cooperatives of India (NUCI) in Sikkim and Bosco Reach Out in Meghalaya emerged as leading NGOs, with more than 80 per cent of the SHG credit links.

In general the lower credit linkages in some of these states can be explained by a lack of concentrated efforts by banks, the inability of banks to identify NGOs with savings and credit group; a lack of motivation among bankers; a lack of large size NGOs with previous background working with SHGs; and the unsuitability of the approach to the region.

Analysis of Banks

Reserve Bank of India and the government lend support to the SHG-Bank linkage programme through policy formation and regulation while the NABARD acts as a facilitator and a refinancing agency. The programme at the grassroots level is executed through a network of commercial banks, regional rural banks (RRBs), district central coopративe banks (DCCBs), and primary agricultural credit societies (PACS).

Commercial Banks

Commercial banks have been found to be more suitable for micro finance because they are regulated and fulfil the conditions of ownership, financial disclosure, and capital adequacy and they have the necessary physical and financial infrastructure, including a large network of branches and well-established internal control and accounting systems. A review of the SHG credit linkages by these institutions indicated that commercial banks had established the maximum linkages. The RRBs had a sizeable coverage but the performance of cooperatives in the programme was minimal (Appendix D).

A study of participation of commercial banks in SHG financing revealed that they were regularly involved in SHG financing and up to 2005 had established 843,473 SHG credit linkages. The State Bank of India (SBI) had the maximum coverage followed by Andhra Bank, Indian Overseas Bank, and State Bank of Hyderabad also had significant credit links. Among the private sector banks, up till 2004 Vysya Bank Ltd. had the maximum credit linkages. But in 2005 with 2988 SHG linked by ICICI Bank Ltd., ICICI Bank now tops the list of private bank credit linkage. However, the overall involvement of private sector banks in the SHG-Bank linkage in minimal.

The commercial banks were predominant across the country, with the highest credit links in 18 states. States like Andhra Pradesh, Tamil Nadu, Maharashtra had the maximum credit linkages.

In the North East commercial bank SHG's credit linkages is not predominant. Figures in Table 16.4 reveals that there is wide variation among the states. The commercial banks are predominant in Meghalaya, Sikkim, Nagaland and Arunachal with the highest credit links in Meghalaya. Sikkim where the SHG linkage programme is relatively weak, commercial banks were found to be the sole financiers. In Assam though commercial banks are not predominant yet it has linked up a considerable number of SHGs with credit. Out of these eight states, Assam tops the list with 12,741 SHGs credit linked by commercial banks.

Table 16.4: SHG-Bank Linkage Agency-wise, Participation State-wise

	States	*Commercial Banks*		*Regional Rural Banks*		*Cooperative Banks*	
		No. of SHGs	*Bank Loan*	*No. of SHGs*	*Bank Loan*	*No. of SHGs*	*Bank Loan*
1.	Assam	12,741	675.1	17210	235.3	1283	31.5
2.	Arunachal	171	5.7	82	4.6	27	1.6
3.	Manipur	349	14	447	16.2	—	—
4.	Meghalaya	119	6.9	117	0.3	13	0.6
5.	Sikkim	36	1.2	—	—	6	0.1
6.	Nagaland	66	1.1	28	3.7	—	—
7.	Tripura	366	7.5	1061	11.1	88	0.5
8.	Mizoram	1	0.1	25	2.6	2	0.2

The average loan per SHG varied across different states. Average loan size is lowest in Mizoram. In Sikkim and Nagaland the loan amount is low, while in Meghalaya, Tripura and Arunachal Pradesh it was relatively higher. Assam received the highest amount of loan followed by Manipur. Under the programme the loan amount is determined on the basis of savings. SHGs with higher magnitude of poverty have lower propensity to save and hence the loans imparted to the SHGs were also smaller.

Regional Rural Banks

The RRBs were established in 1975 to support the rural lending operations of commercial banks. The RRBs responded well to NABARD's initiative for extending their outreach to SHGs. Thirty-five per cent of the SHG linkages were established through the participation of all the 196 RRBs in the country. As one-third of the RRBs are operating in Southern India, the RRBs add maximum linkages there. Out of 563,846 SHGs that were credit linked, almost one-third were in Karnataka, Uttar Pradesh and Orissa.

In the North East the RRBs are relatively more popular in Assam, Manipur, Tripura and Mizoram. In Mizoram where the SHG-linkage programme is relatively weak, RRBs contribute a major share of the SHGs credit. Assam receives the highest amount of loan followed by Manipur and Tripura. In Meghalaya the number of RRBs connected with the programme is nearly the same as the commercial banks but the amount of loan credited to the SHGs is lower than the commercial banks funding. In Nagaland the number of RRBs linked with the SHG-linkage programme is far less than the number of commercial banks involved in the programme, yet the loan amount credited to the SHG by the RRBs is three times that of commercial bank's loan amount. In Arunachal Pradesh also it is found that the funding of RRBs is relatively better than the commercial banks.

Regional rural banks acting as SPIs were more successful in expanding their outreach. As a part of an ongoing search for sustainable institutional mechanism for widening the outreach of financial services to the poor, an experiment was launched in 1994 to test the feasibility of RRBs working as SHPI. After an initial experiment with Cauvery Grameena Bank, 10 more RRBs were encouraged to operate as SHPIs under the guidance and monitoring of its sponsor bank, participating bank, and the NABARD.

Cooperative Banks

The coverage of cooperative banks in the SHG-Bank linkage programme is minimal accounting for only 13 per cent of SHGs linked. The Bidas in Karnataka (44,503) had the maximum linkages, followed by Hooghly DCCB in West Bengal (43,273) and Tamil Nadu and UTP (32,458).

A state-by-state analysis of North East reveals that a majority of the SHGs financed by the cooperative were concentrated in Assam and Tripura followed by Arunachal Pradesh and Meghalaya. The coverage of cooperative banks is minimal in Sikkim and Mizoram and in the rest of the two states, namely Manipur and Nagaland, cooperative banks are totally absent.

Some of the reasons identified for the lower participation of cooperatives were slow reforms, a lack of proper infrastructure, especially training centers, and also specialized staff to pursue micro finance. Furthermore, laws in some states do not allow cooperatives to lend to SHGs.

Conclusion

Micro finance has emerged as a vital approach to meet the heterogeneous needs of the poor. In India, micro finance in the formal sector has assumed the form of SHG-Bank linkage programme. The credit both for introducing SHGs as financial intermediates for the poor as well as for the results achieved so far under the linkage Programme in a major way goes to the NGOs in the state. NGOs have emerged as the major SHPIs. For the NGOs to be able to make a significant dent in poverty alleviation, they need to increase their outreach by forming more and more SHGs within and across the villages. NGOs operating in a particular area must coordinate among themselves. Such a coordination would not only help in orderly growth of SHGs (Osborne 2003) but also in increasing the outreach of SHGs in villages untouched so far by any NGOs. NGOs should try linking their SHGs with the nearby financial system.

The financial institutions and NGOs must enable mature SHGs through training and orientation to launch new savings and credit service which can suit the needs of the members. Providing cash credit facility by the banks to the SHGs could be one way of enabling them to provide bigger and dependable loan services. Equal importance should be given for promoting savings among members by the SHGs. Most of the past attempts like IRDP to provide the poor with easy access to formal credit have had only limited success. The inherent strengths of SHGs for financial intermediation especially in ensuring higher loan recoveries, the proactive involvement of apex agencies like NABARD and also that the NGOs is the major contributory factor in the positive results being seen under the Programme. But the Programme still has a very long way to go. The response of financial institutions to the Programme in general has been very tardy. The weak response of the banks also indicates the major challenge the Programme has to overcome for its future success. The key to the success lies in retaining the basic character and strength of SHGs along with integrating them appropriately with outside systems to meet the needs of the members in an endearing way. A highly co-ordinated effort among all the stakeholders at different levels is what is called for, lest the SHG linkage Programme goes the same way as the past interventions, which were intended to help the poor.

REFERENCES

1. Nanda, Y.C. (2000): Cretical Issues in Micro Finance in K.Basu and K. Jindal (Eds.), *Micro Finance Emerging Challenges.* Tata McGraw Hill Publishing Company.
2. Shylendra, S.L. (2001): "GATS and Financial Sector Reforms: Implications for Rural Sector", Paper published at the National Seminar on "WTO Impact on Indian Agriculture and Rural Sector", October 29-30, 2001 held at the National Institute of Co-operative Management, Gandhinagar.
3. Osborne Matthew Luke (2003): Why do Self-Help Groups Sometime Fail?: A Short Study of Non-Functioning Self-Help Groups in Three Project Areas, Bangalore, MYRADA.

APPENDICES

Appendix A: SHG-Bank Linkage Region-wise Details of Partner Agencies

	Regions	*SHGs promoted by NGO and other agencies*	*SHGs promoted by DRDAs/ DWDA and other Govt. agencies*	*SHGs promoted by VVV Clubs*	*SHGs promoted by Banks*
1.	Northern Region	102,709	61,172	535	1000
2.	North-Eastern Region	93,491	3,541	5	982
3.	Eastern Region	411,219	108,091	5,697	12,645
4.	Central Region	641,436	463,761	2,137	17,391
5.	Western Region	152,828	14,748	880	55,099
6.	Southern Region	1,184,574	661,077	4,765	53,003

Appendix B: Percentage Share of SHGs Provided with Bank Loan, Region-wise

	Regions	*Share of SHGs*
1.	Northern Region	5
2.	North-Eastern Region	2
3.	Eastern Region	11
4.	Central Region	12
5.	Western Region	6
8.	Southern Region	58

Appendix C: SHG-Bank Linkage State-wise Details of Partner Agencies

	States	*SHGs promoted by NGO and other agencies*	*SHGs promoted by DRDAs/ DWDA and other Govt. agencies*	*SHGs promoted by VVV Clubs*	*SHGs promoted by Banks*
1.	Assam	83714	—	—	—
2.	Arunachal	55	—	—	—
3.	Manipur	1956	—	—	—
4.	Meghalaya	4991	3443	—	—
5.	Sikkim	645	70	5	114
6.	Nagaland	590	—	—	—
7.	Tripura	1201	28	—	—
8.	Mizoram	339	—	—	—

Appendix D: SHG-Bank Linkage Agency-wise Participation Region-wise

	States	*No. of SHGs Linked*		
		Commercial Banks	*Regional Rural Banks*	*Cooperative Banks*
1.	Northern Region	42	37	21
2.	North-Eastern Region	40	55	15
3.	Eastern Region	37	42	21
4.	Central Region41		51	8
5.	Western Region	56	25	19
6.	Southern Region	60	29	11

Note: The *Swarnajayanti Grameen Swarozgar Yojana* (SGSY) programme launched by the Government of India has been routing credit of SHGs through the DRDA/DWDA with the active involvement of banks and the NGOs.

17

Impact of New Economic Policy in North Eastern Region

R.P. Bhattacharjee

Introduction

The year 1991 was a watershed year for India. The rule of the game was changed to a more liberalized economy. Though the changes introduced are apparently a response to a distress economy, it is more in tune with the times of the day. India then became a part of the global mega trend of marketization of the economy. The role of the State as a player in the economic sphere is changed to the role of a monitor of the economy and setting the general rules of the game. The hangover of the colonial period viewing multinationals as a front for dominance in the economy and political system of the country is altered to the view that it a vehicle of change in the system. The significant change in the perspective led to changes in the rules governing the business in the country.

In July 1991, the announcement of sweeping liberalization by the minority government of P.V. Narasimha Rao opened the economy and dismantled import controls, lowered customs duties, and devalued the currency. These measures included consistent and co-ordinated steps to reduce protection and liberalise controls over industry and foreign investment and increase competition in areas dominated by monolithic public enterprises. The move virtually abolished licensing controls on private investment, dropped tax rates, and broke public sector monopolies. It was felt as though our second independence had arrived. These policies had serious implications for social sector, as it led to drastic reduction in public subsidies and development expenditure, particularly on social services.

An Analysis

While public opinion in India continues to move towards the view that liberalization has been good, that more of it is needed, and its pace must be accelerated, the view in some scholarly and policy circles has turned skeptical. It is being argued that average annual growth rate of Gross Domestic Product (GDP) had hit the 5.6 per cent mark in the 1980s, well before the launch of the July 1991 reforms. Moreover, the growth rate in the 1990s was not much higher. Therefore, liberalization cannot be credited with having made a significant difference to growth in India or in this part of the region.

The key contribution on expressing this skepticism has come from economic Historian J. Bradford DeLong (2001: 5-6) who writes in an article on growth in India. What are the sources of India's recent acceleration in economic growth? Conventional wisdom traces them to policy reforms at the start of the 1990s. Yet the aggregate growth data tells us that the acceleration of economic growth began earlier, in the early or mid-1980s, long before the exchange rate crisis of 1991 and the shift of the Government of Narasimha Rao and Manmohan Singh towards neo-liberal reforms.

The fragile but faster growth during the 1980s took place in the context of significant reforms throughout the decade and especially starting during 1985. While this liberalization was ad hoc and implemented quietly (reforms by stealth is the term often used to describe them), it made inroads into virtually all areas of industry and laid the foundation of the more extensive reforms in July 1991 and beyond. The reforms in the 1990s were more systematic and systemic and they gave rise to a decidedly more stable and sustainable growth from 1992 onwards (Panagariya, 2004: 2583). It is compared to an elephant which is in the race with the Asian "Dragons" or "Tigers".

The Economic Reforms Policies consisted of LPG, viz. Liberalization, Privatization and Globalization. This was to improve the economic condition of the country. Globalization can be defined simply as expansion of economic activities across political boundaries of a nation or nations. It is a process of increasing economic interdependence between countries in the world economy. The fundamental attribute of globalization is the increasing degree of openness in most countries. A reasonable definition would be free movement of products, money, ideas and people around the globe. At present, the only major obstacles to such movement are national boundaries, so globalization would mean the weakening or eventual elimination of those boundaries (Hensman, 2004). Globalization is seen as the expansion of the market forces beyond the boundaries of nation states and integrating the economies of different countries into the international economy through the markets of goods and services, investments and financial assets, technology and labour services. It is a process associated with increasing economic openness, growing economic interdependence and deepening economic integration between countries in the world economy. Globalization suggests vaguely some increase in international interaction although it is unclear why we should not continue to use the term instead of internationalization.

According to Harris, "The term globalization is not greater interaction between nations (internationalization), but a more robust, if not more measurable, development: the superseding of national economies by the emergence of a single global economy" (EPW, 2003). The concept of globalization makes sense only in terms of the economic interests of the nation state, of sovereignty. We hear of neo-liberal globalization, capitalist globalization and imperialist globalization. In fact, when we ask people what they mean by globalization, they describe capitalism (a system based on the exploitation of workers and production for profits), imperialism (the political, economic, and military domination over some states by others), and neo-liberalism (the policy of allowing the market to determine everything, including wage levels, health care, education etc.). But if capitalism, imperialism and neo-liberalism can all be defined without reference to globalization, should it not be possible to define globalization without reference to them? Globalization is perhaps the free movement of all products, money, ideas, knowledge etc. across the boundaries.

Without going into too much detail, we can list some of the ways in which globalised capitalism is different from imperialism. Imperialism involves military and/or political domination over territories by imperial states, while globalization depends on real political autonomy among its participants. Imperial powers unilaterally dictate the rules in imperialism while globalization would be unsustainable without regulation by multilateral bodies. Imperialism reflects the existence of strong nation states and nationalism, while globalization weakens both. The free and rapid movement of information, which is made possible by information technology, is a key component of globalization but not of imperialism (Hensman, *ibid.*). The fundamental attribute of globalization is the increasing degree of openness in most countries. There are three dimensions, in this phenomenon, like international trade, international investment and international finance. The openness is not simply confined to trade flows, investment flows and financial flows. It also extends to flows of services, technology, information, ideas and persons across national boundaries. The essence of globalization is connectivity. The Economic Reforms Policies consisted of LPG strategies, viz. Liberalization, Privatization and Globalization. This was to improve the economic condition of the country. Globalization ushers faster growth of the economy. Thus globalization refers to the expansion of economic transaction and the organization of economic activities across the political boundaries of nation states. It is a process with increasing economic openness, growing economic interdependence and deepening economic integration between countries in the world economy.

The Effects of Globalization

According to World Development Reports, 1999, "Globalization not only ensures efficiency and growth but also equity and development" (Sengupta, 2004). Goals of globalization should be appropriately viewed as the fulfilment of the rights of the people. At its 96th plenary meeting of December 20, 1995, the General Assembly of the United Nations proclaimed the period of 1997 to 2006 as the "First United Nations Decade for the Eradication of Poverty" (Borocz, 2005). But inequality still persists. For example, poverty in rural areas of NER of India is 40.04 per cent during 1999-2000 (NEC, 2002). One of the basic characteristics of globalization is perhaps inviting foreign direct investment (FDI). In this part of globe especially NER, the impact of FDI is a far cry. There is restriction between countries in this region due to lack of border trade and restrictions within trade. There is restriction within states in this part of world due to imposition of ILP and RAP/PAP. Therefore, for proper globalization, the boundaries of these artificial barriers have to be kept less stringent. But there is some impact of globalization in this region when we think of Information Technology revolution, the uses of internet, the use of mobile-service, the print and electronic media etc. The change in consumer habit is also observed in present day citizens. People like to go Malls/Hubs especially in cities/towns instead of weekly markets. The living condition of people has changed in our society. Now through the electronic media, we can also see the changes occurring in the globe. Globalization is certainly converting the world into a single global village, but it has failed to weed out the inequalities in society in various aspects of life. This has brought the people closer but widened the gap between haves and have-nots, rich and poor. The world today needs a human process of globalization such that the global disparities are not there.

Impact of New Economic Policies

A litmus test to ascertain the health of an economy is to find out how deeply the macro-economic gains percolate to the masses. The distribution of national income to the people takes place through a number of structural, institutional policy, and distributional mechanisms. However, the parameters used to assess the impact of macro-economic gains to individuals need to be clearly established. The ultimate goal is to remove poverty from this region. As stated earlier, in NER, 40.04 per cent of rural people are under below poverty line (NEC: 2002). Human development and better standards of living are not ends in themselves but essential inputs for promoting economic growth and development. They are the dominant routes for inter-generational transfers to ensure the future growth of a country. While in India, there has been a net increase in national wealth both in absolute and per capita terms; it is nonetheless necessary to investigate whether this type of economic prosperity has contributed to human development and the welfare of the masses (Shariff, 1999).

The growth rate of economy is traditional indicator of development and it is growth rate of GSDP/NSDP of the States of this region that will reveal the impact of NEP. This is shown in Table 17.1.

Table 17.1 shows inconsistent growth in the SDP/income of the states of this region. Assam is progressing from its slumber while Meghalaya and Tripura have progressed in recent decade and there is no consistency in the SDP of other states. There is no data available for Mizoram at constant rates with the author and Sikkim's recent data is not available. The consistency we find in the growth rate of all India is not available in NER. The average annual growth of Arunachal Pradesh was 3.6 per cent during 1994-2005, while it was 3.2 per cent in Assam. Manipur had better growth rate of 5.6 per cent (1994-2003) with inconsistency in it. Meghalaya had average annual growth of 7.1 per cent (1994-2004) while Nagaland had highest average annual growth of 9.0 per cent with high inconsistency specially during 2000-2001. Sikkim had average annual growth rate of 7.9 per cent (1994-2000) varying from (-) 2.4 per cent to 14.9 per cent. Tripura's average annual growth rate of 8.7 per cent (1994-2004) has been consistent while all India had an average annual growth of 6.3 per cent.

Globalization as rational outcome of global economic progress, is viewed as a process of (i) expansion of free trade; (ii) more integration of all economies of the world; (iii) more communication amongst different regions; (iv) faster mobility of capital and labour; (v) increasing competition; and (vi) emergence

Table 17.1: Growth Rate of NSDP at Constant (1993-94) Prices of North East Region

States	*1994-95*	*1995-96*	*1996-97*	*1997-98*	*1998-99*	*1999-2000*	*2000-2001*	*2001-2002*	*2002-2003*	*2003-2004*	*2004-2005*	*Annual Average Growth*
Arunachal Pradesh	(-)2.0	14.9	(-)6.0	2.8	2.9	4.2	4.7	4.3	5.4	6.3	2.4	3.6 (1994-2005)
Assam	2.4	2.4	2.4	1.6	(-)0.9	3.5	3.9	4.9	4.1	5.2	5.8	3.2 (1994-2005)
Manipur	(-)2.7	3.3	9.7	9.1	1.7	13.3	(-)1.8	5.0	4.8	NA	NA	5.6 (1994-2003)
Meghalaya	3.4	11.5	3.6	6.5	10.9	8.6	8.2	7.2	4.1	7.0	NA	7.1 (1994-2004)
Mizoram*	8.7	27.7	14.6	4.0	11.4	13.1	26.9	8.7	14.1	NA	NA	14.4* (1994-2003)
Nagaland	7.8	7.2	7.1	8.9	(-)4.7	0.6	38.2	7.0	NA	NA	NA	9.0 (1994-2002)
Sikkim	(-)2.4	10.9	12.1	14.9	9.8	2.1	NA	NA	NA	NA	NA	7.9 (1994-2000)
Tripura	(-)1.1	8.2	10.9	10.9	9.4	8.5	18.4	3.1	8.2	10.1	NA	8.7 (1994-2004)
All India	7.1	7.1	7.8	4.5	6.5	6.1	4.4#	6.0#	3.7#	8.8#	7.7#	6.3 (1994-2005)

Source: 1. SDP Reports of N.E. States. 2. Basic Statistics of NER, 2006. 3. NAS, 2006.
* At current prices as the data for constant is not available. # At constant (1999-2000) prices. NA = Not available.

of global market. And there is no alternative to this. This process leads a strong industrial sector in the economy of the region. Let us find the industrial scenarios of this region in table below.

Table 17.2: Contribution of Manufacturing/Industry in NER during 2002-2003 to NSDP at Constant (1993-94) prices

States	*Registered Manufacturing*	*Unregistered Manufacturing*
Arunachal Pradesh	0.0	2.5
Assam	5.3	2.0
Manipur	NA	NA
Meghalaya	1.4	1.2
Mizoram	0.3	0.5
Nagaland	0.6	0.2
Tripura	0.7	1.0
Sikkim	NA	NA
All India	8.9	5.6

Source: (i) SDP Report of NER. (ii) NAS, 2006.

Here we find that in registered manufacturing sector, only Assam has some industrial base while others are limping. Similarly, in the unregistered sector also, there is not much contribution in line with NEP and its impact for the industry of NER yet.

For industrial development, it is essential that one should have capital and it is mainly available with banks and other financial institutions. The C-D ratio is a basic indicator in this regard. The C-D ratio of this region during 2004 is shown in Table 17.3.

Table 17.3 shows that the banking facilities is not reaching to all the people in the region and the environment is not yet congenial for widespread privatization and globalization in the region.

The UN Human Development Report, 2006 paints a dismal picture of social development in India, which ranks just 126th out of 177 countries. We must be cautious about glowing predictions that India wil! soon become a global economic super power. Without strong social development and human development, the current growth of all India will falter. On the one hand our growth rate is increasing while social development is not progressing in desired path.

Table 17.3: The Credit-Deposit Ratio of NER (as on 31.3.2004)

States	*C-D Ratio*
Arunachal Pradesh	25.4
Assam	32.5
Manipur	34.5
Meghalaya	30.6
Mizoram	39.3
Nagaland	17.9
Tripura	29.2
Sikkim	NA
NER	31.2
All India (as on 30.6.2004)	54.39

Source: (i) NEC, Basic Statistics, 2006, p. 349.
(ii) Economic Survey, 2004-2005.

In the North-Eastern Region, we do not have proper Human Development Report of all the States. We have HDI of NER as follows from the available literature.

Table 17.4: HDI of NER (2001)

States	*HDI (2001)*
Assam	0.386
Arunachal Pradesh	0.328
Manipur	0.536
Meghalaya	0.365
Mizoram	0.548
Nagaland	0.394
Sikkim	0.425
Tripura	0.389
All India	0.472

Source: Demography India.

Here HDI of the States except Mizoram is below the national average. Thus, Human Development as well as social development has not improved much in this region.

Conclusion

The essence of New Economic Policy is to increase economic interdependence between countries in the world without any major barriers in investment, acquirement, ownership etc. The market oriented economic reform programme leads to the process of globalization. In the NER, there is a still restriction between the States in mobility of human being, goods and services, through the restrictions of ILP/RAP etc. and other governmental restrictions on possession of land entrepreneurship and business permit. The provision of basic infrastructure like road, rail, power, market etc. is also not available in the region. We find over 40 per cent of rural population in the region under BPL. The growth rate of States are mostly inconsistent between 3-9 per cent during this period of economic reform. In a recent work of K. Sengupta, we find that HDI for the NER is hovering at 0.431 compared to national average of 0.590. Therefore, the States of this area must open their border both between States and the countries. The border trade with neighbouring Bhutan, China, Myanmar and Bangladesh along with East Asian Countries is a must for globalization of the economy. The look up to East Asian Countries is needed for globalisation of North East Economy. The Look East policy is required to be implemented within a fixed time frame. The insurgency and unrest in NER can be solved through employment generation and this can be achieved by increase in investment from across the borders and within the nation. There is a need for investment in infrastructure of NER such that more border trade can be opened with Bhutan, China, Myanmar and Bangladesh. This will make NER as a part of global village and help in changing the living standard of people of NER.

Recently, Hu Jintao, Chinese President visited our country. He told a delegation of left leaders to adopt a "more pragmatic and positive approach" to developing India's economy and creating infrastructure. He invited Indian leaders to visit China to assess the world's fastest growing major economy. In his view, globalization provides scope for economic prosperity.

But great expectation from the visit of Chinese President in North East ended in great disappointment, as there was no marked progress in the opening of the Stillwell Road for trade between India and China. The border row over Arunachal Pradesh before his visit created such a bad impression that there was no border talks in this region. The only hope for a vibrant trade route to South East Asia therefore lies through Manipur. The Tamo-Moreh route is required to be revitalized so that the Free Trade Treaty with the ASEAN countries can be realized in near future. The peace process with ULFA in Assam has to be successful for development of this region. There must be the end of insurgency in NER to make it investment friendly.

REFERENCES

Boocz, Jozsef (2005): "Redistributing Global Inequality—A Thought Experiment", *EPW,* Vol. XL, No. 9, p. 886.

Delong, J. Bradford, (2001): "India since Independence: An Analytic Growth Narrative" in Dani Rodrik (ed.), *Modern Economic Growth: Analytical Country Studies* (Quoted from Paragariya, 2004).

Hensman, Rohini (2004): "Globalisation, Women and Work", *EPW,* Vol. XXXIX, No. 10. p. 1030.

Harris, Nigel, (2003): "Globalisation and the Management of Indian Cities", *EPW,* Vol. XXXVIII, No. 25, p. 2535.

IAPS, "Demography India", Vol. 33, p. 229.

NEC, "Basic Statistics, 2006", p. 333, 2002, p. 400.

National Accounts Statistics, 2006, CSO, New Delhi, pp. 1-194.

Paragariya, Arvind (2004): "Growth and Reforms during 1980s and 1990s", *EPW,* Vol. XXXIX, No. 25, pp. 2581-83.

SDP Reports of all NER States.

Sengupta, Arjun, "Managing Globalisation", *EPW,* Vol. XXXIX, No. 6, 2004, pp. 549-51.

Sengupta, Keya (2006): Assám University, Quoted from *The Times of India,* dated 15 June, 2006.

Shariff, Abusaleh, (1999): *India Human Development Report,* Oxford University Press.

The Arunachal Times, dated 4th December, 2006.

18

Tourism as a Strategy for Economic Development of North East India

B. Francis Kulirani

The concentration of communities having Scheduled Tribe status in the North East Region of India is a known fact. It is also a fact that North East has taken the character of a socio-political entity (Shimray, 2004). The data available with the Anthropological Survey of India estimates that there are about 305 communities in the North East and out of that 166 are Scheduled Tribes. In some of the states like Meghalaya, Nagaland and Arunachal Pradesh majority of the communities are Scheduled Tribes. The developmental achievements of the region in other words are directly proportionate to the development achieved by the tribes of the region. The region is richly endowed with natural resources of water and rainfall, fossil fuel, coal, uranium, limestone and unique flora and fauna, but the region is struggling to evolve the right strategy for economic development. The problems of under-development experienced by the communities of the region are common in terms poor industrial growth, communication, poor health services, unemployment, inter-ethnic clashes and militancy.

At the very outset, the very description of North East as 'tribal' itself is being considered objectionable by certain sections of the communities of the region, who are bestowed with the ST status in the region. It is their view that by categorizing them as 'tribals' along with all diverse communities of India who differ among themselves in terms of ethnic origin, language/dialect and religion, a conspiracy is being hatched by the dominant communities to suppress the unique ethnic characteristics of North East India (cf. Kathar, 2002). Use of the word 'tribals' to denote the STs is also not grammatically correct as the word is an adjective of tribe. But the anthropological usage of the term 'tribes' in the context of India basically refers to all those communities who are ascribed with constitutional status of 'ST' and ethnic groups having characteristics of socio-economic, cultural, linguistic and religious traits. Considering the sentiments of the people of the region against the term 'tribe' I would like to use the neutral term community instead of 'tribe' as in any case the ST population of the region constitute the largest (57.3%) demographic group of the region during 1991 census.

The concept of development in the context of distinct community identities of North East, who are mostly Scheduled Tribes, itself need to be examined from social, political, economic, and geographic dimensions. The very formation of the states of North East region itself was based on the dominant features of ethnicity and language. The ethnic differences and political aspirations within the states are so divergent that there is a perpetual state of ethnic unrest within. Intra-regional disparities of growth and development between ethnic groups in the plains and hills are also evident. Sharing of land resources, sharing of funds for regional development, sharing of employment opportunities and sharing of power and authority all lead to claims and counter claims. At the same time internal revenue generation within the states and per capita income at the level of individuals also remain low. One of the reasons that can be cited as the cause for the state of affairs can be the 'landlocked nature of North East'. Prabhakara (2004) has examined the multi-dimensional aspects of 'landlockedness' of the North East region. According to Prabhakara 'unlike the other landlocked states of the Indian Union the states of North East are not surrounded by Indian territory, on the contrary the North East is almost entirely surrounded by foreign countries, which is a unique location feature. Further an even more unique aspect is the fact that each of these states is also internally locked and locking out others, unable to connect with each other physically in terms of poor transport links and more seriously, unable to make connections intellectually and emotionally with their closest neighbours or even with and among their own people' (*ibid.*). The reason for this can be found in the region's political history.

Community Development Planning for Economic Development of North East

The people of the North East are longing for a self-reliant, communitarian and spontaneous development, which is not happening at the ground level. Development no doubt has been occurring but not suitably adapted to address the problems specific to small geographic pockets within the region and the ethnic groups living therein. In short development planning has to be community specific because communities occupy specific territories. Communities should be the 'micro' unit for development planning and there should be a working definition for the concept of community itself. In the context of 'tribal/community' development of North East the communities can be viewed as ethnic geographic units. Macro planning for the region as a whole alone may not yield positive results. The ethnic groups may be feeling threatened by the domineering nature of exogenous development planning and implementation that is submerging the indigenous. At one extreme is the vision of India as a global player and at the other is the marginalized region grappling with localized visions. The fear of the marginality originates from the fear of being swallowed up by the globalizing forces.

The North East is not an exception to the influence of the 'new economy' and its globalizing forces. The 'new economy' is the all-concurring force of capitalism powered by competition. The simple subsistence economies of the communities of the North East need to be protected against the marauding 'new economy', though in economic terms the market forces constitute the core and the weaker economies constitute the 'periphery'. But in the context of North East the 'core' is now the periphery because of the widening gap between rich and poor. In such a context the appropriate strategy for development planning is 'globalization from below' (Falk, 1993 quoted by Reid 2003: 58). The notion of globalization from below being defined as 'an array of trans-national social forces animated by environmental concerns, human rights, hostility to patriarchy and a vision of human community based on the unity of diverse cultures seeking an end to poverty, oppression, humiliation and collective violence' (*ibid.*). This sort of movement has been frequent in recent times as a reaction to corporate globalization that is affecting poor regions of the world. In the concept of 'globalization from below' the central theme is coalition building in and between communities, which are the smallest political units and the place where most people spend the greatest part of their lives. In the North East such coalition building can have wonderful benefits; it can occur through the leadership of community interest groups with compatible goals (Community development through tourism development could be the focal point for this coalition building). The working definition provided by Reid is most appropriate for conceptualizing community development or tribal development (especially in the context of North East) which suggests that the focus is on change, indigenous problem identification, participation of all concerned community members in the activities and process of development of the community having the notion of self-help and community control of the process and outcome (Reid, 2003: 90). The overarching principle is the stress on process than product.

The development of the capacity of the people to establish any project is more important than a given project at a given time, stressing the process over product. (But, the scope of community development/tribal development in North East or for that matter in the whole of India appears to have been increasingly weighed in favour of community economic development (CED). In the initial stages community development planning, in the second half of the 20th century, was a combination of approaches. According to Sanders (1970), it was viewed as a programme, as a process, as a method and as a movement. The development initiative was a movement and process so that it could lead to the empowerment of the people involved in the process. Empowerment itself is a process not an enactment and can only be achieved in stages of powerlessness, awareness, connecting and learning, motivation, and finally, reaching a stage at which the people are able to make a creative contribution. The desirable outcome of community development could be intellectual and emotional development of the individual and the community.

The approach to community development/tribal development in the context of North East or for that matter in the whole of India appears to have undergone shift in ideology. This shift is very much visible as the focus of attention has moved towards economic issues and hence the perspective now seems to be 'community economic development' (CED) or 'tribal economic development'. All problems of community underdevelopment are attributed to economic issues. It became fashionable for all the players involved in community development to focus on economic issues rather than on social issues. National and international funding agencies also shifted their policies. The outcome is too stark and devastating 'over-exploitation of natural resources' and 'individualism' which is detrimental to the concept of community and tribe that are integral to the tribe dominated North East context. Instead the correction that is required is that development should be driven by the community and not outside forces, from 'community economic development' to 'community-based economic development' (CBED). Even in CBED model there is limitation of being dealt with a single domain, as the goal remains intervention only at economic realm.

Yet another recent initiative has been the use of 'social capital' as an input for economic development of communities. Reid (2003) quotes Schuller (2001) to define 'social capital in terms of networks, norms and trust and the way these allow agents and institutions to be more effective in achieving a common objective. It is understood as a matter of relationships, as a property of groups rather than the property of individuals.

The concept of community development, which began as a holistic approach to community problem-solving by communities with a stress on process over product, has moved exclusively into economic realm. This is detrimental to the collective psyche of any community, its mental health, intellectual and social capacities. Communities are passing through a fast phase of change in the

North East and in the process many of the tangible and intangible aspects of their heritages are going out of use or being lost for ever. This is the prize being paid by communities in the North East for development.

Community based Economic Development through Tourism Development

The tourism potential of the North East is a very well known fact in spite of the prevailing climate of tensions in the area and the restrictions imposed on travel for domestic or international tourists. The scenario of community development and tourism development in North East is gloomy mainly because the planning and implementation is in the administrative control of centralized and corporate agencies. Tourism at present provides only fringe benefit to people in the region and communities are only indirect beneficiaries as only some of the individual entrepreneurs or operators are benefited.

The multiple advantages of North East as a tourist destination are the region's geographical features and the unique and diverse cultures and lifestyles of the people living in a close proximity. The pulling power of both ecological and cultural heritages of the region has to be combined to frame the approach to tourism development planning in the region. The 'eco-cultural tourism development model' appears to be best suited for the region as it permits incorporation of the richness and diversity of local lives into the equation (Russel and Wallace, 2004). What is urgently required is participation of Social Anthropologists to provide a holistic approach for representing environment, local people, and tourists as interlinked components of 'responsible tourism' in policy-making and planning. If Anthropologists and Geographers can engage with communities and policy-makers, responsible-tourism-approaches to suit the specific requirements of any given community and locality of the region can be designed.

There is a traditional mindset of considering communities as obstacles to development, not partners in the process, and have been subjected to the negative consequences of business driven tourism development. But the communities in pockets of Assam, Meghalaya, Arunachal Pradesh and Sikkim are becoming increasingly aware that 'community development approach is an option for tourism development'. Communities and NGOs who are already involved in environmental and development issues are able to make the connection between their interests and the welfare of the people living in the areas concerned. The awareness that if environmentally sensitive areas of North East are to be preserved and protected, then the communities living in each area need to make a living from efforts to achieve the desired outcome. 'Eco-cultural tourism' is an appropriate model for inducing development from within. Thus community development becomes a method for focusing on communities and their development, with the secondary outcome of preserving an eco-cultural system, rather than a pure economic approach to community development.

Community development and tourism development conceptually are multi-disciplinary fields which utilize various academic perspectives, theories and methods. In the first part of this paper multi-disciplinary field of community development has been discussed. Treaties on tourism development are concerned with geographical issues, such as spatial and environmental analysis of destination sites. Sociology contributes a focus on social class and leisure analysis, psychology throws light on individual behaviour, economics is concerned with issues of supply and demand and tourism market; and hospitality study concerns itself with product development; while planning concerns itself with process of deliberate intervention in the human, social and environmental system. Thus tourism is a sub-discipline of development studies (Ried, 2003: 74).

The modernizing pressures experienced by the traditional communities of the region have been demonstrated by the studies of Miri (1980, 1993), Nag (2002), Subba and Ghosh (2003). At the centre of the debate is the choice between traditions *vs.* modernity and this has been an ongoing one in the region. The modernization theories are concerned primarily with how traditional values, attitudes, practices, and social structures break down and are replaced with modern ones (Martinuseen, 1997: 56).

In contrast the core economic values and the worldviews of the traditional societies of North East rest on cooperation and community-first principles. They have a unique culture, adhering to an economic system often based on direct commodity exchange. They have an existence at subsistence level by following shifting cultivation coupled with hunting, gathering and fishing. While the core of the Scheduled Tribe groups may be maintaining traditional social system, the younger members are on a fast road of modernity. In spite of the contrast, many of the tangible and intangible heritages do persist and flourish in the region. What should be the major concern is not the issue of modernization or change, but who is in control and how change in social structures is motivated. Is it mainly controlled and driven by endogenous influences or exogenous influences?

Proponents of modernity would agree that change might be disruptive in the short-term but progressive in the long-term by way of increased materialism, resulting in extended life expectancy and various technological conveniences that are preferable to the persistence of poverty and disease.

While promoting tourism in the North East the planners can ensure that the traditional communities can maintain the integral elements of their culture through the tourism activity, because that is what the visitors would love to see and experience. There is a hidden danger in this approach. This selective approach to preserve and promote some elements and abandoning other elements may lead to commodification of the favoured practices by the tourism activity. For the practitioners' point of view the elements that are being abandoned may be vital to the actual practice. This is an issue that can be resolved only through dialogue. The 'eco-cultural tourism model' for North East needs to be considered from the 'inside out' rather than from the 'outside in' approach. Let us consider some specific cases, the community specific Bihu festivals in Assam are ceremonial occasions in their own right. Same is the case of Nongkrem dance in Khasi Hills, Behdienkhlam dance of Jaintia Hills, Motsu in Ao Naga Areas and Chavang Kat festival of Mizos. On the occasion of the event other communities are invited to view and participate in the side lines of the celebration.

Such events are marked by lot of singing, music and dance performances. Traditional craft objects and cusine are also essential components and they are designed for community specific and occasion specific utility. Even if these events are promoted for tourism development proper community participation will prevent commodification of the event and will also turn it as an occasion for the people of the community to generate income by organizing it.

Strategy for Development

The need for community development in the North East and the potential for tourism development in the region have to be addressed as a combined strategy for regional economic development. The initiative for this strategy has to develop within the region, what has been termed as 'globalization from below' by reasserting the role of communities in development process. There are certain internal strengths in the communities of the region that are very significant:

1. The communities have certain exclusive rights provided to them under the 6th Schedule.
2. The traditional political institutions have survived and are respected by the people.
3. Community specific autonomous areas are struggling to achieve development.
4. Exclusive community specific village organizations, as in Nagaland, hill districts of Assam, Arunachal Pradesh, and Manipur are 'republics' on their own.

The above strengths can be used to balance the economic, environmental and socio-cultural aspects of both community development and tourism development provided the approach is bottom-up, community-driven and community planned and the objectives for development are integral, sustainable and long-term.

The weaknesses are well known:

1. Land locked region and poor connectivity with outside.
2. Internally locked between states and countries and poor internal connectivity.
3. Insurgency and ethnic unrest.
4. Human resource development.

The potential of development and alternatives that development can provide will help in the amelioration of these conditions.

Phases of Project Development

The strategy can be implemented in two phases:

Phase of Community Empowerment

Stage 1

The community and its members become concerned with issues and the problems that confront them. This can also be called the conscientious state.

Stage 2

Connecting and learning to identify and analyze the problem in detail through communicative action.

Stage 3

Mobilization, creating on organizational network and the political skills necessary to act.

Stage 4

Contribution in collaboration with others to use the skills to address the problem.

Project for Formulation and Implementation Phase

The tourism development project for the communities of North East states calls for the application of the social learning and social mobilization approaches in order to ensure that communities are willing partners and stakeholders in the process. Continuous monitoring and diagnosis can help to incorporate correction in the dynamics if required. The model quite often used in tourism development project is the entrepreneurial approach. As a departure Reid and others (1993) have developed a model that lays stress on tourism as a strategy for community development.

Community Development Phase through Tourism

Stage 1 : Gearing Up Phase

The gearing up phase is achieved through the programmes in the community empowerment by availing services of process catalysts and their interaction with community partner.

Stage 2: Community Assessment

The participating communities take a realistic assessment of their strengths and weaknesses as to initiate and implement the project.

Stage 3: Organization and Planning Stage

The expected outcome of the previous stage is the rise in community awareness and identification of right values to focus on things which can lead to framing as organization structure, product development and marketing.

Stage 4: Monitoring Phase

The project is implemented and is continuously monitored and evaluated and the feedback is given to organization aspects. Thus the 3rd and 4th stages are ongoing.

The unique feature of this model is the fact that unlike the entrepreneurial model, wherein there are only two interest groups—the supplier of the product destination (tourism operator and Government/corporation) and the customer (the travel agents and the tourists), the producers of the product of eco-cultural tourist activity is included in the planning process. The biggest mistake in tourism development planning in India as a whole is the tendency of the Tourism Ministry (Central/State) to sell off cultural and environment locales cheaply to entrepreneurs and global operators. Unless social, political, and entrepreneurial capacity is built in the communities, they cannot take charge of their own development.

Conclusion

People will learn social and entrepreneurial skills most effectively if they can see some short-term advantages as well as long-term benefits. The developmental initiative will become participatory only when communities are in charge of their development and it is unambiguously clear to them that the ownership of the eventual tourism project will remain in their hands and that they will benefit from it. The project must be based on a comprehensive vision of future and on both short-term and long-term objectives of the community. The implementation of the vision must be accomplished in incremental steps. Caution must be exercised in implementation of the vision in incremental steps, in order to avoid setting in the frustration. Any failure to accomplish part of a plan may sabotage the entire process. Equally, the steps must be sufficiently small to assure success and not so small that they do not seem to make significant progress towards the overall goal. Finally, the community must have access to a variety of resources in order to implement their goal; these may include development funds to assist them with their tourism project. It is important for the government not to dictate the conditions of the tourism project or to micro-manage the plan, but simply to support the ingenuity and resourcefulness of the community.

I conclude the paper by submitting that the ideas projected above are neither utopian nor unachievable. One can draw attention of all concerned to a success story in this field in North East region in Kewzing village in Ravangla sub-division of South Sikkim which made this a reality through their 'Village Home Stay' programme (Jamwal, 2004). The villagers have set up an elected registered body—the Kewzing Tourism Development Committee (KTDC). The KTDC regulates tourism, ensuring that the profits are evenly distributed among the participating families. The whole initiative to integrate tourism into the rural economy of Kewzing came from Sikkim Development Foundation a Gangtok based non-governmental organization. Hopefully, if the model can succeed in Sikkim it can succeed in the other states of the North East region as well.

REFERENCES

Bandyopadhyay, P.K. (1985): *Leadership among the Mizos.* Delhi: B.R. Publishing Corporation.

Bareh, Hamlet, (1964): *Khasi Democracy.* Shillong: Ri-Khasi Press.

Bhattacharjee, J.B. (1989): *Sequences of Development in North East India.* New Delhi, Cosmo Publications.

Falk, R. (1993): 'The making of Global Citizenship'. In *Global Visions: Beyond the New World Order,* Jeremey and Others (Eds.). Boston: South End Press.

Kathar, J.I. (2003): *Mongolians of North East India* (Paper presented in the G.J. Seminar of An. S.I., NERC, Shillong).

Martinuseen, J. (1997): *Society, State and Market: A Guide to Competing Theories of Development.* Halifax: Fernwood Publishing.

Miri, Sujata (Ed.) (1980): *Religion and Society in North East India.* Vikas. New Delhi.

Miri, Sujata, (1993): *Communalism in Assam: A Civilizational Approach.* Har-Anand. New Delhi.

Nag, Sajal (2002): *Contesting Marginality: Ethnicity, Insurgency and Sub-nationalism in North East India.* Manohar, New Delhi.

Prabhakara, M.S. (2004): Is North East India Landlocked? *EPW* 39(42): 4606-4611.

Reid, Donald G. (2003): *Tourism, Globalization and Development.* Pluto Press, London.

Russel, Andrew and Wallace, Gillian, (2004): Irresponsible eco-tourism, *Anthropology Today,* 29(3) 1-2.

Saikia, P.D. (1968): *Changes in Mikir Society.* Jorhat: Agro-Economic Research Centre for North East India.

Sanders, I.T. 'The Concept of Community Development'. In *Community Development as a process,* L.J. Carey (ed). Columbia, MO. University of Missouri.

Schuller, T. 'The Complementary Roles of Human and Social Capital'; *ISUMA,* Canadian Journal of Policy Research, 2(1): 18-24.

Shimraey, U.A. (2004): 'Socio-Political Unrest in the Region Called North-East India'. *EPW* 39(42): 4637-4643.

Singh, K.S. (1972): *Tribal Situation in India* Simla: Indian Institute of Advance Study.

Singh, K.S. (1982): *Tribal Movements in India.* Vol. I, New Delhi: Manohar Publications.

Subba, T.B. and G.C. Ghosh (2003): *The anthropology of North East India.* Orient Longman, New Delhi.

19

Economic Growth in the Regime of Reforms: Nagaland's Experience

Mithilesh Kumar Sinha

India started adopting economic reforms since 1991 with a view to have speedy economic growth in the economy. The economic reforms can have effect on the two sectors of the economy: (1) on the real sector, (2) on the financial sector.

Nagaland has made less strides in the real sector during reform period but has made impressive strides in the reform period, particularly, in areas such as attainments in literacy, health related indicators, health care services, water and sanitations, power and fiscal reforms. The unique initiative of 'Communitisation' of public institutions and services, in the sectors of education, health care and power distribution, has enhanced accountability and involvement of both the community and the Government towards greater effectiveness.

In this paper, we look at a close range the relative growth performance of Nagaland economy after the country made a paradigmatic shift in its basic economic policy towards liberalization and introduced a number of market-oriented economic reforms. We also attempt a critical assessment of the claim of the end of lopsided development and emergence of the "virtuous cycle of development" during the regime of reforms in Nagaland. If the claim is found lacking in clear empirical support, it is important to identify major constraints that the state faces for acceleration of economic growth matching with the achievement in human development. In doing so, the concept of lopsided development is defined not only in the sense of the riddle of high social development with low income growth, but also in some enigmatic structural sense (e.g., concentrated sector-composition of output and growth) and the impact on sustainability of the growth momentum for the future. In specific terms, we review growth trends in the macro-economic after the implementation of reforms in the neo-liberal features of lopsided development, and recommend some pragmatic approaches to achieve accelerated growth in Nagaland.

Growth Trajectories

We begin with an assertion that studies on long-term growth trends in Nagaland's macro-economy are generally based on the analysis of net state domestic product (NSDP) and have put forward statistical evidence supporting the inference of different growth trajectories. One trajectory is marked by a phase of stagnation since the early 1970s, and the second one a phase of recovery in the late 1980s which continued in the 1990s and thereafter, and put the economy on a high growth path. Admittedly, the inferences drawn from the analysis of SDP have to be taken with a pinch of salt. In particular, the methodology of estimation is based on income generation (and not income accrual) within the geographical boundaries of the state. Hence, it is inadequate to reflect the real picture of the economic status as it ignores remittance from the Nagas working in other states and outside the country. Besides, there are differences in the estimation methods actually practiced by the statistical offices of different states though they are required to follow uniform guidelines issued by the central statistical organization. In the case of gross state domestic product (GSDP) the incidence of the data drawback is relatively less as compared to net state domestic product as values of depreciation are not required to be estimated. We, therefore, look closely at the growth rates in GSDP (instead of NSDP) recorded in the present phase of "high" growth trajectory which coincides with the policy regime of ongoing economic reforms in Nagaland.

We restrict the analysis to period from 1993-94 to 2001-2002 on the following grounds:

1. There is rationale in considering periods for analysis based on the timing of shifts in policy-framework.
2. Although the shift in India's basic economic policy towards neo-liberal approach was formally announced by the national government in June 1991, the states effectively started implementing market-oriented economic reforms by the middle of 1990s only.
3. The choice of starting the period of analysis in 1993-94 is made on the consideration of the availability of new SDP data series with 1993-94 as the base ending it in 2001-02. It is on the consideration that the data for subsequent two years are either provisional or quick-estimates and hence its conclusion in the time series is likely to give a biased picture of growth trend.

Have reforms led to a growth turnaround and "virtuous cycle of development"? In Table 19.1 we have recorded Annual trend of growth rates of gross domestic product (GDP) of Nagaland.

Table 19.1: State Gross Domestic Product and its Growth Trend of Nagaland

Year	*GSDP (in Rs. Lakh)*	*Trend Growth (Annual Per Cent)*
1993-94	137463	11.36
1994-95	—	11.36
1995-96	—	11.36
1996-97	202410	—
1997-98	232410	14.82
1998-99	238523	2.63
1999-2000	254713	6.79
2000-01	367936	44.45
2001-02	413688	12.43
All India		6.01

Note: Trends growth rates from 1993-94 to 1996-97 are calculated from Geometric Mean.

Source: Calculation-based on Data from Statistical Hand Book of Nagaland, Government of Nagaland.

The estimated values for Nagaland broadly indicate a higher growth rate of the present growth trajectory. In other words, Nagaland has achieved a higher growth performance in the post-reform period. To illustrate, what Nagaland achieved during 1994-95 to 2001-02 is an average annual growth rate of 14.4 per cent as against 6 per cent at all-India.

We also note that Nagaland's performance in terms of growth rate in real per capita SDP (at 1993-94 constant price) present a remarkable picture though the state has not witnessed steady growth rate in real per capita SDP in different years. In 1998-99 the growth rate in real per capita SDP was negative, i.e. –4.5 per cent; in 1999-2000 it was only 1.6 per cent. This trend shows much fluctuation in the growth rate in real per capita SDP because from 1993 to 1997 its growth rate was more than 40 per cent, i.e. 41.7 per cent and it was in 2000 and 2001, 37.14 per cent and 16.97 per cent. Average annual growth rate per capita SDP in Nagaland (20.08) is higher than all-India record (4.26 per cent) during the period under review (Table 19.2).

Table 19.2: Average Annual Growth in Per Capita GDP

Years	*Per Capita GDP (in Rs. Lakhs)*	*Average Annual Growth (in Per Cent)*	*All-India (in Per Cent)*
1993-94	10033	—	—
1994-95	—	41.7	5.13
1995-96	—	41.7	5.26
1996-97	—	41.7	5.79
1997-98	14196	—	2.8
1998-99	13552	–4.5	4.51
1999-2000	13770	1.61	4.45
2000-01	18926	37.14	2.21
2001-02	20246	6.97	3.95
All India	—	20.08	4.26

Source: As in Table 19.1.

The point for emphasis is straight and simple. Nagaland economy in the present growth trajectory is growing faster than its record in the earlier trajectories, but there is an element of exaggeration in the growth turnaround and the dawn of 'virtuous cycle of development' with mutually reinforcing spiral of high human development and high economic growth. Nagaland is not growing sufficiently high enough in income generation matching with its achievement of the high order in human development. We would, therefore, argue that Nagaland continues to present some characteristics of lopsided development due to imbalanced economic growth, notwithstanding the implementation of reforms under the neo-liberal policy perspective.

Lopsided Structural Transformation

Viewed in the conventional sense, the macro-level growth record in an economy is expected to bring about significant structural changes in terms of diversification in the composition of output and employment of economic activity sectors. This question needs to be addressed in the evaluation of growth process inasmuch as the prospect for a long-term growth as well as its sustainability depends significantly on the pattern of change in the economic structure defined as the sector composition of output, employment and labour productivity on the lines of Kuznets (1957). This implies that a lopsided structure with the dominance of a few economic activity sectors is not conducive for maximizing and sustaining the overall growth of the macro-economy. Does the sector growth pattern and structural changes witnessed in Nagaland during the period under review fit into Kuznets' conventional pattern?

The relative shares of different economic activity sectors and sub-sectors in the aggregate output (GSDP) of Nagaland assume imporance in any analysis. Table 19.3 shows tertiary (service) sector as the dominant component of GSDP in 1993-94 and it continued to be so, and in fact expanded its importance, over-time. The relative share of the primary sector (especially agriculture) increased from 19.57 in 1993-94 to 28.20 in 2001-02 and the relative share of the secondary sector declined (especially, manufacturing). In fact, the share of manufacturing activity in GSDP declined from 3.29 per cent in 1993-94 to 1.17 per cent in 2001-02.

Table 19.3: Share of Sector and Sub-sector in GSDP Nagaland

(in Per Cent)

Sector and Sub-sector	*1993-94*	*2001-02*	*1993-94 to 2001-02*
Agriculture	19.57	28.20	24.24
Forestry and Logging	4.44	2.71	3.15
Fishing	0.36	0.60	0.54
Mining and Quarrying	0	0.06	0.05
I. Primary Sector	24.38	31.58	29.78
Manufacturing	3.29	1.17	1.69
Registered	0.86	0.63	0.69
Unregistered	2.42	0.54	1.01
Construction	8.11	10.38	9.82
Electricity, Gas and Water Supply	2.54	0.56	1.05
II. Secondary	13.94	12.12	12.57
Transport, Storage and Communication	16.35	19.09	18.41
Railways	0.03	0.02	0.02
Transport by Other Means	16.07	18.66	18.03
Storage	0.01	0.01	0.01
Communication	0.24	0.40	0.36
Trade, Hotels and Restaurants	5.68	5.78	5.76
Banking and Insurance	1.28	1.39	1.36
Real Estate, Ownership of Dwelling and Business Service	11.69	9.04	9.70
Public Administration	18.94	13.56	14.91
Other Services	7.74	7.43	7.51
III. Tertiary Sector	61.68	56.30	57.64

Source: As in Table 19.1.

The process of such a lospisded structural transformation in output becomes clearer when we compare sector growth rates in Nagaland with all-India averages during the post-reform period under review (Table 19.4). Interestingly, the growth rates recorded in Nagaland are higher than all-India averages both in agriculture and industry. In tertiary (service) sector, the growth rate was also higher than all-India average. Nagaland's tertiary sector enjoyed a share larger than all-India at the close of the period under review. Thus viewed, the tertiary (service) is found leading the growth process in Nagaland during the post-reform period.

Within the tertiary (service) sector, the growth process is shared by a number of sub-sectors like (1) Communication, (2) banking and insurance, (3) storage, (4) transport by means other than railways, (5) trade, hotels and restaurants, and (6) public administration. In a sense, the high growth in the service sector was marked by a diversified structure. Here one is tempted to make a quick observation on the public administration sub-sector which has recorded higher growth rate relatively to all-India record. This characteristic feature certainly values the rationale of adopting of the State Government's participation in favour of the private sector (meaning thereby, the commercialization) in social services like health and education under the neo-liberal policy perspective presently being pursued in Nagaland.

Table 19.4: Average Annual Growth Rate (1994-95 to 2001-02) of GSDP

(in Per Cent)

Sector/Sub-sector	*Nagaland*	*All-India*
Agriculture	15.4	3.01
Forestry and Logging	6.3	1.85
Fishing	17.4	4.5
Mining and Quarrying	75.2	4.56
I. Primary	14.9	3.11
Manufacturing	0.9	6.97
Registered	8.2	7.12
Unregistered	–4.1	6.74
Construction	14.5	6.12
Electricity, Gas and Water Supply	–4.3	6.21
II. Secondary	10.2	6.68
Transport, Storage and Communication	13.5	9.73
Railways	0.3	4.88
Transport by Other Means	13.5	6.99
Storage	9.7	1.72
Communication	17.8	19.39
Trade, Hotels and Restaurants	12.0	8.51
Banking and Insurance	12.7	8.92
Real Esstate and Business Service	8.9	5.81
Public Administration	8.1	6.93
Other Services	11.2	8.45
III. Tertiary	10.8	8.15

Source: As in Table 19.1.

Reverting to the issue of structural change in output composition, the manufacturing activity as such is seen to have recorded only a low growth rate (0.9%) in Nagaland as against a high rate (around 7%) at all-India level during the reform period under review (Table 19.4). The share of manufacturing in GSDP of Nagaland (1.69%) at the close of the period under review is less than what it was (3.29%) at the beginning of the period. It stands to reason that the implementation of ongoing economic reforms characterized by liberalization, privatization and globalization (LPG) has resulted in putting the state more into a process of "de-industrialization" than accelerated industrialization. In no sense, ongoing economic reforms can be said to have put Nagaland on the path of industrialization. It also follows that the critical issue of concern in the recent development experience of Nagaland is the paradox of lagging manufacturing industry in a growing macro economy with high levels of human development achievements.

Growth and Structural Changes in Employment

The pattern of change in the size and structure of employment that accompanied the growth performance during the post-reform era in Nagaland is pertinent. As the question has been under serious scrutiny in the earlier studies, we do not intend to make any new exploration. We only need to contextualize the major findings of earlier studies on the structural change in employment. When we do that we are led to draw the conclusion of some positive effect on the overall growth in employment during the post-reform era. However, the growth rate in employment was not adequate enough to make any significant impact on redressing the acute problem of unemployment especially of the educated men and women in the state. Further, some lopsided structural features biased against the interests of women and marginalized sections of the society marked the growth trend in employment.

Sustainability of the Growth Momentum

We now turn to question raised earlier on the sustainability of growth momentum without developing a dynamic manufacturing industry in Nagaland. Is the growth performance influencing pattern of structural transformation marked by the slow growing manufacturing-based industrial sector with a low share in GSDP and the domination of the service sector witnessed during the 1990s sustainable in the long-run? To some extent the answer depends upon the income-elasticity of the services and the prospects of a continuous rise in the purchasing power (disposable income level) of the people. It must be noted that service covers a broad spectrum of activities, some conducive to production, some for consumer satisfaction or an amalgam of the two. The basic question is whether or not the sub-sectors having large shares in the service sector consist of services linked to commodity production. If it is promoting interlinkages, the sustainability of the growth pace in the aggregate service sector and thereby the sustainability of the growth momentum of the overall economy is not at risk. If not, the sustainability of the growth momentum in the long-run would be doubtful.

An empirical analysis is needed of the sustainability of the growth momentum in the macro-economy of Nagaland, which at present is propelled by the service (tertiary) sector. It is an interesting exercise and can leave useful lessons for designing a growth accelerating development strategy. The task, however, is difficult due to non-availability of detailed data on the nature of use to which the services are rendered. Some of the activities in the service sector are multi-dimensional in the sense that a service can be linked to commodity production or to final consumption in varying degrees across the states. The use of transport service or communication service can generally be conceived to have more linkages with production than consumption. However, the communication sub-sector renders mainly the consumer services and does not have strong linkage with the commodity production in Nagaland. Notwithstanding such analytical problems, we categorize on the lines of RBI's Report on *Currency and*

Finance (RBI, 2002) "sub-sectors including trade, transport and communication, financing, insurance, real estates and business services, as producer services with hotels and restaurants and other services as consumer service" (pp. III-39). On the line of RBI we may also have a third cateogy called, government service comprising of public administration, which provides intermediary services. The share accounted by these three categories of services, viz. (1) producer services; (2) consumer services; and (3) government services in the total GSDP of a state tell us their relative importance in shaping that GSDP.

It can be derived from the Table 19.3 that the average share of producer service category (13%) is smaller than that of the consumers' service category (30%) in the total GDP of Nagaland during the post-reform period under review (1993-94 to 2001-02). In other words, the largest part of the service sector in Nagaland is accounted by the consumers' services category. The fact that the share of producers' service category is lower than that of the consumer services in GSDP is suggestive of the limited interlinkages between services and commodity producing sectors in Nagaland.

Concluding Observations

In the light of the findings of our foregoing analysis we close our discussion by suggesting some pragmatic approaches for accelerating the growth rate in Nagaland.

- Given the inevitability of a neo-liberal policy perspective in the context of present-day strides in technological revolution and global integration, there is a logic in seeking a pragmatic approach of developing a new vision on the choice-mix of patterns for development based on modern manufacturing led industrialization.
- The new vision, however, should not ignore in its strategy the potential for development of employment-intensive and knowledge-using service sector. What is stressed is the risk in relying upon an unbalanced growth strategy based

on service sector. The strategy to transform Nagaland as mere service provider without building upon its dynamic comparative advantage in skill- and technology-driven commodity production, as is currently being done, is to miss an opportunity to grow in a balanced way by removing the lopsided structural features of present-day development.

- It is not the state but the private sector that can take more efficiently the initiative for a balanced growth in a competitive environment and push Nagaland deep into the new economy guided by increased investment and modular production of 'sun-rise' industries and manufacturing based on biotechnology and genetic engineering.
- In the product structure envisaged in the new pattern of manufacture-based industrialization, there is a systematic advantage in terms of organization structure. The pattern of industrialization is amendable to small- and medium-scale production with large scope for flexible specialization and opening up space for the emergence of a new class of entrepreneurs and new dimension to competition in the market-structure.
- In short, Nagaland society has to modify its mindset on treating private capitalist including foreign capital as a labour exploiting class alone. Instead, it has to adopt a proactive approach towards foreign capital and private sector investors to for attracting investment in new industrial activities to the mutual advantage of capital and labour as integrated components of a new society.
- In the development strategy the initiative and dynamism of private capital including multi-national corporations should get the right focus. However, the state still has to play a major role. The pragmatic approach is to transform the State not as an active participant entrepreneur but as a monitor and regulator to correct the market-failures so that the lopsided development is corrected, and as a facilitator striving to ensure economic growth

on a sustained basis through manufacture-based industrialization.

We conclude with the hope that our discussion here has the power to persuade meaningful debate to come up with pragmatic approach in a development strategy that helps nullifying the ill-effects of the current forms of liberalization, privatization and globalization and promoting accelerated growth by remaining within the regime of reforms.

20

Economic Reforms and Employment in Nagaland: Issues and Challenges

Manoj Kumar Singh

Profile of Economic Reforms

Since 1990s the Indian economy was passing through a period of an economic crisis. In order to place the economy back on the path of high and sustainable growth the government introduced certain economic reforms including privatization, liberalization and marketisation from June 1991, and even now the reforms are being continued. According to Manmohan Singh, champion of economic reforms in India, "we are creating a macro-economic environment in which industry speeds ahead with growth rates of 12 per cent or more, generate more jobs and higher levels of wages and incomes through increased productivity". In order to achieve these objectives, a series of outward oriented policy changes, industrial, fiscal, monetary and trade policies were introduced for attracting by multinationals as wells as for the reduction of fiscal deficit. In addition, food and fertilizer subsidies were cut down and the public expenditure was also cut down considerably. The new trade policy has liberalized exports and imports, exchange rate was devalued, licensing and control on industries were removed and acceleration of investment was encouraged. In order to get technological upgradation in Indian industries, free flow of foreign investment was permitted and the multinationals were allowed to invest up to 51 per cent in all areas of production without prior governmental permission and in exceptional cases upto 100 per cent foreign investment was also permitted. Private sectors have been encouraged, even privatization of profit making public enterprises has also been done. Fiscal deficit has been reduced to certain limit. In short, the new policies have shown a strong preference for market oriented economy for solving the various problems of the economy. The purpose of this paper is to highlight the impact of economic reforms on employment generation in Nagaland.

Growth of Labour Force

Unemployment is a normal feature of market economies and Nagaland is no exception. During the last two decades the population of Nagaland has grown at the rate of 6.4 per cent, but the employment opportunities have failed to increase in line with the growth of population (Table 20.1). Hence, there has been continuous rise of persons seeking employment.

Table 20.1: Growth of Population in Nagaland

Years	*Population*	*Decadal Growth Rate (%)*	*Growth Rate of Population (%)*
1971	516449	39.88	3.98
1981	774930	50.05	5.00
1991	1209546	56.08	5.60
2001	1988636	64.41	6.44

Source: Statistical Hand Book of Nagaland, 2004, p. 41.

There is a large gap between the rate of growth of labour force and availability of employment. During, 1994 to 2000 the average rate of growth of labour force is 4 per cent, whereas growth rate of employment during the same period is 1.13. The workforce constitutes 42.74 per cent of the populaton in Nagaland. Though in absolute number, the total number of workers has increased 5.16 lakhs in 1991 to 8.49 lakhs in 2001, the percentage of worker to population has remained at 42.7 per cent. However, among the workers the share of main workers is falling from 42.29 per cent to 35.62 per cent, while the share of marginal workers has increased from 0.39 per cent in 1991 to 7.12 per cent in 2001. The near stagnant proportion of workers and increasing share of marginal workers is indicative of increased prevalence of unemployment and disguised unemployment in the state (Table 20.2).

Table 20.2: Percentage of Total Workers, Main Workers and Marginal Workers to Total Population During 1991 and 2001

(Percentage of Total Population)

	Total Workers		*Main Workers*		*Marginal Workers*		*Non-Workers*	
	1991	*2001*	*1991*	*2001*	*1991*	*2001*	*1991*	*2001*
Persons	42.68	42.74	42.29	35.62	0.39	7.12	57.32	57.26
Males	46.86	46.83	46.69	40.73	0.17	6.10	53.14	53.17
Females	37.96	38.25	37.32	30.01	0.64	8.24	62.04	61.75

Source: State Human Development, Report 2004, p. 243.

Another feature of workforce is that in Nagaland unorganized workforce is very high that is 73.68 per cent. The percentage of organized workers is 26.32 per cent. We have observed that under non-farm workers the percentage of organised workers is very high, that is 70.78 (Table 20.3).

Table 20.3: Share of Unorganised Sector Workers in North East Region: 1999-2000

(In Percentage)

State	*All Workers*		*Non-Workers*	
	Organized	*Unorganized*	*Organized*	*Unorganized*
Assam	22.04	77.96	22.12	77.88
Nagaland	26.32	73.68	70.78	29.22
Mizoram	14.46	85.54	43.07	56.93
Meghalaya	7.56	92.44	32.24	67.76
Manipur	11.22	88.78	30.73	69.27
Arunachal Pradesh	12.98	87.02	48.97	51.03
Sikkim	20.04	79.96	47.84	2.16
Tripura	17.87	82.13	22.14	77.86

Source: Computed from Unit level records of employment—Unemployment Survey, 55th Round of NSS, 1999-2000.

Growth of NSDP and Employment

There is a positive relation between the NSDP and Employment growth rates. The NSDP growth determines the demand for labour force. The average annual growth of employment in Nagaland has been around about 1.3 per cent over past twenty years. As far as the NSDP growth is concerned during the post reform period, it is found to be about 11.6 per cent but employment generation has further fallen to 0.91 per cent per annum.

Sectoral Growth of Employment

A study of the trend in the growth rates of employment between organized and unorganized sectors reveal that the both the sectors have experienced a deceleration in employment growth. The growth rate of employment, in the organized sector has not shown much satisfactory growth rate. In joint sector the growth rate of employment is decreasing. In Nagaland the percentage of contract workers is very high that is 46.80 (Table 20.4).

Table 20.4: Workers Employed by States of North East Region in Three Sectors and by Category. Distribution of Total Workers

(in per cent)

State	*By Sectors*						*By Category of Workers*		
	Public		*Joint*		*Private*		*Men*	*Women*	*Workers*
	2001-01	*2001-02*	*2000-01*	*2001-02*	*2000-01*	*2001-02*	*2001-02*	*2001-02*	*2001-02*
Nagaland	0.98	1.0	1.23	0.31	97.79	98.64	47.63	5.58	46.08
Manipur	9.78	0.20	0.58	7.06	89.64	92.74	64.62	35.08	0.30
Tripura	0.73	0.99	17.60	13.73	81.67	85.28.	31.25	1.02	67.74
Meghalaya	0.00	3.35	28.28	19.42	17.72	77.22	46.10	3.43	50.47
Assam	8.69	9.15	13.96	11.20	77.35	79.65	89.62	2.887.	28

Source: Report on Absenteeism, Labour Turnover Employment and Labour Cost in Census Sector, Annual Survey of Industries 2000-01 and 2001-02, Volume II, Ministry of Labour and Employment, Labour Bureau—Chandigarh/Shimla.

The latest survey on India's employment situation conducted by National Sample Survey Organisation (NSSO) published in September 2006, finds that in urban Nagaland, 404 workers out of every 1000 were employed in trade, hotel, restaurant, sector in 2004-05 against 117 in 1999-2000. In the rural sector the figures have increased from 28 to 49 during the same period. The highly dominant area of employment is still agriculture in Nagaland. In rural Nagaland 793 workers out of every 1000, were employed in agriculture sector in 2004-05 against 797 in 1999-2000. It also shows that this sector is giving a declining trend of employment.

In urban sector the figure has increased from 84 to 129 during the same period. Nagaland has also witnessed a marginal increase in the share of 'manufacturing' sector during this period. Number of workers employed in Agriculture has declined by 4 heads in every 1000 from 797 in 1999-2000 to 793 in 2004-05 in the rural sector. This was because of higher employment in construction, trade, hotel, restaurant and public administration and education (Tables 20.5 and 20.6).

Table 20.5: Sector-wise Total Rural Employment in Nagaland (Per 1000 distribution of Working Persons in the Principal and Subsidiary Status taken together by Industry—Rural)

Sectors	*1999-2000*	*2004-2005*
Agriculture	797	793
Mining and Quary	1	0
Manufacturing	6	21
Electric, Water	7	4
Construction	8	17
Trade, Hotel, Restaurant	28	49
Transport	13	14
Finance, Business	1	3
Public Administration, Education	139	100

Under the economic reforms more emphasis in diversification of agriculture is given. However, these developments are only limited to horticulture, floriculture, and agriculture. No doubt, these developments will improve the returns per unit area, generate more employment in secndary and territory sectors and foreign exchange earnings.

Table 20.6: Sector-wise Total Urban Employment in Nagaland (Per 1000): Distribution of Working Persons in the Principal and Subsidiary Status taken together by Industry—Urban)

Sectors	*1999-2000*	*2004-2005*
Agriculture	84	129
Mining and Quary	0	0
Manufacturing	62	66
Electric, Water	7	13
Construction	52	35
Trade, Hotel, Restaurant	117	404
Transport	3	51
Finance, Business	21	8
Public Administration, Education	654	294

Source: (For Tables 20.5 and 20.6): Employment and Unemployment situation in India, 1991-2000 and 2004-025 (35th Round and 61st Round)—NSSO.

The other sub-sectors of Primary sector, viz., forestry, bee-keeping and Mushroom farming etc. are also required to be encouraged, so that with less capital investment, more employment generation can be promised in rural sector.

Employment Exchange Statistics

Besides the above-mentioned observation, the employment exchange statistics also reveal a declining trend in placement, in comparison to the total registration (Table 20.7). In the year 1999, 35463 were registered in 7 employment exchanges of Nagaland.

Table 20.7: Number of Persons on Live Register of Employment Exchange

	Years				
	1999	*2000*	*2001*	*2002*	*2003*
No. of employment exchange	7	7	7	7	7
No. of persons on live register	35463	37090	37546	35041	42764
Placements	50	74	163	61	54

Source: Statistical Hand Book of Nagaland, 2004.

But the number of placement was only 50. In 2000, the number of candidates registered an increase by about 2000 and it was almost stagnant in 2001. Again it declined around 2000 in 2002 but in 2003 there was sharp increase in the number of candidates registered (about 7000). But placements are very negligible as compared to the number of candidates registered. The placements were 50, 74, 163, 61 and 54 in years of 1999, 2000, 2001 and 2002 and 2003 respectively.

Thus, it is quite obvious that the economic reforms have not even addressed the problem of unemployment and hence the economic reforms are not conducive for the growth of employment in Nagaland.

Impact of Economic Reforms

Despite economic growth during the post-reform period, there is low labour absorption is the Nagaland economy. The declining trend in employment particularly in the organized sector of the economy may be due to (i) Rise in the growth rate of population and labour force; (ii) Use of more and more capital intensive techniques of production; (iii) Use of labour savings devices; (iv) Dearth of Industrial activities in the state etc.

Even though lot of encouragement is given by the Government of Nagaland for the growth of the industries during the post-reform period, the number of small scale industries was 1360 in 2000-2001 and by end of the March 2000 there were 1014 establishments in organized sectors. Despite government efforts, the employment situation is not encouraging. Further, privatization and globalization are aggravating the worst fear on account of their inherent bias against labour intensive techniques. Hence, from the point of view of labour absorption, present policy changes may not help.

Policy Suggestions

Harnessing of the resources and potentials—mineral, forests, agriculture, land, industry and the opportunities in trade, the new sector of IT or Bio-technology require not only investments but also policy interventions to encourage such investments. The state should develop a comprehensive agriculture policy and promote agro-forest and mineral based industry in accordance with the available natural resources, so that these two sectors may absorb the labour force of the state.

Further entrepreneurial skills should be promoted for encouraging more self-employment opportunities. All these developments will have an effect on the employment in the service sector. Similarly, social service should be given due importance through which employment generation is possible in short as well as in long run.

REFERENCES

1. Adi, S. Mukta (1999): "Impact of economic reforms on employment in India", Conference Volume, 1999, The Indian Economic Association, p. 771.
2. State Human Development Report, 2004, Government of Nagaland; p. 243.
3. Statistical Hand Book of Nagaland, 2004, Directorate of Economics and Statistics, Government of Nagaland, Kohima.
4. Mishra, Baidy Nath (1997): *Economic Profile of India,* A.P.H. Publishing Corporation, New Delhi.
5. National Sample Survey Organization (NSSO), 35th Round and 61st Rounds, 1999.

21

Impact of Globalization on Industrial Sector of India's North-Eastern Region with Special Reference to Assam

Pranay Jyoti Goswami

In simple economic term, globalization refers to the process of integration of the world into one huge market. Such unification calls for removal of all trade barriers among countries.

The process of globalization started in Indian economy since 1991 when Government of India announced structural and financial reforms measures in order to integrate our economy into the global economy. Though from the very beginning till date debates are going on in the academic circle on concept and various issues of globalization as well as economic reform, it cannot be denied today that globalization became a reality more particularly when WTO came into existence in January 1995 and India was one of the signatories. Even the countries like China and Taiwan who were skeptical on globalization in the beginning realized its merits later on and became members of WTO in 2003. Russia had also taken decision to join in the WTO within 2006.

India's North-Eastern region is characterized by abundant natural resources and large manpower resources on the one hand, and poor infrastructure facilities, low per capita income, low level of industrialization, power problem, transport bottleneck, dominance by agricultural problem, unemployment problem, lack of technical manpower etc. on the other hand.

The main objective of the paper is to throw light on the impact of globalization on industrial sector of India's Noth-Eastern region with special reference to Assam.

What is the impact of globalization in household and other manufacturing industries? What is the employment scenario? Is there any structural change that has emerged in the North-Eastern region? One of the objectives of the present paper is to answer these questions. The paper also suggests various measures in order to strengthen the industrial base so that the people of this area can reap the fruits of globalization in order to raise their standard of living.

For the sake of proper understanding the paper is divided into two sections. Section 1 deals with industrial sector of the North-Eastern region. The employment scenario is also highlighted in this section. The section 2 is devoted to conclusion and suggestions.

The data sources of the present paper are secondary covering various Governmental and non-Governmental publications like census report, NSSO report, SIA statistics, books, journals, newspapers and various magazines.

In order to know the impact of globalization on our economy, 1991 may be marked as cut off year. The reason is that data on 1991 or early years will reveal the conditions of North East part of India before globalization which can be compared with the available recent data in order to know the impact of globalization in our economy more particularly in industrial sector.

SECTION 1

For economic development, industrial development is most important. Government of India in 1991 announced new industrial policy in order to remove the shackle of bureaucracy from the industrial sector. Major reforms initiated during the decade in the industrial sector are de-licensing, curtailment of public sector, and automatic approval for foreign equity in some areas, replacement of FERA by FEMA. Moreover, MRTP was almost scrapped, Companies Act was introduced, and Indian companies were allowed to make overseas investment up to certain limits. India's rupee was made fully convertible on current account for further consolidating the links of India's industry with the global industry. Apart from this in the new century, second generation reforms were also initiated including amending labour laws partially, bringing duties structure at the global standard in 2005 etc. Hence the obvious question has been before the researchers as to whether industrialization in India with special reference to North East has achieved its objective or not. Here some indicators have been taken to test the above statemetns.

Structural and Qualitative Change

Since 1991, the agricultural sector is no more a major contributory to India's GDP. The share of primary sector in India's GDP is gradually decreasing but the share of tertiary sector is gradually increasing. The share of secondary sector in the context of India has slightly declined. The contribution of secondary sector in 2001 was 26 per cent as against 29 per cent in 1993. Thus the reforms have failed to give impetus to Indian industries.

Coming to the North-Eastern region the share of agricultural sector is still much higher than India as a whole. In all the states of North-Eastern region contribution of primary sector is much higher than that of India as a whole. The contribution of secondary sector in all states except Manipur is much lower than India as a whole. But unlike India except Meghalaya the sign of improvement in the secondary sector is there. In case of Meghalaya no structural change is visualized in the last decade. In some states like Tripura, Assam, Manipur, Mizoram and Arunachal Pradesh contribution of primary sector to their NSDP has slightly fallen. In all other states of North-Eastern region except Meghalaya the contribution of secondary sector has risen slightly but it is much less than that of India. In Manipur and Tripura the contribution of tertiary sectors has declined (Table 21.1).

Table 21.1: NSDP at Factor Cost by Identity of Origin

States/Country	*Primary Sector*		*Secondary Sector*		*Tertiary Sector*	
	1993	*2001*	*1993*	*2001*	*1993*	*2001*
Tripura	38.0	34.18	8.19	14.01	53.81	51.81
Assam	48.03	44.56	13.40	15.17	38.59	40.27
Manipur	37.8	32.6	15.7	26.0	46.5	41.4
Meghalaya	31.86	31.08	11.92	11.12	56.22	57.80
Mizoram	33.23	27.73	94.5	13.08	57.32	59.18
Nagaland	25.8	29.82	12.2	15.4	62	54.78
Arunachal Pradesh	37.11	31.26	NA	NA	NA	NA
India	31	23	29	26	40	53

Source: Calculated for NEDFI Databank Quarterly, July 2002 and other issues.

Table 21.2 reveals that like India the proportion of cultivators to main workers has increased in all states of North-Eastern region except Tripura. Except Arunachal Pradesh the proportion of

Table 21.2: Main Worker by Industrial Categories

(in per cent)

States/Country	*Year*	*Cultivator*	*Agri-cultural Labour*	*House-hold Workers*	*Others*	*Total Main Workers*
Arunachal Pradesh	1991	60.35	5.12	.18	34.35	100.00
	2001	68.15	4.49	1.0	26.36	100.00
Assam	1991	50.90	12.0	.87	36.23	100.00
	2001	52.8	18.2	4.6	24.4	100.00
Manipur	1991	61.8	3.28	5.80	29.12	100.00
	2001	65.1	16.0	12.9	6.00	100.00
Meghalaya	1991	55.3	12.5	.40	31.8	100.00
	2001	61.5	23.2	2.4	12.9	100.00
Mizoram	1991	61.3	3.28	1.0	34.42	100.00
	2001	69.5	7.5	1.8	21.2	100.00
Nagaland	1991	72.6	1.4	.38	25.62	100.00
	2001	76.8	4.77	2.5	15.93	100.00
Tripura	1991	38.09	23.38	1.4	37.13	100.00
	2001	34.34	30.70	3.6	31.36	100.00
India	1991	38.4	26.4	2.4	32.8	100.00
	2001	40.75	34.30	5.23	19.72	100.00

Source: Sratistical Outline of India 2002-03.

agricultural labourer has increased in all states of North-Eastern region along with the country as a whole. Percentage of household workers to total main workers has increased much in Manipur that is from 5.80 per cent to 12.9 per cent. But little improvement has taken place in all other North-Eastern states. The proportion of other workers has declined in all states of North-Eastern region along with the country as a whole.

Performance of Industrial Sector

Performance of industrial sector in the period of liberalization in India has been better in comparison to agriculture but still it is far below the desired level. The overall index has increased by 176.4 points in 2003-04 by taking 1993-94 as base year. Obviously the growth is still single digit and lot of efforts is required to achieve double-digit growth. But in the North-Eastern region many industries more particularly tea is struggling hard for their survival. The biggest hurdle in the way of industrialization is stagnation in power generation. There is power cut varying from 5 hours to 10 hours in most of the states of North-Eastern region. In spite of huge hydro-electric potential more particularly in Arunachal Pradesh even one per cent of this potential is not exploited.

During liberalization period, Maharashtra, Gujarat, Tamil Nadu have further strengthened their share but North-Eastern states continue to lag behind due to lack of proper infrastructure, terrorism, absence of law and order and poor industrial relation etc. Data regarding industrial entrepreneur memorandum implemented during 1992 to April 2004 reveal that the industrialists are not attracted in the North-Eastern region to start their industries. Though in some of the states, a number of industrial proposals are there (Table 21.4), but due to red tapism, corruption, lack of sincerity of bureaucracy, etc. the rate of implementation of these proposals is very poor (Table 21.5). The growth rate of large scale and medium industries in Assam is around 5 per cent. In some states growth rate is zero or negative (Table 21.7).

Employment Scenario

In order to portray the employment situation let us first see whether unemployment rate is rising or falling during the period of globalization. For these purpose NSS 50th, 55th Round and 60th Round data are taken into consideration. Table 21.3 shows that compared to 1993-94, during 2004 (Jan.–June) the unemployment rate in terms of usual principal status has remained almost the same, except for females in rural areas. In urban areas, no significant change in this rate in terms of *cws* is noticeable between the earlier round and the present one. In terms of CDS the rate is found to be higher in 2004 by about 2 per cent points in both rural and urban areas than that obtained in 1999-2000 (55th Round), except for urban males. As per 60th Round of NSS data it reveals that out of 1000 usually working persons the number of people dependent on secondary sector in North-Eastern region is much

Table 21.3: Unemployment Rate (Number of Persons Unemployed Per 1000 Persons in the Labour Force) for 50th and 60th rounds of NSS (All India)

Rural	*Male*				*Female*			
	US	*US**	*CWS*	*CDS*	*US*	*US**	*CWS*	*CDS*
60	24	18	47	90	22	13	45	93
	(13)	(10)	(25)	(47)	(5)	(4)	(12)	(19)
55	21	17	39	72	15	10	37	70
	(11)	(9)	(21)	(37)	(4)	(3)	(10)	(15)
50	20	14	30	56	14	8	30	56
	(11)	(8)	(17)	(30)	(3)	(3)	(8)	(13)
Urban	*Male*				*Female*			
60	46	40	57	81	89	67	90	117
	(25)	(22)	(32)	(45)	(12)	(11)	(14)	(16)
55	48	45	56	73	71	57	73	14
	(26)	(24)	(30)	(38)	(9)	(8)	(10)	(12)
50	45	40	52	67	83	62	84	105
	(24)	(22)	(28)	(36)	(11)	(10)	(12)	(14)

Note: Figures within brackets indicates the Rate of unemployed per 1000 persons.

Source: NSSO Different Rounds.

Table 21.4: Industrial Invetment Proposals State-wise

Name of the State	*IEM+LOI+DIL*		*Industrial Entrepreneur Memorandum*						*Latter of Intents of Interest + Direct Industrial Licences*					
	Numbers	*Per Cent*	*Numbers Field*	*Per Cent*	*Proposed Invest-ment (Rs. crore)*	*Per Cent*	*Proposed Employment (Numbers)*	*Per Cent*	*Numbers Granted*	*Per Cent*	*Proposed Invest-ment (Rs. crore)*	*Per Cent*	*Proposed Employment (Numbers)*	*Per Cent*
Maharashtra	11007	19.57	10449	19.97	237559	19.70	7860733	17.48	558	14.24	14567	13.11	129482	15.28
Gujarat	6986	12.42	6548	12.52	201053	16.69	1041087	10.19	438	11.18	21028	18.92	71700	8.46
Tamil Nadu	5076	9.03	4340	8.30	62143	5.16	660307	6.46	736	18.79	11273	10.14	129056	15.23
Uttar Pradesh	4837	8.60	4484	8.57	70350	5.84	2085856	20.40	353	9.01	9752	8.77	97750	11.54
Andhra Pradesh	3922	6.97	348	6.67	131844	10.94	562240	5.50	434	11.08	10715	9.64	79775	9.42
Haryana	3303	5.87	3070	5.87	37786	3.14	454158	4.45	233	5.95	4318	3.89	63120	7.45
West Bengal	2944	5.24	2854	5.46	48309	4.01	466813	4.57	90	2.30	4047	3.64	19112	2.26
Rajasthan	2639	4.69	2542	4.86	40461	3.36	466718	4.57	97	2.48	1626	1.46	15455	1.82
Punjab	2434	4.33	2251	4.30	50904	4.23	504209	4.93	183	4.67	4887	4.40	54035	6.38
Karnataka	2297	4.08	2064	3.95	61135	5.07	324254	3.17	233	5.95	9598	8.64	71599	8.45
Madhya Pradesh	2180	3.88	2039	3.90	43753	3.63	388966	3.81	141	3.60	3160	2.84	30163	3.56
Dadra and Nagar Haveli	1763	3.14	1729	3.30	25642	2.13	184236	1.80	34	0.87	314	0.28	3917	0.46
Chhattisgarh	866	1.54	839	1.60	54815	4.55	192379	1.88	27	0.69	550	0.49	3738	0.44
Daman and Diu	799	1.42	776	1.48	4625	0.38	55895	0.5	23	0.59	94	0.08	3535	0.42
Orissa	582	1.03	545	1.04	42697	3.54	19239	1.46	37	0.94	5444	4.90	11882	1.40
Pondicherry	581	1.03	562	1.07	6957	0.58	48022	0.47	19	0.48	1304	1.17	2894	
Kerala	554	0.99	487	0.93	8232	0.68	74841	0.73	67	1.71	2782	2.50	14326	1.69
Goa	543	0.97	507	0.97	7257	0.60	49468	0.48	36	0.92	168	0.15	3526	0.42
Himachal Pradesh	527	0.94	494	0.94	10601	0.88	100730	0.99	33	0.84	477	0.43	6142	0.72
Delhi	501	0.89	480	0.92	6503	0.54	47563	0.47	21	0.54	30	0.03	1652	0.19

(Table 21.4 contd.)

Name of the State	IEM+LOI+DIL		Industrial Entrepreneur Memorandum						Latter of Intrents of Interest + Direct Industrial Licences					
	Numbers	Per Cent	Numbers Field	Per Cent	Proposed Invest-ment (Rs. crore)	Per Cent	Proposed Employment (Numbers)	Per Cent	Numbers Granted	Per Cent	Proposed Invest-ment (Rs. crore)	Per Cent	Proposed Employment (Numbers)	Per Cent
Uttaranchal	490	0.87	464	0.89	7550	0.63	69018	0.68	26	0.66	257	0.23	7404	0.87
Jharkhand	424	0.75	409	0.78	12561	1.05	67780	0.68	15	0.38	359	0.32	2118	0.25
Assam	292	0.52	280	0.54	5688	0.47	40434	0.40	12	0.31	2433	2.19	4538	0.54
Jammu & Kashmir	209	0.37	202	0.39	2297	0.19	49754	0.49	7	0.18	76	0.07	2074	0.24
Bihar	177	0.?1	144	0.28	3036	0.25	16948	0.17	33	0.84	1462	1.32	13674	1.51
Meghalaya	159	0.28	157	0.30	1652	0.14	14580	0.14	2	0.05	5	neg	201	0.02
Chandigarh	38	0.07	37	0.07	4.58	0.04	6103	0.06	1	0.03	0	0.00	9	Neg
Tripura	24	0.04	24	0.05	1883	0.16	2662	0.03	0	0.00	p	0.00	0	0.00
Andaman & Nicobar	21	0.04	17	0.03	224	0.02	2826	0.03	4	0.10	1	neg	522	0.06
Sikkim	14	0.02	13	0.02	46	neg	IIOI	0.01	1	0.03	5	neg	204	0.02
Nagaland	13	0.02	12	0.02	16242	1.35	301803	2.95	1	0.03	0	0.00	0	0.00
Andaman & Nicobar	9	0.02	9	0.02	322	0.03	2810	0.03	0	0.00	0	0.00	0	0.00
Lakshadweep	1	neg	1	neg	4	neg	278	neg	0	0.00	0	0.00	0	0.00
Manipur	1	neg	1	neg	3	neg	125	neg	0	0.00	0	0.00	0	0.00
Mizoram	0	0.00	0	0.00	0	0.00	0	0.00	0	0.00	0	0.00	0	0.00
Location in More than one State	24	0.04	1	neg	0	0.00	0	0.00	3	0.59	404	0.36	3596	0.42
Total	**58236**	**100.00**	**52318**	**100.00**	**1204732**	**100.00**	**10219516**	**10.00**	**3918**	**100.00**	**111136**	**99.99**	**847219**	**100.00**

Note: Figures of three States include those located in districts originally falling within the respective parent States.
Source: SIA Statistics April 2004. Ministry of Commerce and Industry (GoI).

Table 21.5: Industrial Entrepreneurs Memoranda Implemented During 1992—April 2004

State/UTs	*Industrial Entrepreneurs Memoranda Implemented (Investment in Rs. crore)*										*% Share in Total*		*% Change*	*IEM Filed Implement (%)*	
	1992-96	1997	1998	1999	2000	2001	2002	2003	Jan-April 04	1992-94	1992-96	1992-04	1992-04	Upto 2004	Upto 2004
Andhra Pradesh	145	36	27	37	44	51	74	22	3	438	5.65	7.54	202.1	3510	17.48
Arunachal Pradesh	0	0	0	0	0	0	0	0	0	0	0.00	0.92		17	0.00
Assam	3	4	2	2	3	12	13	10	2	51	0.12	0.11	1600.00	282	18.09
Bihar	4	0	1	0	0	1	0	0	0	6	0.16	0.94	50.00	144	4.17
Chhattisgarh	27	4	4	3	0	4	5	5	0	52	1.05	1.56	92.6	873	5.96
Goa	22	4	7	4	11	17	12	5	4	86	0.86	17.61	290.9	508	16.93
Gujarat	465	146	66	46	47	85	60	45	11	971	18.10	6.42	108.8	6603	14.71
Haryana	184	57	12	13	14	29	28	9	8	354	2.17	0.60	92.4	3084	11.48
Himachal Pradesh	11	3	2	2	0	11	3	0	1	33	0.43	0.20	200.0	498	6.63
Jammu & Kashmir	5	2	C	1	1	0	1	1	0	11	0.19	0.85	120.0	213	5.16
Jharkhand	14	5	3	2	3	4	2	2	1	36	0.55	2.88	157.1	414	8.70
Karnataka	88	19	8	6	7	20	5	5	1	159	0.43	1.38	80.71	2974	7.67
Kerala	40	8	9	7	5	4	2	1	0	76	1.66	5.11	90.0	492	15.45
Madhya Pradesh	163	31	20	21	17	14	13	3	0	282	6.35	15.78	73.0	2047	13.78
Maharashtra	487	72	48	38	21	104	55	37	8	870	18.95	13.78	78.6	10505	8.28
Manipur	0	0	0	0	0	0	0	0	0	0	0.00	0.22		2	0.00
Meghalaya	0	1	0	0	0	3	6	2	0	12	0.00	0.00		159	7.55
Mizoram	0	0	0	0	0	0	0	0	0	0	0.00	0.00		0	0.00
Nagaland	0	0	0	0	0		0	0	0	0	0.00	0.63	218.7	12	0.00
Orissa	11	0	4	1	0	6	9	1	3	35	0.43	4.79	88.6	561	6.24
Punjab	140	31	7	15	20	22	24	3	2	264	5.45	6.04	129.7	2264	11.66

(Table 21.5 contd.)

State/UTs	Industrial Entrepreneurs Memoranda Implemented (Investment in Rs. crore)										% Share in Total		% Change	IEM Filed Implement (%)	
	1992-96	1997	1998	1999	2000	2001	2002	2003	Jan-April 04	1992-94	1992-96	1992-04	1992-04	Upto 2004	Upto 2004
Rajasthan	145	54	10	24	17	44	29	9	1	333	5.65	0.00		2560	13.01
Sikkim	0	0	0	0	0	0	0	0	0	0	0.00	7.54	70.9	14	0.00
Tamil Nadu	237	39	18	12	17	57	20	2	3	405	9.22	0.07		4366	9.28
Tripura	0	0	0	0	0	0	2	2	0	4	0.00	0.47	225.0	24	16.67
Uttranchal	8	6	1	0	2	1	2	4	2	26	0.31	7.78	125.4	479	5.43
Uttar Pradesh	192	42	21	26	24	67	28	17	12	429	7.48	6.44	367.1	4511	9.51
West Bengal	76	27	16	23	33	54	73	39	14	355	2.96	0.00		2880	12.33
Andaman & Nicobar	0	0	0	0	0	0	0	0	0	0	0.00	0.07	100.0	9	0.00
Chandigarh	2	1	1	0	0	0	0	0	0	4	0.08	1.25	263.2	37	10.81
Dadra and Nagar Haveli	19	3	11	5	4	6	17	3	1	69	0.74	0.82	4.7	1734	3.98
Delhi	43	1	1	0	0	0	0	0	0	45	1.67	0.73	166.7	481	9.36
Pondicherry	15	2	4	0	2	5	12	0	0	40	0.58	1.25	213.6	566	7.07
Daman and Diu	22	7	5	7	9	5	4	9	1	69	0.86	0.00		779	8.86
Lakshadweep	0	0	0	0	0	0	0	0	0	0	0.00	0.00		1	0.00
Total	**2568**	**605**	**308**	**294**	**301**	**626**	**499**	**236**	**78**	**5515**	**100.00**	**100.00**	**114.8**	**52703**	**10.46**

Source: Economic Times, 12 August, 2004.

lower than that of India as a whole. Table 21.6 reveals that whereas 145 persons worked in the secondary sector in rural India, it is 82 for North East as a whole and 34 for Assam. This shows poor industrial employment in this area. In urban areas, 338 persons out of 1000 worked in secondary sector in the country as a whole whereas in North-Eastern region it is only 137. The same figure is also valid for Assam. However, number of persons working in the tertiary sector is much higher in Assam as well as in North-Eastern states compared to the country as a whole. However, over the years in all India level the number of people working in primary sector is gradually decreasing and in secondary and tertiary sector it is gradually increasing. In case of North-eastern region though the

Table 21.6: Per 1000 Distribution of Usually Working Persons by Broad Group of Industry by State

		Male			*Female*		
		Primary	*Secondary*	*Tertiary*	*Primary*	*Secondary*	*Tertiary*
Assam	Rural	715	34	251	745	33	222
	Urban	54	137	810	72	147	781
North-East	Rural	667	82	252	676	85	239
States	Urban	150	137	713	167	143	689
All India	Rural	703	145	152	724	136	139
	Urban	72	338	589	83	339	578

Source: NSSO 60th Round.

Table 21.7: Number of Large and Medium Scale Industries in North-Eastern Region (1991-2000)

State	*1991*	*1994*	*2000*
Arunachal Pradesh	9	17	17
Assam	116	118	129
Manipur	6	6	12
Maghalaya	7	7	10
Mizoram	0	1	1
Nagaland	16	16	7
Tripura	1	1	2
Total	**154**	**166**	**178**

Source: Basic Statistics Relating to North-Eastern Region.

same trend is emerging, still the number of persons employed in the secondary sector is much lower than that of India as a whole (Table 21.8).

Border Trade

The contribution of North-East region in border trade is even less than 1 per cent of India's total export in spite of the fact that some trade liberalization measures have been taken by the Government of India in order to boost up trade among the members of the SAARC Countries. In order to connect this part of the country with the South Asian countries like Myanmar, China etc. the Government is trying to reopen Stilwel Road.

SECTION 2

From the foregoing analysis, it can be concluded that the globalization of Indian economy fails to bring any change in the industrial scenario of North-Eastern region. Majority of the people still depend on agricultural sector in order to maintain their livelihood. A very little structural change has been observed in this part of the country. The condition of some states like Meghalaya remains more or less same. However, a marginal positive improvement has taken place in secondary or household sector in the state like Manipur. In urban areas people depend heavily on tertiary sector. There is an uneven sectoral growth rate in the states of North-Eastern region. The growth rate of tertiary sector is much more than other sectors.

There is much scope of industrialization in North-Eastern region. The region is rich in natural mineral and forest resources. But the prerequisite of industrialization in the region is improvement of power scenario, transportation and law and order. So Governments of North-Eastern region must take measures in order to set up hydro-electric projects in this area. Raw materials of Ayurvedic medicines are there in the forests of North-Eastern region. The expertise of MNCS can be utilized in order to exploit the mineral resources of NER. Measures may be taken to export

Table 21.8: Unemployment Rate (Number of Persons Unemployed Per 1000 Persons) in the Labour Force for 50th, 55th and 60th of NSS Round (North-Eastern States and All India)

States	*NSS Round*	*Rural*								*Urban*							
		Male				*Female*				*Male*				*Female*			
		US	US*	CWS	CDS	US	US*	CWS	CDS	US	US*	CWS	CDS	US	US*	CWS	CDS
Andhra Pradesh	50	17	16	18	19	3	2	4	4	17	17	17	18	77	73	72	73
	55	9	8	11	13	1	1	1	1	14	14	24	22	100	100	91	65
	60*	19	26	28	32	14	13	14	15	35	27	33	34	22	21	23	43
Assam	50	62	46	54	70	143	77	111	124	62	55	57	65	289	256	267	256
	55	42	32	45	60	119	66	88	125	91	77	84	99	223	189	197	219
	60	21	5	23	23	33	14	11	17	18	19	24	18	23	30	33	23
Manipur	50	19	12	17	22	11	7	7	11	53	48	48	50	44	32	27	31
	55	24	21	25	24	25	15	27	26	74	69	66	66	103	62	68	76
	60*																
Meghalaya	50	4	4	5	6	0	0	0	2	13	10	14	16	32	31	27	31
	55	5	5	5	6	3	3	3	5	34	34	34	35	68	62	68	76
	60*																
Mizoram	50	16	14	14	10	6	4	5	5	5	5	2	4	5	5	4	5
	55	21	14	18	19	5	3	4	5	44	34	29	38	26	24	24	31
	60*																
Nagaland	50	21	21	20	21	0	0	6	6	69	69	69	69	70	64	68	67
	55	30	26	26	28	38	20	22	31	93	93	97	98	108	87	98	104
	60*																
Tripura	50	15	14	21	34	84	58	85	104	62	60	70	82	201	174	203	215
	55	8	7	9	17	46	44	46	57	55	54	57	57	88	85	89	96
	60*																
All India	50	20	14	30	56	14	8	30	56	45	40	52	67	82	62	84	105
	55	21	17	39	72	15	10	37	70	48	45	56	73	71	58	73	94
	60	13	10	25	47	5	4	12	19	25	17	22	45	12	11	16	45

* State-level Data except Assam are not available. NER Data as a whole may be used in the Inidividual States.
Source: NSSO (50th Round), NSSO (55th Round), NSSO (60th Round).

the produce of cottage and small scale industries of NER. Moreover, some fruit processing units may be established.

REFERENCES

Ansari, A.Q. Aziz and Khan Amriulla, Indian Economy Beyond 2005 on the Fast Track in the *Indian Journal of Commerce,* July-September 2005.

Basic Statistics of NER, 2002 and other issues published by NEC Secretariat, Shillong.

Bezbaruah, M.P.: A Review of Economic Trends in India's N.E. Region Since Independence, *Journal of North East India Council for Social Science Research,* Shillong, 2001.

Dubey, Amaresh, Das, Smita and Pala, Veronica: Migration in North East States of India. The paper was presented in a seminar on Globalization at NEHU, Shillong in 2002.

EPW Research Foundation: National Accounts Statistics of India, 1950-51 to 1996-97, Published in 1998.

Goswami, Pranay Jyoti: Agricultural Development in North East India with Special Reference to Settled Agriculture in Alam, K. (ed.) *Agricultural Development in North East India: Constraints and Prospects,* Deep & Deep Publication, New Delhi, 1993.

Goswami, Pranay Jyoti: Electrification in North East India in Athparia, R.P. and others (ed.) *Energy and Energy Resource Management,* Deep & Deep Publication, New Delhi, 1999.

Goswami, Pranay Jyoti: Health and Nutritional Status of People of N.E. Region in Datta Ray, B. (ed.): *Agenda for North East India,* Concept Publishing Company, New Delhi, 2002.

Goswami, Pranay Jyoti: Industrial Development Needs: Entrepreneurial Development in North East India in Datta Ray, B., (ed.): *Sociological Constraints to Industrial Development in North East India,* Concept Publishing Co., New Delhi, 1998.

NSS Reports, 50th, 55th and 60th Round.

Panda, Sudhakhar: Globalization and Challenges of Poverty, Unemployment and Social Development in North East States. The paper was presented in a seminar on Globalization at NEHU Shillong on Nov. 2002.

Pandey, M.C. and Langistia, B.S.: Growth of Population and Literacy in the District of North-Eastern States in *Journal of North East India Council for Social Science Research,* Shillong, 1994.

Pradhan, H. Prasad, Globalization: A Saga of Poor Understanding *EPW,* January 20, 2001.

Rana Kulwant *et al.,* Indian Industry in the Era of Reforms in the *Indian Journal of Commerce,* July-September 2005.

Roy Burman, B.K.: Land, People and Demographic Indicator of North East India, *Journal of North East India,* December 1999, p. 63.

Various Census Reports.

22

Impact of New Economic Policy on Tea Industry of Assam

Biswajyoti Dasgupta

Tea is the cheapest hot beverage which is popular worldwide. It is consumed by a large section of society and by people in almost all age groups in some countries. India is leading tea producer in world market to meet the demand. In India, Assam plays a dominant role in the country's tea-map by producing more than half of the total tea production of India. The geographical factor helped the development of tea industry in Assam. The encouragement by the colonial government and initiatives by private tea planters made rapid flourishing of tea industry in the state. The production of tea in Assam has been consistently dominant in whole of India since the early years of inception. At present, Assam is the biggest producer of Tea in India whose share ranges between 53-60 per cent of India's total tea production. Assam alone produces approximately 29 per cent of the world tea production.

To make a big push to each and every sector of the economy, the New Economic Policy was introduced by the Government of India on its full wave in 1991 by incorporating the concepts of Liberalisation, Marketisation, Privatisation and Globalisation for the first time. Tea industry especially the Assam Tea Industry being the major contributor to the foreign exchange earning of the country, gets a special place in the context of new economic policy.

The present paper throws light on the impact of new economic policy on the tea industry of Assam in two sections. The Section I deals with analysis of some parameters such as annual tea production, yield rate per hectare, area under tea plantation, number of tea estates, income, employment and also sickness to understand the impact of new economic policy on the tea industry of Assam. The Section II is devoted to conclusion and suggestion.

Secondary sources of data were used for the paper from Tea Board of India, Tea Auction Centres, books and journals etc. To depict the impact of New Economic Policy, 1991 is taken as cut-off year to make a comparative analysis of the situation of tea industry in Assam with the available recent data.

SECTION I

Assam, in the far North East of India, is the world's largest distinct tea growing area. The weather conditions here are both extreme and, for the tea plant, ideal. The mix of sun and rain, heat and humidity, offers the native tea plant its perfect habitat and produces the instantly recognisable, rich, malty, full-bodied, bright tea that have established itself as favourites around the world. Being the home of Indian tea, Assam produces about 425 million kilograms of tea annually, more than any other country except China.

It was hoped that the launch of new economic policy would boost every indicator of the economy. But, picture is dismal in some sectors specially Tea Industry of Assam.

The opening up of markets due to liberalisation has resulted huge arrival of foreign tea in Indian markets which is rich in quality (Table 22.1). The elasticity of domestic demand for tea is high with respect to domestic income. As a result, a sizeable portion of erstwhile domestic demand for Indian tea has shifted to the foreign tea.

On the other hand, the demand for tea in the international market is both price elastic and income elastic.

Due to supply of mainly quantity-tea (not quality tea), the poor demand for Indian tea in the international market over the period offers lower price. This generates less income to the Indian tea industry.

Further, the income elasticity of Indian tea is comparatively less than that of foreign tea.

Table 22.1: Import of Tea into India (Financial Year)

Years	*Quantity (M. Kgs.)*	*Value (Rs. Crs.)*	*Unit Price (Rs./Kg.)*
1992-93	1.37	5.14	37.52
1993-94	0.87	3.99	45.86
1994-95	0.20	1.10	55.00
1995-96	0.45	2.41	53.56
1996-97	1.25	6.21	49.68
1997-98	2.61	17.79	68.16
1998-99	8.93	64.73	72.49
1999-2000	10.36	61.97	59.80
2000-2001	15.35	96.67	63.00
2001-2002	16.14	83.73	51.86

Source: Tea Digest, Kolkata, different years.

Assam being the largest producer of tea in India, the stiff competition being faced by the Indian tea in the international market naturally affects the tea industry of the state. The income earned from the tea sector of the state has been gradually decreasing in the last few years due to this reason.

On the one hand, lesser income and on the other, increasing cost of production, resulted sickness in a number of tea estates. Further, there is also downsizing of workers and lesser incentives for increasing production.

All these have resulted in poor performance of tea industry in Assam in the post-New Economic Policy period. Here, some parameters have been taken to test the statements.

Production of Tea

To get a picture of the impact of new economic policy, let us see the trend of production of tea in Assam since 1991.

Assam produced around 53 per cent of total tea production of India in 1991. It remained same in 1998. In 2002, the share of Assam to total tea production of India slightly declined to around 52 per cent.

In this context, it is evident that the growth of tea production in Assam in 1998 was 16.60 per cent over 1991. But in 2002, there was a negative growth of 7.22 per cent over 1998 (Table 22.2).

Table 22.2: Production of Tea (in Assam and India)

(Figures in thousand Kgs.)

Years	*Assam*	*India*	*Growth of Production (%) over previous year in Assam*	*Share of Assam (%) in India*
1991	400554	754192	—	53.11
1993	410430	760826	2.47	53.95
1998	467046	874108	13.79	53.43
2002	433327	838474	(-)7.22	51.68

Source: Tea Digest, Kolkata, different years.

Thus , it shows that the new economic policy has failed to give any impetus to the tea production of the state of Assam.

In this context, it is interesting to note that after the introduction of New Economic Policy especially in recent years, the share of India in total tea production of the world has slightly declined. In 2001, India produced around 27.63 per cent of total tea production of the world. It reduced to 26.65 per cent in 2002 (Table 22.3).

Table 22.3: Production of Tea (India and World Total)

(Figures in millions Kgs.)

Years	*India*	*World Total*	*Share of India (%) in World Total*
2001	854	3091	27.63
2002	826	3099	26.65

Source: Tea Digest, Kolkata, different years.

Average Yield Rate

On yield rate, the picture is also not very hopeful. In 1991, average yield of tea per hectare in Assam was 1818 kg. It got reduced to 1688 kg. in 2000 and again reduced to 1601 kg. in 2002; whereas average yield of tea in India was 1794 kg. per hectare in 1991, reduced to 1679 kg. in 2000 and further to 1625 kg. in 2002.

Thus, it is found that the trend of yield rate of the tea production is negative for both Assam as well as all India. However, it is fascinating to note that average yield of tea per hectare for both Assam and all India is higher than that of the world total (Table 22.4).

Table 22.4: Average Yield of Tea

(Kg. per hectare)

Year	*Assam*	*India*	*World Total*
1991	1818	1794	1026
2000	1688	1679	1127
2002	1601	1625	1157

Source: Tea Digest, Kolkata, different years.

Area under Tea

There is almost a stagnant position in the share of total area under tea plantation in Assam to that of all India level. In 1991, Assam had 47.08 per cent share of total area under tea plantation in India. It increased to 53.08 per cent in 1998, but declined to 52.76 per cent in 2001. On the other hand, growth of area under tea plantation in Assam gives us a fluctuating figure which is not congenial for any type of industrial activity. In 1998, there was 27.10 per cent growth of tea area over 1991. But, in 2001, the same rate got reduced to only 6.90 per cent over 1998 (Table 22.5).

Table 22.5: Area Under Tea Plantation

(In hectares)

Years	*Assam*	*India*	*Growth of area under tea (%) over previous year in Assam*	*Share of Assam (%) in all India*
1991	197970	420470	—	47.08
1998	251625	474027	27.10	53.08
2001	268983	509806	6.90	52.76

Source: Tea Digest, Kolkata, different years.

Thus, in post-New Economic Policy period, the share of area under tea plantation in Assam gives us a fluctuating picture, nay a jolt by the new economic situation, which may cause further problem in future.

Number of Tea Estates

One interesting feature in the tea industry of Assam in post-New Economic Policy period is the ever increasing number of tea gardens since 1998. This is due to operation and recognition of small growers in different tea producing districts especially in Dibrugarh and Sibsagar districts.

The total number of tea gardens in Assam was 727 in 1991. It rose to 2472 in 1997. Further, it rose to 25708 in 1998 and to 40795 in 2001. The share of tea gardens in Assam of all India level is also showing an increasing trend over this period (Table 22.6).

Table 22.6: No. of Tea Estates (including Small Tea Growers)

Year	*Assam*	*India*	*Share of Assam (%) in India*
1991	727	13873	5.24
1997	2472	38707	6.39
1998	25708	88115	29.18
2001	40795	N.A.	—

Source: Tea Digest, Kolkata, different years.

Thus, in terms of number, it is an impressive feature and is also generating self-employment and income opportunities to a good section of youth in Assam.

Income

Although Assam produces more than 50 per cent of the country's total tea production, the income earned from the tea sector of the state has been gradually decreasing in the last few years due to stiff competition being faced by the Indian tea in the international market.

The export of tea from India has been fluctuating over the period since 1998 to 2002. There is almost constant fall in export price of Indian tea during the period. The picture is almost same in the case of North Indian Tea in which Assam plays a dominant role.

The marketing of Indian tea is primarily done at auction centres of India. There has also been a fall in the price of tea at Indian auction centres during the same period (Table 22.7).

Table 22.7: Export Quantity and Prices of Tea (both export and auction prices)

Year	*North India*				*All India*			
	Export (incl. instant tea)		*Sold in Indian auctions*		*Export (incl. instant tea)*		*Sold in Indian auctions*	
	Qnty. (th. kg.)	*Unit price (Rs./kg.)*	*Qnty. (th. kg.)*	*Avg. price (Rs./kg.)*	*Qnty. (th. kg.)*	*Unit price (Rs./kg.)*	*Qnty. (th. kg.)*	*Avg. price (Rs./kg.)*
1998	100361	122.01	295680	80.22	210338	109.80	442359	76.43
1999	95254	122.11	321589	80.56	191719	102.54	480768	72.79
2000	95727	121.22	337154	70.34	206816	91.80	507527	61.71
2001	85420	119.63	305020	69.80	182588	92.13	463688	61.66
2002	94381	111.87	311030	62.66	201002	87.23	456549	55.96

Source: (i) Tea Digest, Kolkata, different years.
(ii) Different Tea Auction Centres, India.

Coming to the Tea Auction Centre at Guwahati, it is found that price of tea (per kg.) was Rs. 80.53 in 1993 which got reduced to Rs. 68.45 in 2000 registering a 15 per cent fall (Table 22.8).

Table 22.8: Sale and Price of Tea at Guwahati Tea Auction Centre

Years	*Sale (thousand kg.)*	*Price (Rs./Kg.)*	*Change in price (%) over previous year*
1999	145055	80.53	—
2000	146847	68.45	(–) 15

Source: Tea Auction Centre, Guwahati, Assam.

It is further found that there has been more or less gradual fall in the average price of both CTC and Orthodox types of tea in Assam since 1998 (Table 22.9).

Table 22.9: Quantity and Average Price of Tea Sold in Guwahati Tea Auction Centre

(Quantity in lakh kgs.)

Year	*Leaf*				*Dust*			
	CTC		*Orthodox*		*CTC*		*Orthodox*	
	Qnty.	*Avg. price (Rs.)*	*Qnty.*	*Avg. price (Rs.)*	*Qnty.*	*Avg. price (Rs.)*	*Qnty.*	*Avg. price (Rs.)*
1998	924	79.70	8.0	74.08	467	77.12	3.0	56.25
1999	1023	81.55	4.0	74.18	470	78.58	0.4	48.22
2000	974	72.51	8.0	67.56	432	70.90	1.0	39.97
2001	943	70.58	6.0	59.22	427	64.68	0.7	38.32
2002	908	63.06	7.8	56.06	398	57.44	0.2	29.69

Source: Guwahati Tea Auction Centre, Assam.

Thus, it seems that there has been a rapid fall in the export and auction prices of Indian as well as Assam tea in the post-liberalisation period specially in recent years. This may be due to the fall in the demand and or market crunch for Indian tea in contrast to the foreign tea. This results in reducing income to the tea industry of the country as well as the state Assam.

Employment in Tea Estates

During the post-liberalization period, there is almost stagnant employment position of tea workers in Assam, when presumably population is increasing geometrically among this section.

In 1995, the growth of average daily number of labour employment in tea plantation was just 2.32 per cent over 1991.

Further, in 1997, the same is only 2.19 per cent over 1995.

On the other hand, in 1991, the share of Assam of the average daily number of labour employment in tea plantation of all India level was 55.64 per cent which got reduced to 55.15 per cent in

1995 and again slightly increased to 56.17 per cent in 1997 (Table 22.10).

Table 22.10: Average Daily Number of Labour Employed in Tea Plantation

Years	*Assam*	*All India*	*Growth in employment (%) over previous year in Assam*	*Share of Assam (%) in all India*
1991	554536	996735	—	55.64
1995	567398	1028787	2.32	55.15
1997	579803	1032267	2.19	56.17

Source: Tea Digest, Kolkata, different years.

Thus, it is evinced that the New Economic Policy has failed to give an impetus to the employment situation of the tea industry in Assam.

Sick Gardens

Due to rise in cost of production and fall in the price of tea, a number of tea gardens in Assam is going to be sick or already sick.

The sick gardens have shown huge liabilities; lands have been encroached, factory machineries and transport have been disposed off. Old and unhealthy tea bushes have been dying thereby creating vacancies in Sections and most of the shade trees have been cut off. The labour payment, medical treatment, ration etc. are irregular.

Though the exact number of sick tea gardens in Assam on date could not be made available, yet it is found that in 2001, there are 22 sick tea estates alone in the Barak Valley only (Singh, R.K., 2001).

SECTION II

From the foregoing analysis, it is clear that there is crisis in the tea industry of Assam during the post-New Economic Policy period especially in the last few years. This is mainly due to declining price realisation coupled with rising cost of production. Further, the growing threat of new entrants in the tea industry of the country after liberalisation from the high quality and low cost producers needs constant innovation so as to stay ahead of competitors.

It is a reality today that globalisation cannot be denied. In the days of liberalisation and globalisation, the tea industry of Assam has to compete on both price front and quality front. For competition on price front, there is a need for reduction of cost. The following measures may be taken for reduction of cost and quality fronts.

Large Scale Production

In many gardens, about one-fourth of the total area in unutilised. In order to reap the economies of large scale production, it is necessary to find possible scope for extension of area under plantation.

Production of Green Manure

Many gardens can take measures for production of green manures by utilising water-borne plants, leaves of leguminous trees and cow-dung. This will reduce the cost of chemical fertilisers and improve the quality of soil as well as product.

Diversification of Product

By product diversification, it is also possible to increase the scale of tea products. Research and Development (R&D) Wing should invent more products from tea which can be used for different purposes.

Government Role

In order to revamp the tea industry of the state, Government of India as well as the State Government should take initiative. In this context, cess and excise duty as well as *ad valorem* tax can be reduced to bring a reduction in price of tea. Further, Government of India should discover new markets in the international arena for Indian tea.

Source of Extra Revenue

The tea gardens by utilising its many unutilised area can earn revenue. For example, if the unutilised marshy lands of tea estates are converted into fisheries, the income of the gardens can be increased.

Moreover, efforts should be taken in order to create demand for tea by advertisement, exhibition etc.

All these steps may revitalise the tea industry of the state of Assam and can also provide a scope to retain the past glory again.

REFERENCES

Banerjee, Sarada and Banerjee, G.D., 'Sustainable Tea Plantation Management', *IASSI Quarterly* Vol. 22, January-March, 204, Vol. 22, No. 3, New Delhi.

Das, R., *The Tea Industry in India—Threats, Opportunities and Challenges,* Centenary Souvenir of Surma Valley Branch, Indian Tea Association, 1901-2001, Silchar, Cachar, Assam.

Goswami, Pranay Jyoti, *Problems and Prospects of Indian Tea Industry in the Liberalised Economy,* the paper was submitted to a Seminar on Survival and Growth of Tea and Other Industries in the Liberalised Economy, ICWAI, Silchar Chapter of Cost Accountants, District Library, Silchar, 20th April, 1997.

Mishra, S.P. and Sharma, Ashwani, 'Revival of Tea Industry in Weak Tea Estates', *Yojana,* December 3, 1994.

Mitra, Neelanjana, Indian Tea Industry: Problems and Policies, *EPW,* November 30, 1991.

Purnendu Kumar, *State and Society in North East India: A Study of Immigrant Tea Plantation Labourers,* Regency Publications, New Delhi, 2006.

Reddy, V.N., 'Global Tea Scenario: 2001 AD', *EPW,* November 30, 1991.

Singh, S.N., (Kr.) Amarendra Narayan, Purnendu Kumar, *Socio-Economic and Political Problems of Tea Garden Workers,* Mittal Publications, New Delhi, 2006.

Singh, R.K., *Cachar Tea and Attitude of Small Holdings and Sick Units,* Centenary Souvenir, Surma Valley Branch, Indian Tea Association 1901-2001, Silchar, Cachar, Assam.

Tea Digest, Tea Board of India, different issues, Kolkata.

Tea Auction Centres, Statistics of different years, India.

23

Impact of Globalization on Tea and Silk Industry of Assam

Ganga Rani Das

Globalization has now become a buzzword for any economy. No country or region can escape from the effects of globalization. An economy has to depend on other economy to fulfil the demand as the taste and preferences of the consumers increase. The more we are approaching modernity, the more we are getting dependent on others. The extent of international trade relation is getting enlarged. No modern economy can claim to be self-dependent. Globalization's ideology is treating the entire world as one Country for trading of commodities, goods and services. It is not static but a continuous process. Exports and imports of even capital goods, and technology are permitted. The world becomes a village, globalization is neo-liberalism. Once we decide to follow a liberal economic policy we must be ready to face a lot of stringent international norms and practices in the sphere of internal trade. We should be able to build up a collective approach along with other developing countries and should be able to project our own interest in the international body like WTO.

Tea Industry of Assam

Tea is the only industry worth the name that kept us in the industrial map of the country. Tea industry, being the largest industry of the state, is playing a dominant role in the economy of Assam. It is the largest single industrial sector in the state, which is contributing a big share in the state income of Assam. The importance of tea industry can be realized from the fact that Assam alone produces more than 50 per cent of country's total tea production.

The first tea garden in Assam was established by the East India Company in 1835. Again in 1844 this garden was sold to Assam Company. Since then the number of tea gardens has started to increase gradually and it was spread over a large part of Assam Valley and also to a considerable part of Surma Valley. The total number of registered big tea estates in Assam has increased from 751 in 1970 to 777 in 1980 and finally to 790 in 2006.

Another recent development in the history of tea plantation in Assam is the inclusion of small tea growers for production and supply of green leaf to the tea factories owned by the bigger tea gardens. As per records of All Assam Small Tea Growers Association, total number of small tea growers in Assam increased considerably from 5064 in 1983 to around 40,000 in September 2003.

The tea industry is a labour-based industry. It has employed nearly eleven lakh labourers in Assam. Many industries like plywood, alluminium, tea, rubber, fertilizer etc. have also grown up along with the tea industry. The Government of Assam collects the highest amount of agricultural income-tax from the tea industry. In Assam, the tea garden labourers together receive Rs. 2 crore daily as wages.

But presently, more than one century old tea industry of Assam is facing certain problems like age old gardens, scanty rainfall, sharp fall of price in international market, increasing cost of production etc. and which have resulted in a fall of production through years gone by.

Impact of Globalization on Tea Industry

Impact of Globalization coupled with import threats and rising competition from other beverages has adversely affected the tea industry of Assam. The price level has been declining since 1994 and though there was marginal improvement in the first quarter of

2001, the level is still below the comparative position in 1998. We can see it from the following Table 23.1:

Table 23.1 shows that the average price level of tea in 1997-98 was Rs. 76.67 per kg., then it started to decline to Rs. 72.72 in 1998-99 and finally to Rs. 61.07 per kg in 2005-06.

The fall in tea prices in recent times at this auction centre and declining trend of tea prices through out the country has created a serious unfavourable impact on the tea industry in general and on the small tea growers of Assam in particular. The concern felt by the small tea growers has posed a serious problem as the falling prices and lack of demand need to be addressed with great urgency because any delay to tackle the problem may act as a disincentive to small tea growers and a good number of persons directly or indirectly related to these small tea growers.

Tea exports from Assam have been decreasing since 2000-01. The neighbouring country Pakistan has been consuming about 140 million kg and USA has been consuming another 120 million kg of tea imported from the world market, but only two per cent has been exported from India to these countries.

The following Table 23.2 shows the decreasing rate of tea exports.

Table 23.2 shows that the amount of tea exported from Assam was 14,768,905.4 kg. in 2000-01, which declined to 8,346,649.5 kg. in 2005-06. The trend of export of tea since 2000 to 2006 has been decreasing by 44 per cent. Export is decreasing due to emergence of new competition, fall in quality, high cost of production etc. Mainly the cheap tea from Sri Lanka, Kenya and China in the international market is a potential danger for the tea industry of Assam. Since both internal and external tea markets demand quality control at all the tea production levels. The entry of duty free inferior quality Sri Lanka tea is partly responsible for the general fall in tea prices and exports. In the prevailing general climate of globalization and dismantling at tariff barriers, it is quite difficult to impose duty on Sri Lanka tea being imported to our country. Despite the declining scenario of export of tea from Assam, it has now been observed that the small tea growers are adding fair amount of raw production (green leaf) to sustain the domestic demand.

Table 23.1: The Price Level of Tea in Guwahati Tea Auction Centre

Year	CTC		Orthodox		Dust		Total	
	Qnty. in Kgs.	*Avg. Pr.*	*Qnty. in Kgs.*	*Avg. Pr.*	*Qnty. in Kgs.*	*Avg. Pr.*	*Qnty. in Kgs.*	*Avg. Pr.*
1997-1998	87,602,577.7	77.26	973,401.0	88.10	47,763,303.3	75.34	136,339,282.0	76.67
1998-1999	96,659,065.0	74.42	840,530.2	71.02	49,358,602.9	69.42	146,858,198.1	72.72
1999-2000	110,104,337.5	79.51	409,209,8	76.66	49,077,971.0	77.99	159,591,518.3	79.03
2000-2001	97,474,897.9	72.51	814,148.9	67.56	43,344,637.2	70.83	141,637,684.0	71.97
2001-2002	96,784,462.5	65.44	642,667.9	58.48	43,532,537.6	58.21	140,959,667.1	63.17
2002-2003	88,298,431.1	65.00	680,343.7	58.30	36,229,986.4	58.21	125,208,761.2	64.04
2003-2004	92,150,519.0	58.56	477,599.4	53.87	39,931,780.4	57.53	132,559,898.8	58.24
2004-2005	91,453,923.4	68.84	443,125.3	74.16	36,784,854.4	68.48	128,681,903.1	67.76
2005-2006	99,793,315.6	61.79	638,561.5	60.71	40,113,292.6	59.26	140,545,169.7	61.07

Source: Guwahati Tea Auction Centre—Year Book (2001-2002, 2003-2004, 2005-2006).

Table 23.2: Exports of Tea from the Guwahati Tea Auction Centre

Year	CTC		Orthodox		Dust		Total	
	Kg.	*Pr.*	*Kg.*	*Pr.*	*Kg.*	*Pr.*	*Kg.*	*Pr.*
2000-2001	14,365,185.0	79.64	130,977.6	66.69	272,742.5	57.13	14,768,905.4	79.10
2001-2002	12,682,361.6	71.50	154,219.9	55.44	440,324.8	51.21	13,276,906.3	70.69
2002-2003	13,650,963.7	72.56	187,237.8	48.25	330,924.8	64.84	14,169,126.3	72.05
2004-2005	8,991,984.4	74.78	20,171.7	63.57	498,818.9	73.85	9,510,975.0	74.71
2005-2006	7,725,443.9	70.70	37,588.4	66.31	583,617.2	59.52	8,346,649.5	69.89

Thus, to face the challenges, the tea industry of Assam must now meet the strategies like export promotion and marketing, diversification of market portfolio, value addition to the product, quality control at international level, proper input base, cost reduction etc. The brand name of Assam tea, which has been developed by Tea Board needs to be popularized more. Thus, what is important at the moment is to frame a defnite strategy to boost up exports of tea in diversified markets on the one hand and also to keep alive its built in image in the global market.

Silk Industry of Assam

Weaving is one of the biggest and oldest industries in Assam. Assam produces three unique verities of Silk: the Golden Muga, the White Pat and Warm Eri. Silk grown all over the state find their way to Sualkuchi, 32 kms from the state capital Guwahati. It is the largest village in Asia and is the largest silk producing village in the world. The village of nearly 50,000 people employ over 20,000 weavers and helpers. 60 per cent of the workers in the industry are women. It produces over six million metres of muga and pat fabrics every year which are exported to Japan and other countries.

The silk industry in Assam is one of the major contributors to state revenue. It is also a major source of employment particularly in rural areas. Eri contributes Rs. 31.5 crores, whereas muga contributes Rs. 40 crores, and pat silk contributes Rs. 120 crores.

The tassar silk is posing a serious threat to muga silk due to high cost of muga yarn and time consuming method of its production. The price of muga yarn varies from Rs. 3200.00 to Rs. 5000.00 per kg. while tassar cost ranges from Rs. 1500.00 to Rs. 2000.00 per kg.

The daily demand for pat thread is estimated over 1000 kg, with a market price of Rs. 1.5 million. This demand was met by importing raw material from China and Japan till 1963. Thereafter fabrics from Karnataka fulfilled the demand. However, liberalization of silk trade in recent years paves the way for the Chinese fabrics, which has competitive advantage in terms of quality and price. This negatively affected the domestic business of silk fabrics particularly in Karnataka.

Impact of Globalization on Silk Industry

The Multi-Fibra Agreement (M.F.A.) is an instrument designed to regulate imports of textile products from developing countries. But, the Multi-Fibra Agreement (FMA) of 1974 has been replaced by the Agreement of Textile and Clothing (ATC) in 1994. The new agreement eliminates all remaining textile and clothing quota restrictions from developing countries by 1st January, 2005 and thus infuses more competition among countries such as China, India, Bangladesh, Sri Lanka, Vietnam etc. to increase market share in global textile market. The elimination of restrictive quota system by the developed countries may affect the textile business in the developing and the least developed countries of South East Asia in a positive or in a negative way. The positive features may be reflected in:

1. New employment opportunities resulting from higher demand and market share.
2. Enhanced wage structure, which may lead to better standard of living.
3. Development of related business, etc.

The negative effect of Globalization of the industry may be reflected in:

1. More pressure on workers to produce more in less time.
2. Exploitation of women and child labour.

Indian silk exports witnessed an increasing trend both in terms of value as well as share in total exports. In 1971-72, silk exports amounted to Rs. 75.9 million. However, exports increased multifold to reach a level of Rs. 22,413.4 million in the year 2000-01. In terms of percentage share in textile exports as well as in total exports also, silk exports enjoyed an increasing share over this period. In 1971-72, the share of silk exports in total export was 0.5 per cent, which has increased to 1.2 per cent in 2000-01. Similarly, the share of silk exports in textile exports also increased from 5.1 per cent in 1971-72 to 5.6 per cent in 1991-92. However, it came down slightly to 4.4 per cent in 2000-01. The female work participation rates has increased in most of the North Eastern states between 1991 and 2001 (Census of India 2001). However, majority of the women workers are in low-paid occupation such as in farms, handloom, sericulture, jute craft, silk industry, brick klin, factories and sales women whereas number of self-empoyed women are relatively low. Although women wage earners are increasing, in most of the cases they do not have control over what they produce because of poor education and technical skills and poor social status. Without adequate technological upgradation the workload on the ordinary workers will be tremendous. However, in several cases the increase in daily wage against their added workload is not in proportion to the rising product price. The wage is relatively less for the unskilled labourers. As most of the unskilled workers in the industry are women, they are the worst sufferers. This may deteriorate further the already poor working condition of workers. So, globalization of the textile industry may result in economic gain for many Asian Countries at the cost of society in general and women workers of the industry in Assam. The process of globalization may increase employment opportunity of women for paid works as casual labourers. However, it increases job insecurity, deteriorates working conditions, right and status of workers.

Gloabalization may have some negative effect in our domestic market. This is becoming prominent particularly in the yarn business in the North Eastern states of India. Till 1963, raw materials for the industry in the North Eastern states have been imported from China and Japan. Thereafter the import has been declining drastically and fabrics from Southern Indian states fulfilled the demand. However, liberalization of silk trade in recent years paved the way for the Chinese fabrics, having competitive advantage in terms of quality and price. This negatively affected the domestic market of silk fabrics particularly in Karnataka. Without adequate competitiveness in price and quality of domestic products, the economic gain from globalization of the industry may not be properly harvested.

Another negative effect of globalization is that lives of women are changing rapidly in North East India. They are no more dependent totally on traditional dresses, rather they have started depending more on readymade garments. Their work pattern started changing from weaving to tailoring, embroidery and computer related works, etc., and many of such works are outsourced on contractual basis. Although these have generated some jobs on casual basis, risk of losing a job is relatively high as most of them are temporary in nature and women are used here mostly as cheap ordinary labour.

Conclusion

The impact of globalization of Tea and Silk industry in Assam is bound to be crucial. In case of tea industry the process may result in the negative because our export is declining. On the other hand, in case of silk industry, the process may result in positive economic gain from rapid growth of export in terms of generation of employment opportunities, more earning capacity for the rural people, etc. However, negative sociological features like child labour, poor working conditions etc. are also increasing.

REFERENCES

Baisy, Prabin, *The Silk Industry of Assam.*

Dhar, P.K., *The Economy of Assam.*

Guwahati Tea Auction Centre—*Year Book* (2001-02, 2003-04, 2005-06).

Import threats hit tea consumption—*The Economic Times,* Dated: Friday, November 23, 2001.

Indian Silk Industry—A Sector Study, Export-Import Bank of India.

24

Resource Mobilisation and Local Products of Garo Hills in the Perspective of New Economic Policy

Anjan Jyoti Borah

Introduction

The New Economic Policy with its fundamental features of liberalization, privatization and globalisation was launched by the Government of India with the aim of economic reforms towards global economy. New policies were promulgated substantially modifying the restrictions placed on foreign investment, industrial licensing etc. and abolished import licensing and removed certain constraints imposed by Foreign Exchange Regulation Act (FERA) 1973.

Globalisation as perceived by the modern world is a form of world society. It involves a breaking through from the rigid national walls to an international community where diverse societies and national economies merged together. Thinking broadly on global terms help people share their ideas for the common good and welfare of the community. This involves a worldwide mobility of technology and a continued supply of goods and capital. Broadly speaking the term globalization means integration of economies and societies through cross-country flow of information, ideas, technologies goods, services, capital finance and people. The essence of globalization is connectivity.

In the era of liberalization, privatization and globalization, the Garo Hills region of Meghalaya remain untouched. With its abundant resources the region has the potentiality of fast development *vis-a-vis* national and international markets. It is enriched fairly with different resources, some of them are over utilized but most of them are not properly utilized. In the age of science and technology most of the resources of the region are not mobilized for which the region and the state is lagging behind. Hence an attempt has been made to study the mobilization and utilization of resources of Garo Hills in the context of New Economic Policy.

Minerals

Minerals occupy a significant place from the point of view of planning for rapid economic development. The Garo Hills are rich in mineral resources. The coal reserves in Meghalaya are estimated to be 63,880 million tonnes out of which more than two-thirds are available in this region alone. The most important coalfields of this region are West Darranggiri coalfields, Kaylash coalfields, the Balpakram Pendengiri coalfields, Nongal coalfields etc. Large deposits of white clay are found at Tura, Khera and Nangalbibra in the Garo Hills. Limestone deposits are also found near Siju, Simsang Valley (Rongrenggiri) and Darang Era Aning in the West Darranggiri coalsfields which constitutes good quality limestone suitable for manufacture of cement.

The estimated limestone in the Garo Hills is 25,778 million tonnes while in Meghalaya it is 45,000 million tonnes. Glass sand feldspar, gypsum and other minerals and different kinds of road metals and building stones are occurring around Siju, Tua and Nanglabibra. Mica being useful mineral is found at Nengkhra in the Garo Hills. Iron ore is available at Aradonga and Athiabari.

But the economic exploitation of these minerals has been hindered by a good number of bottlenecks such as poor transport and communication, non-availability of cheap labour, lack of capital and lack of sincere effort on the part of the government.

Agriculture

Agriculture is the mainstay of the bulk of the population in the Garo Hills. The principal crops such as rice, wheat, pulse, oilseeds, cotton, jute, banana, papaya, pineapple, lichi, orange, mango, jackfruits, betelnut are grown abundantly in Garo Hills. Among the crops cotton, banana, orange, pineapple, jackfruit are worth mentioning. The Darranggiri banana market which is largest in Asia largely depends on Garo Hills banana. The cotton production of the region is more than 5000 bales annually. Orange and jackfruit are also grown abundantly which are sent outside the region. Among the horticultural crops pineapple is the main crop of Meghalaya. It is also remarkable that Meghalaya is the second largest in production of ginger in India next to Kerala.

The region produces good amount of rubber. Rubber plantation is being encouraged by the Rubber Board in the Garo Hills. But no effective steps have been taken in buying rubber from the farmers at reasonable price. In the whole Garo Hills only the Mendi Pathar Co-operative Society is trying its best in support of these farmers.

The fundamental problems of agriculture in Garo Hills are lack of uniformity in soil condition, practice of jhuming, difficulties in undertaking irrigation projects, lack of marketing facilities and complexities of land tenure system.

Handicraft and Handloom

The people of Garo Hills are skilled in making different craft items. The people domestically produce hand made items like *moora, sweeping broom* and different craft items which they sell in the market as a part of their earning. Apart from that the women are good weavers. They produce beautiful traditional garments like *shawl, gamocha, dakbandha* (a sort of women's wear), for livelihood which also attract domestic and outside customers. As the people are poor, they cannot go to the extent of large scale production for commercial purpose.

Hydel Power

The state of Meghalaya has a number of fast and meandering rivers, hot streams from which cheap hydro-electric power can be generated. It has great potentiality for the development of hydro power as it receives adequate rainfall.

Other energy resources such as coal, hydropower, bio-gas and solar energy are yet to be utilized economically and scientifically.

Meghalaya has plenty of potentiality for conventional energy but her need for energy cannot be met by conventional energy source alone. Today power is synonymous with economic development. However, development of hydel power is one of the most efficient and less expensive methods of producing electric power.

Efforts are to be taken in this direction to identify suitable industries for the state and at the same time steps should also be taken to remove those hurdles which hamper possible industrialization. The Garo Hills has no easy access to specialized consultancy service, flexible labour market, communication facilities and air connections to metropolitan markets which are some of the real bottlenecks failing to motivate the industrial units. The limited size of the home market for the products arising out of widespread poverty and structural obstacles constitute an inbuilt impediment to Meghalaya's industrial growth. Further, the pattern of consumption expenditure in a state like Meghalaya is highly connected to food items and the state is overwhelmingly rural.

Suggestions and Conclusion

To achieve accelerated growth it is felt that:

1. The Government should set up a State Export Regulatory Board which will fix the prices of locally produced goods to be exported. Most of the time farmers do not get due price and the benefit goes to the middleman only. If this Board is to be formed farmers will get return according to their quality of products.

2. For the mobilization of resources there should be better infrastructure. The transportation system must be improved. The state should be well connected with the commercial hub of the country. At the same time, communication technology must be improved for easy transmission and flow of information.
3. There should be administrative flexibility in granting trade permission. Generally, in areas covered by the 6th Schedule certain limitations are faced in getting licence and carrying out any trade by people from outside the area. As a result it becomes a hindrance in free movement of people, ideas and scientific technologies.
4. Effort should be made to set up different agro-based industries. For the purpose, Government should find out priority areas to attract the big companies to invest in different sectors. The Government should also provide adequate security and flexibility in terms and conditions. For example, soft beverage producing factory could be set up as Meghalaya produces adequate amount of banana throughout the year. Ginger processing unit is another aspect of agro industry.
5. Last, but not the least proper emphasis has to be given on conservation and plantation of medicinal plants. Meghalaya is one of the sub-tropical North Eastern States of India and home of variety of medicinal plants. The state is losing out economic benefit on this account due to lack of awareness and research. So there is an urgent need for conservation and development of agro-technology for the medicinal plants.

REFERENCES

Globalisation and Its Impact in Economic Development, Academic Foundation, New Delhi, 2003.

Journal of the North-Eastern Council, Vol. 22, No. 2 and 3, April to June and July to Sept., 2002.

Kapila, Uma, *Understanding the problems of Indian Economy*, Academic Foundation, New Delhi, 2003-04.

Meghalaya District Gross Domestic Product, Directorate of Economics and Statistics, Government of Meghalaya (1993-94 to 1999-2000).

25

India's Look East Policy and Youth of Manipur

Th. Binarani Devi

The third world developing countries have greatly contributed to the demand for the creation of a New International Economic Order. They have consistently insisted on the regulation of economic relations among various nations in terms of equality and demanded an effective share in the determination of the international commercial, monetary and financial policies. Today, there is surely a great awareness in the world about inequality between the developed and under-developed countries and the injustice of this economic order. But it would be wrong to believe that a new international economic order would be realised very easily. It will take effort and struggle on the part of the third world to achieve this new economic order.

Generally trade and aid are the two means for improving the financial position of the countries. But the trade relationship between the North and South is not a channel for improving the economic resources of the Southern countries. It gave more opportunities to the Northern countries. To buy technology and other things which the third world countries need most, it needs money or capital. Third world countries are poorer and short of capital. So it is believed that trade does not reduce the unequal relations between the North and South. Another channel of getting resources is aid. It is true that developed countries give aid to the developing countries under varying types of arrangements. But sometimes aid is given in such a way that the economy of the aid receiving country becomes economically dependent on that of the donor country. Also quite often when a developed country provides economic aid, it asked for political advantages in return. This is called aid with strings. It is like saying to the poorer country that you would have economic aid only if you act according to the dictates of the donor. Thus both trade as well as aid relationship with the developed countries have failed to make the third world countries self-reliant. So there is an awareness that there should be greater cooperation among themselves and should try to help each other out.

As a leading third world country India after July-Augugst 1991 followed a new trade policy within this new global economy by giving a sweeping change in the existing trade scenario of the country. It embodied elements that are working to alter the very functioning of the economy for good. The then Government of India under the leadership of P.V. Narasimha Rao, the B.J.P. led (NDA) Government, and also the present Congress led UPA Government fully supported the Look East Policy of India. As a result, a number of bilateral and multilateral agreements were made which had provided the foundation for India's growing relations with South East Asian Countries in particular and beyond these countries in general, but most of them belong to the third world group. This new policy will give ample scope for expanding our trade, economic and cultural relationship with the South East Asian Countries which are belonging to the same group.

Indo-Myanmar trade relationship is the stepping stone for promotion of trade between India and other South East Asian countries. The eventual success of India's Look East Policy will depend on India's ability to control both a maritime and a continental thrust in its Look East Policy.

The Government of India and the Myanmar Government signed a border trade agreement on June 1994 for exchanging locally produced commodities by people living along the border. But on 12th April, 1995 the Indo-Myanmar cross border trade was formally opened by P. Chidambaram, the then Indian Union Minister of Commerce and Myanmar counterpart Lt. Gen. Tun Kyi, Minister of Trade. Since then the continental trade between the two countries have started formally with the expectation of extending beyond Myanmar to other South East Asian Countries. At present two trade centres—one in Manipur at Moreh-Tammu sector, since Apirl 1995, and another in Mizoram at Chaimphai Rih sector since January 2004 are operating between the two countries.

Trading system between India and Myanmar may be broadly categorized into official or legal and unofficial or illegal. The official or legal multi-lateral or bilateral trade is synonymous with international trade while the unofficial trade is popularly known as smuggling.

A major portion of the trade between the two countries are unofficial. Businessmen or traders from Imphal, Kohima, Silchar, Aizawl, Shillong, Guwahati and Kolkata work through the local agents at the different trade centres like Moreh, Champhai and Lungmalong in Myanmar Border. In the Myanmar bordering state of India, a large section of the population, including people in public life and administration, educated unemployed youth, common men, women and children are involved in unofficial trade as a means of their earning. For this purpose, the introduction of new trade routes like the proposed railway link between Delhi and Hanoi (Veitnam) will create more job opportunities for both the educated and uneducated youth of North East India, especially in Manipur, will uplift the socio-economic conditions of the region and mitigate the insurgency problem in general and will check illegal cross border trade of the region in particular.

The North Eastern Region of India is known for its social and economic backwardness as well as never ending story of social and political instability and poor political delivery system. There is a great need for a participatory human development, the investment in human beings themselves by means of education and training, i.e. human capital is quite necessary. Again in the pattern of human capital accumulation, youth constitutes the latent resource of human resource development. At the stage of youth, we can impart, train, nurture skills and help them maintain good health. Unfortunately, substantial section of the youth does not get the opportunity to go for training or better higher education. Even those who do get the training and education do not get employment. Today, the trend of unemployed youth signals a major crisis in the human resource development. The crisis sometimes responds negative human capital investment. The number of unemployed youth registered in the employment exchange was 5,75,605 in October 2006. The negative responses arising as a result directly make an erosion in the human capital. Such erosion in the human capital is caused by drug abuse, addiction of alcohol, tobacco and infection through HIV virus. It sets a major social and economic problem as well as neglect of human resource development.[1]

Impact of Look East Policy on the Youth

India can be regarded as a developed country when the socio-economic and political conditions of all parts/regions are developed in an equal way. Mooted as a path breaking initiative to bring development to the North Eastern Region, India's Look East Policy aims to further the country's buoyant trade with South East Asia.[2] The present effort in connection with Look East Policy to make the North Eastern Region a transit point with an attempt to enhance the productive forces of the region for its economic regeneration and development underlines the utility of the policy. The structure of India's Look East Policy is characterized by free flow of capital, commodities, financial fluidity, loosening of national political economic frontiers and increasing geographical mobility. The ongoing project of the Government of India for constructing a new rail link between Jiribam-Imphal-Moreh and further linking it to Tamu-Kalay-Segji and Cabinet Committee on Economic Affairs' clearance to the proposal to augment the road network in the North East which also includes the connectivity of the capitals of Nagaland, Meghalaya and Sikkim with the East-West Corridor will enhance the policy.[3]

The proposed Trans Asean Highway from Singapore to Istambul through India, Myanmar and Thailand will further develop the trade relationship between India and Myanmar and other South East Asian Countries and with the introduction of this new highway the most chronic problems of the youth of North-Eastern Region, i.e. the problem of unemployment will be solved to some extent. They will get job directly as well as indirectly. The location of the region is also more favourable to have a trade relationship with South East Asean Region which is closer to the market of this region than that of the mainland markets of India in Delhi, Mumbai, Chennai etc. The ethnic origin of the people is also more similar to the people of the South Asean Region than that of the Indian mainland.

There is an ample scope and potential for hydro power resources, oil, gas, tea, herbal medicinal plants, fruits etc. in North East India. If all these goods are fully harvested and exported through Myanmar to other South East Asean countries, it will give direct and indirect job opportunities to the educated and uneducated youth of the region, which will result in the massive growth in the economy of the region.

India, being a member of World Trade Organisation, there will be no restriction on Multi-National Companies' entry into India. This will further increase the volume of trade between India and the South East Asean countries.

Problems of the Youth of Manipur vis-a-vis the Look East Policy of India

The location of Manipur is in the extreme corner of North East India bordering Myanmar on the east. After signing the Indo-Myanmar cross border trade in 1995, Manipur is considered as gateway to South East Asean countries. So Manipur is witnessing both benefits and weaknesses of India's Look East Policy directly.

When the border trade was opened in 1995 between India and Myanmar it covered 22 items. But the official legal trade has been dying slowly over the years, while the unofficial trade has been flourishing. Businessmen or traders from Imphal, Kohima, Silchar etc., work through the local agents at the different trade centres like Moreh, Champhai and Lungwa along Myanmar border.

The increase in illegal trade specially of drug trafficking is largely responsible for the fast degeneration of social environment in states of North East India bordering Myanmar such as Manipur,

Mizoram, Nagaland and Arunachal Pradesh. North East India is a heroin trafficking route. Different chemicals which are used in producing heroin No. 4 from raw opium are smuggled from Kolkata and other parts of the country to Tamu, Mandalay, then to the North-Eastern part of the Shan States. After refining, heroin No. 4 is smuggled to North East India and then into the world market.[4] In connection with this problem, another surprise information relate to security personnel who are directly and indirectly involved in this trade. Among the security personnel, the Myanmarese army, the Indian Customs Department officials, the BSF etc. are focused in the media. Keeping this fact in view, any sort of free trade between India and South East Asia entails the risk of opening a floodgate of immigrants and with it hordes of heroin smugglers from across the border.[5] The opening of more roads and railways through Myanmar are sure to bring along drugs and infectious diseases. The impact of the golden triangle is badly felt particularly in Manipur and other North East States and India in general where the number of drug addicts is increasing. In fact, the number of drug addicts in Manipur is increasing day by day. Manipur AIDS Control Society checked 1,65,747 samples. Out of those persons, 24,198 were found to be HIV positive.[6] Consequently, the HIV positive cases are also increasing day by day. Not only the local people, the Armed security personnel who are posted in the border areas are also suffering from this evil. The Inspector General, BSF, Assam, Nagaland, Meghalaya, Manipur, Joyti Prakash Sinha expressed to the UNI, Shillong that six Jawans in B.S.F. are found HIV positive in N.E. India and 94 persons in India as a whole.[7] The figure of the HIV affected persons is increasing so quickly in the state of Manipur when it is compared with the all India figure. The rich middle class people from other parts of India and abroad rush towards this region for the business of this high value but low weight item. But this business gives direct impetus to the youth of the region so badly.

For reaping the benefits of India's Look East Policy, industrialisation of the state is quite necessary for the state of Manipur. But, more than a decade after the initiation of India's Look East Policy, there has been no serious introspective effort on the part of the state to change the infrastructure and industrial policy. The present efforts in connection with India's Look East Policy to make the North-Eastern Region a transit point with no serious attempt to enhance the productive forces of the region for its economic regeneration and development will be meaningless without any serious step for the infrastructural and industrial development in the region. India's Look East Policy will further generate an array of marginalisations linked to the economic development through the neo-liberal methods and understanding. The middle class elite and a small group of capitalists in the region may benefit from the programme. The availability of huge consumer goods and items-brought from other parts with the full operationalisation of Look East Policy may usher in the economically weaker sections of our society a retreating behaviour.

With the opening of new trade routes in the region in a liberalized economy, the forceful flow of massive migrant population has led to serious complications in the fragile economic, political and cultural life of the indigenous people. The presence of mainland immigrants and illegal foreigners is not only a threat to the indigenous population of the region but also a security risk for the country as a whole. Immigration on a large-scale has created an environment conducive to communal and linguistic problems. The emergence of collusive networks of smugglers, organised criminal gangs and religious extremist groups operating in the North East greatly accentuated the problems of illegal immigration. Apart from the problems of drug smuggling, human trafficking, gun running etc., generally associated with cross-border immigration, another security concern is the infiltration of foreign intelligence agencies along with the hordes of espionage and other clandestine operations.[8]

The benefits of free trade should reach the people of North East rather than going to the business houses in big cities. The Look East Policy of India should not be a mere tool to use North East as a corridor for free trade with neighbours. The knowledge of trade with full technical infrastructure is quite necessary. Over and above, there is a need for more universities and technical and management institutes for the youth of the region. Introduction of new and relevant courses in the Universities would help talented students to pursue courses of their choice. The number of higher and technical educational institutions is very low in this region when it is compared with other parts of the country. The following figures show the minimal infrastructure of N.E. India in the field of technical and non-technical education.[9]

Universities		*Engineering Institutes*	
North East	15	North East	10
Delhi	17	Madhya Pradesh	61
Maharashtra	42	Gujarat	37
Karnataka	23	West Bengal	54
Tamil Nadu	35	Uttar Pradesh	89
Uttar Pradesh	34	Punjab	45
Bihar	14	Maharashtra	155
Rajasthan	20	Karnataka	118
Gujarat	17	Andhra Pradesh	236
West Bengal	20	Namil Nadu	254

In the name of the maintenance of law and order, and security in the region, a number of armed personnel are deployed. On the other hand a number of underground organisations are operating in the region, mainly in National Highway 39. The situation not only gives disturbances to the traders, it also creates problems for the local innocent people.

From the above, it is very clear that sixteen years of India's liberalized economic policy and eleven years after signing trade pact with Myanmar, one questions is still with us—will it be boon or curse to the younger generation of North-Eastern Region in general, and Manipur in particular? Here I would like to draw the attention of the Central and State Government that if proper steps are not taken in time it will create total chaos and confusion in the region instead of development. Only making policy and programme is not enough for development. For achieving the real fruits of the India's NEP, I want to mention a few suggestions:

(i) Controlling illegal trade along the 1640 km. long border with Maynmar and increase the number of official trade items like bicycle, fertilizers, medicine etc.

(ii) Improving the insufficient infrastructural facilities such as road, transport and communication, banking, insurance, warehouse, hotel facilities etc.

(iii) Initiating measures for improving the present law and order situation of the North-Eastern states in general and bordering states of Manipur and Nagaland in particular which has caused the slow pace of development and disrupted the normal volume of trade.

(iv) Facilitating certain programmes to encourage the involvement of local people in the infrastructural and trade development.

(v) Opening of new secondary and tertiary sectoral industry in the area which will give more job facilities to the youth of the region.

As an impact of liberalization, privatisation and globalization generally and Indo-Myanmar border trade especially there is a ray of hope for the socio-economic and political development of the region which will give direct result to the youth of the region. But it is right time for understanding the impact of the above-mentioned policies and programme on the youth. The youth are the backbone of the society and if they are damaged, society cannot develop at all.

NOTES

1. *The Sangai Express,* Imphal dt. 15.11.2006, p. 2.
2. *Alternative Frames—Economy, Polity, History and Cultrue,* Vol. 1, Issue II, June-March, 2006.
3. *The Hindu,* 24.10.2005.
4. *Eastern Frontier.* A Monthly News Magazine, Bikay Loitongbam, Kwakeithel Thiyam Leikai, Imphal, Manipur, Vol. I, Issue No. 6, June 2006, p. 7.
5. *Alternative Frames—Economy, Polity, History and Culture,* Vol. I, Issue II, June-March, 2006, p. 42.
6. Manipur AIDS Control Society Report, Poknapham (Manipur local daily paper) dt. 29.11.2006.
7. Poknapham, dt. 5.12.2006.
8. *Alternative Frames, op. cit.* p. 32.
9. *The Times of India,* dt. 6.11.2006, p. 3.

26

New Economic Policy and Poverty Alleviation Programmes in Manipur
An Overview

N. Tejmani Singh and *Th. Jitendra Singh*

The present study examines NEP and Rural Development in the State of Manipur. Poverty eradication is one of the most prominent objectives of the development planning in India. To achieve this goal various programmes/schemes have been implemented by the Central Government in our country. The researchers have selected two schemes, namely Indira Awaas Yojana and Sampoorna Grameen Rozgar Yojana and analysed their financial and physical performance in the state. The study is based on secondary data which have been compiled from various journals, books and concerned officers of Monitoring Cell Department, Government of Manipur. These two programmes are playing a very important role to develop standard of living of rural poor like STs/SCs, small and marginal farmers, widow and disabled personnel etc. by providing additional and supplementary wage employment, infrastructural development in rural areas.

It has been just over a decade since the launching of New Economic Policy in July 1991 by the Government of India. The main objective of this policy was to place India on a high growth path. There are various aspects of the New Economic Policy, for instance, the issue of globalization is an important one. It means that the Indian economy is responsive to the developments taking place at the global level and is also moving in the direction of India trying to play greater role in the world economic environment. Thus, globalization of the Indian economy is the need of present times in the backdrop of the unsatisfactory economic record of previously closed economies.

Indian economy must prepare itself for moving on non-traditional lines to achieve the goal of macro balance between aggregate demand and supply, saving and investment, revenue and expenditure, exports and imports etc. It is essential to totally transform the Indian economy to solve its basic problems of poverty, unemployment and equality. Liberalisation or globalization of the economy is a remedial measure for all these ills. Therefore, India has decided to participate in process of globalisation.

Different scholars have given a variety of definitions of globalisation. But briefly, globalization means adoption of market-friendly approach thereby making the economy more open. In other words, globalisation of the Indian economy means integration of it with the world economy.

New Economic Policy (NEP)

In June 1991, Indian economy was in the grip of a drastic economic crisis characterised by acute balance of payment deficits, low foreign exchange reserve, high rate of inflation, lumping credit worthiness with mounting pressure of debts and debt serving burden and sharp increases in money supply due to large budgetary deficit. Considering the graveness of the situation, the Government came with a package of comprehensive economic reforms known as New Economic Policy (NEP). The reform package has often been characterised as an attempt to globalize our economy in the sense of its being moved closer to an effective integration with the world economy. As India enters global competitiveness, various sectors of its economy will have to assess the impact of globalization in their own context.

Objective of the Present Study

The present study focuses on the following main objectives:

- To evaluate the performance of IAY in both financial expenditure and physical achievement in Manipur.

- To analyse the financial and physical performance of SGRY in the state.
- To make recommendations concerning to the financial and performance of both the schemes so as to promote economic development of the rural poor.

Methodology

The present study is based on relationship between NEP and Rural Development. For this secondary data were collected from the related books, journals, research articles, Government offices and library etc. For the purpose of analysis yearwise data from the Monitoring Cell Secretariat, Government of Manipur, were also collected and have been examined intensively with the help of different statistical techniques such as percentage etc.

Implementation of Indira Awaas Yojana (IAY) and Sampoorna Grameen Rozgar Yojana (SGRY) under the NEP of Eradication of Poverty in Manipur

From the beginning of planning in India, various poverty alleviation programmes have been introduced to alleviate poverty through providing more opportunities for involving the poor in the economic process. Improvement in the quality of life of the economically weaker section of the society is also one of the basic objectives of development planning. To achieve this objective a variety of programmes, namely SGSY, JGSY, EAS, IAY, PMGY, PMGSY, SGRY etc. have been under implementation in the state. These programmes provides minimum wage to rural workers and enable them to acquire assets to evaluate various development schemes and programmes launched in the state for uplifting the standard of living of the rural population of Manipur.

Indira Awaas Yojana

Housing is one of the basic requirements for human survival. A normal citizen owning a house enjoys significant economic security and status in society. The origin of the Indira Awaas Yojana (IAY) can be traced to the programmes of rural employment which began in the early 1980s. The National Rural Employment Programme (NREP) began in 1980 and the main activity was the construction of houses. The Rural Landless Employment Guarantee Programme (RLEGP) also began in 1983. As per announcement made by Government in June 1985, a part of RLEGP fund was earmarked for the construction of houses for SCs/STs and freed bonded labourers. As a result of it, IAY was launched during the year 1985-86 as a sub-scheme of RLEGP. Thereafter IAY continued as a sub-scheme of Jawahar Rozgar Yojana (JRY) since its launching in April 1989. JRY funds allocated to IAY formed only 6 per cent out of the total fund. From the year 1993-94 the scope of IAY was extended to cover Non-Scheduled Castes/Scheduled Tribes below the poverty line families in the rural areas. Then fund allocation to IAY was increased from 6 per cent to 10 per cent of the total resources available under RJY at the national level, but subject to the condition that the benefit to non-STs/SCs poor should not exceed 4 per cent of the total JRY allocation. IAY has been made an independent scheme with effect from 1st January, 1996. The main objective of IAY is to give assistance in construction of dwelling units by members of SCs/STs, freed bonded labourers and inclusion of non-SC/ST rural poor below the poverty line by providing them with grant-in-aid.

Target of IAY

IAY targets rural people below poverty line who are either totally houseless or living in unserviceable *kutcha* houses. From the year 1995-96, the IAY benefits have been extended to widows or next-of-kin of defence personnel in some conditions and also to ex-servicemen and retired members of the paramilitary forces as long as they fulfil the normal eligibility condition of IAY and have not been covered under any other shelter rehabilitation scheme. 3 per cent is earmarked for the benefit of disabled persons below poverty line of IAY. Under the scheme, a maximum assistance of Rs. 25,000 per house for plan areas and Rs. 27,500 per house for hilly or difficult areas is given to BPL family to construct house. Assistance is also given for upgradation of *kutcha* house at the rate of Rs. 12,500 per unit. 60 per cent of the houses are for SC/ST beneficiaries. In the next 4 years (2006-2010), the number of construction houses will be 60 lakh and investment in rural housing will be about Rs. 12,000 crore. Now IAY has been made part of the Bharat Nirman by UPA Government.

Achievements of IAY

The physical and financial achievement under IAY in Manipur is given in Table 26.1, which shows the fund allocation of Central and State Governments, O.B. (Opening Balance), and fund released by Central and State Governments. In the year 2001-02, an expenditure of Rs. 138.98 lakhs was incurred and a total number

Table 26.1: Performance of IAY for Four Years (2001-2002 to 2004-2005)

(Rs. in lakhs)

Year	*Fund Allocation*			*Open-ing Balance on 1-4-2001*	*Fund Released*			*Total available Funds (5+8)*	*Expenditure*	
	Central	*State*	*Total*		*Central*	*State*	*Total*		*Financial*	*Physical*
1	*2*	*3*	*4*	*5*	*6*	*7*	*8*	*9*	*10*	*11*
2001-02	662.82	220.60	883.42	224.23	299.15	220.60	519.75	743.98	138.98	319
2002-03	679.51	226.50	906.01	143.62	247.62	220.60	468.22	611.84	551.34	2571
2003-04	748.47	249.47	997.94	87.71	267.42	180.85	448.27	*550.49	286.30	1656
2004-05	984.83	328.27	1313.10	120.53	763.18	205.45	968.63	1089.16	913.04	6066

* In the year 2003-04 total available funds was 550.49 including other receipts 4.51 lakhs.

Source: State Level Rural Development, Department Monitoring Cell, 2005.

of 319 beneficiaries were covered under this scheme. In the year 2002-03 and 2004-05 the financial expenditure has been increased to Rs. 551.34 lakhs and 913.04 lakhs respectively. As a result of this, physical performance has also been increased, i.e. 2571 beneficiaries in 2002-03 and 6066 beneficiaries in the year 2004-05. But decrease in the number of beneficiaries in the year

2003-04, i.e. 1656 was due to the decrease in fund released from Central and State Governments. In Manipur, the hurdles of implementation of IAY are absence of proper planning, non-conducting of survey for identification of beneficiaries, underutilisation of the allocated funds and non-release of Central assistance etc. All these factors affected to achieve the objective of this programme.

Sampoorna Grameen Rozgar Yojana (SGRY)

Creation of employment opportunities with food security has also been an important objective of development planning in India. Relatively, the higher growth of population and labour force has enhanced the volume of unemployment and under-employment from the one plan period to another. The aim of Government of India is to create employment through wage and self-employment into a larger focus with the goal of reducing unemployment and under-employment to a negligible level and of providing food security against hunger. To obtain the objective, it is also necessary that efficient use of available human and other resources is done in the most effective way of alleviating poverty, reducing inequalities, improving nutritional levels and sustaining a reasonably high pace of economic growth.

To provide a greater thrust to additional wage employment, food security and infrastructural development in the rural areas a new scheme with an annual outlay of Rs. 10,000 crores was launched which would be in term of cash and foodgrains. The Ministry of Rural Development reviewed the hitherto ongoing schemes of the Employment Assurance Scheme (EAS) and the Jawahar Gram Samridhi Yojana (JGSY). By 25th September, 2001, these two schemes merged in one new scheme that is Sampoorna Grameen Rozgar Yojana (SGRY).

EAS is the only additional wage employment scheme and JGSY a rural infrastructure development scheme. From the year 2001-02, SGRY has been divided into two streams, i.e. 1st stream EAS and 2nd stream JGSY. Sampoorna Grameen Rozgar Yojana has the following two objectives:

1. The primary objective of the scheme is to provide additional and supplementary wage employment and thereby provide food security and improve nutritional levels in all rural areas.

2. The secondary objective is the creation of durable commodities, social and economic assets and infrastructural development in rural areas.

Fig. 26.1: View of the Road constructed in a Village of Tribal Area Under SGRY

Status and Target Group of SGRY

The programme will be implemented as a centrally sponsored scheme sharing cost in the ratio of 75:25 between the Centre and the State Governments of the cash component of the programme. For the UTs, the Centre would provide entire (100%) funds under the scheme and foodgrains would also be provided to the state or UTs free of cost. This programme will facilitate all rural poor who are in need of wage employment and desire to do manual and unskilled work in the around his village or habitat.

While providing wage employment, preference shall be given to agricultural wage earners, non-agricultural unskilled wage earners, marginal farmers, the persons affected due to calamities, women, members of SCs/STs and parents of child labour withdrawn from hazardous occupations, parents of handicapped children or adult children of handicapped parents who are desirous of working for wage employment.

Work to be Done

The works which ought to be done will be labour intensive, leading to the creation of additional wage-employment, construction of village infrastructure like roads, primary school building, dispensaries, veterinary hospitals, marketing infrastructure, panchayat building, watershed development and promoting of traditional water resources etc. All these works should not be permitted to the contractors, middle men or intermediate agencies employed for executing these schemes. The full benefit of wage to be paid should, at all times, reach the workers.

Works Prohibited

The works which should not be done under these schemes were construction of Monuments, Idols, Arch Gate, Memorials, Statues, Buildings relating to religious, Big Buildings and Bridges, Government Office Buildings and Compound Walls, Buildings for Higher Secondary Schools and Colleges.

Fig. 26.2: Strengthening of Infrastructure in a Rural Area Under SGRY

Performance of SGRY

The financial and physical achievement under SGRY in Manipur are given in Tables 26.2 and 26.3. And the financial and physical achievements for India are also shown in Appendix

(Tables 1 and 2). The total fund available of SGRY and its cumulative expenditure to the different sections of the society for the years 2003-04 to 2004-05 respectively are highlighted in Table 26.2. The total fund available under SGRY has increased to huge amounts in the year 2004-05 compared to 2003-04 which indicates that the Centre and State Governments have released more fund under this scheme with the objective to provide additional wage employment, rural infrastructure development and alleviating poverty. Cumulative expenditure was enhanced for all the sections except disabled in the year 2004-05. The highest expenditue was Rs. 1114.54 lakhs for SC/ST and lowest was Rs. 10.51 lakhs for training in 2004-05. Training facilities were provided to implement this scheme smoothly.

Table 26.2: Financial Performance of SGRY for the Years 2003-04 to 2004-05

(Rs. in Lakhs)

Year	*Total fund available*	*Cumulative Expenditure*						
		General	*SC/ST*	*Disabled*	*Maintenance*	*Training*	*Others*	*Total*
2003-04	1778.57	492.72	472.60	6.13	69.53	—	30.11	1071.19
2004-05	2873.88	1105.41	1114.54	—	89.75	10.51	66.99	2387.20

Source: State Level Rural Development, Department Monitoring Cell, 2005.

The physical performance of SGRY for the years 2003-04 to 2004-05 is shown in Table 26.3. It is quite evident that total number of mandays generated in the year 2003-04 was 14.004 lakhs which rose to 31.93 lakhs in the year 2004-05. It is due to the increase in

Table 26.3: Physical Performance of SGRY for the Year 2003-04 to 2004-05

(Employment Generated in Lakhs Mandays)

Year	*SC*	*ST*	*Others*	*Total*	*Out of Column 5*		
					Women	*Landless*	*Disabled*
2003-04	1.464	9.359	3.181	14.004	3.732	—	0.077
2004-05	2.170	19.127	10.633	31.930	8.504	—	5.665

Source: State Level Rural Development, Department Monitoring Cell, 2005.

total availability of funds and also for imparting the training facilities in the year 2004-05. The highest mandays generated for STs was 19.127 lakhs in 2004-05 but for landless it was nil.

Suggestions for Improvement

- It is essential to prepare proper planning and conduct survey for identification of right beneficiaries.
- Allocated funds ought to be utilised fully and must direct a segment of funds for training for rural youth for self-employment.
- Central and State Governments should release the fund in time. The outlay of Government must be increased at the possible level though there is the restriction on public expenditure consequent upon the adoption of the NEP.
- To achieve the desired objectives, a massive awareness generation campaign should be launched in rural areas.
- The training needs of DRDAs, PRIs and implementing agencies should be analyzed and identified.
- Under IAY, the land for construction of house is provided by the beneficiary but many of the landless labourer do not get house under this scheme. Hence, it should also be rectified so that the most marginalised section of the society could benefit from the scheme.
- An effective housing policy could play a crucial role in employment generation and arresting migration of population from rural to urban areas. So, the Government could consider making housing activities an integral part of the National Rural Employment Guarantee Scheme.

Conclusion

Since independence, one of the most prominent objectives of development planning in India has been the ultimate removal of poverty. Since early 1970s various poverty alleviation programmes have been operating till now. These two programmes have succeeded to some extent in providing assistance to the rural poor, particularly to the SCs/STs. But there is sufficient evidence to show that the programmes have not gone down smoothly among the people. In fact, the State Government is not serious to release its share of funds and as a result, huge cash balances are lying unutilized.

Abbreviations Used

IAY = Indira Awaas Yojana.
SGRY = Sampoorna Grameen Rozgar Yojana.
SGSY = Swarnajayanti Gram Swarozgar Yojana.
JGSY = Jawahar Gram Samridhi Yojana.
EAS = Employment Assurance Scheme.
PMGY = Pradhan Mantri Gramodaya Yojana.
PMGSY = Pradhan Mantri Gram Sadak Yojana.
NEP = New Economic Policy.
DRDAs = District Rural Development Agencies.
PRIs = Panchayati Raj Institutions.
SCs/STs = Scheduled Castes/Scheduled Tribes.
BPL = Below Poverty Line.

REFERENCES

Annapurna Jha (2006): I.A.Y. Under Bharat Nirman, *Kurukshetra,* Vol. 54, No., 12, pp. 48-49.

Atmanand (1997): *Globalisation and Dimension of Management in India,* Shipra Publications.

Department of Monitoring Cell, Government of Manipur, "Annual Reports of State Level Rural Development".

Directorate of Economics and Statistics, Government of Manipur (2002-03): "Economic Survey Manipur".

Government of India, Ministry of Rural Areas and Employment, New Delhi, (1988): "Indira Awaas Yojana Guidelines".

Government of India, Ministry of Rural Development, Krishi Bhawan, New Delhi, (with effect from 1-4-2004): "Sampoorna Grameen Rozgar Yojana, Guidelines".

Hari Shankar Singhania: *Economic Issues Global and National: A Business Perspective.* Vikas Publishing House Pvt. Ltd., pp. 312-315.

K.R. Gupta (1995): *Liberalization and Globalisation of Indian Economy,* Atlantic Publishers and Distributors, pp. 36-37, 83-87.

Pawan Kumar (July 2006): Rural Infrastructure : Thrust Area in Rural Development, *Kurukshetra,* pp. 17-19.

APPENDIX

The Financial and Physical Achievement for India under SGRY

Table 1: Financial Performance under SGRY for Whole India (For the Years 2001-02 to 2002-03)

(Rs. in crores)

Year	*Stream*	*O.B.*	*Total allocation (Centre + State)*	*Total release (Centre + State)*	*Other Receipts*	*Total available funds*	*Expenditure*	*%age expenditure*
2001-02	1st	435.37	2496.74	2414.56	40.46	2890.39	2020.85	69.92
	2nd	346.02	2493.01	2521.87	—	2867.89	2171.22	75.71
2002-03	1st	710.26	2371.10	1536.98	51.59	2298.82	1159.75	50.45
Upto November	2nd	531.50	2364.00	1464.01*	37.07	2032.57	1009.77	49.68

* Includes Central Releases upto 31-12-2002

Source: Planning Commission and Other Concerned Departments.

Table 2: Physical Performance Under SGRY for Whole India (For the Years 2001-02 to 2002-03)

(Lakh Mandays)

Year	*Stream*	*Scheduled Castes*	*Scheduled Tribes*	*Others*	*Total*	*Women*	*Works completed (Nos.)*	*Works in Progress (Nos.)*	*Foodgrains Released (Lakh Tonnes)*
2001-02	1st	822.96	596.24	1175.00	2605.54	750.43	170928	94593	16.93
	2nd	881.76	559.17	1183.31	2626.24	693.77	936261	284731	17.56
2002-03	1st	533.23	344.38	706.09	1583.70	390.13	115578	143167	13.64
Upto November	2nd	574.01	281.80	691.56	1547.37	369.03	384869	367292	13.62

Source: Planning Commission and Other Concerned Departments.

27

Harvesting Prosperity by Look East Policy

Kaustubh Lahiri

'To convince people in poor countries about the benefit of Globalization, we must take a more enlightened view in liberalizing trade in services and labour intensive manufacturing in which developing countries are productive'—Dr. Manmohan Singh in his address at Cambridge University as recipient of D.Lit.

Promises that Encourage

Look East Policy brings an opportunity in the perspective of glorious Indian heritage of embracing the neighbours through cultural bonds. This is more particularly for South East Asian countries in the context of Indian History.

Today the emphasis is on sharing our attainments in developing our nation and also learning their experiences to absorb rectifications. Resource whether human or natural, symbiotic sharing is also required to be organized to induce a harmonious growth pattern. A democratic form of governance is another crucial asset which can provide inspiration for reforms towards activating peoples' participation.

The Reality Check

In the context of practical situation ASEAN nations do not display a cohesive democratic governance system as also a uniform financial management pattern. With revolutionary concepts no more playing active role in trans-border dimensiŏn, the disiilusionment of the citizens with the elected Governnment in removing their livelihood constraints was picked up by the men in uniform to capture absolute power. Though Professor Gunnar Myrdal advocated 'hard state' as catalyst for rapid growth, in reality it has proven to be opposite.

Look East Policy deserves a phase oriented approach with priority to be assigned. This is applicable in both nations to be selected as also policy to be emphasized. In this perspective Malaysia and Singapore are the two dependable destinations with rich potentiality.

Malaysia : The Value of Asia

The Watershed in Malayan Economy has been introduced by New Development Policy termed as Vision 2020 during their Sixth Five-Year Plan (1991-1995). Outline Perspective Plan (OPP 2) encouraging a strong link between Public and Private Sector by mobilizing people around a collective project holds out the promise of future reward to the community. Auxiliary significance is a ruling by Malaysian Central Bank by which it has been established that FDI acquiring can only be given by if the Project can earn foreign exchange to foreign debt servicing to avoid building up of high level of private foreign debt that led to the Stock Exchange Crisis in Indonesia, Thailand and South Korea.

Basically Malayan economy thrived by successful adoption of Japanese System of Function which according to William Lockwood is 'a web without spider'. This is a "web of influence and pressure interweaving through Government and Business rather than a streamline pyramid of authoritarian control". But equally important is the paradigm value shift towards collective effort instead of Anglo-Saxon personal approach cultivated under former Prime Minister Mahatir through UNMO political organization.

Singapore: The Springboard of Asia

S. Nordin in his book, *Towards a New Asia* attributed the rise of Singapore to the collaborative foundation of race, ethnicity and religion cultivated during its colonial period serving as a key social marker to attract foreign investment. Since 1960 the People's Action Party by astute utilization of this foundation by high level social and political control along with export oriented industrialization has turned Singapore the promising growth pole.

The Long Shadow of Army Brass

Both of Indonesia and Phillippines democracy is in volatile stage ravaged by ethno-religious instability and therefore, lives on tactical support from men in uniform.

The situation is worst in Myanmar completely jacketed under Military rule with no transparency. It is more alarming because Myanmar being the adjacent neighbour through which land based trade linkages are being planned where arm deal happens to be the determining factor in providing space for infrastructural expansion. Thailand though at present under the siege of army but with His Majesty King Bhumibal at the helm of affairs the situation is expected to turn to normalcy soon.

And the Ameliorating

Specifically noteworthy is Vietnam where a consistent transformation is sponsored by the ruling Communist Party for ensuring accountability in the growing business sector. The very recent step has been the decision to decentralize business from ruling party functionaries.

Towards a Deductive Assessment

Situational description provides the impression that Malaysia and Singapore can be designated as two dependable destinations to start with Look East Policy. Indonesia with its trembling democratic system but with buoyant Stock Market is posing a contradiction but still the situation is worth exploring essentially with surveillance. The scope in Vietnam is promising but with outsourcing playing the vital role, opportunities are to be formulated.

This descriptive profile needs to be evaluated through adoption of certain macro-economic and human resource parametric indicators.

Table 27.1: Differential Ranking in Selective Macro-Economic Parameter

Sl. No.	*Nations Selected ASEAN Nations*	*GDP Growth Rate at Constant Price*	*PPP Index*	*Unemployment Rate*		*Inflation Rate*	*Fiscal Balance*
				Gen,	*15-24 Years*		
1.	Indonesia	5.3(4)	3.1(4.5)	9.9(2)	13.4(2)	8.4(3)	1.2(3)
2.	Malaysia	4.4(6)	2.2(6)	3.6(6)	4.7(4.5)	3.4(6)	4.3(6)
3.	Myanmar	5.0(5)	10.8(1)	4.0(5)	Ab	57.3(1)	Ab
4.	Philippines	4.1(7)	4.5(3)	10.9(1)	19.0(1)	7.1(4)	3.9(5)
5.	Singapore	5.4(2.5)	1.1(7)	5.3(4)	4.7(4.5)	0.5(7)	1.1(2)
6.	Thailand	5.4(2.5)	3.1(4.5)	1.5(7)	6.6(3)	5.6(5)	0.1(1)
7.	Vietnam	7.7(1)	4.8(2)	5.6(3)	Ab	7.6(3)	2.0(4)

Source: ASEAN statistics as on 31-12-2006 and ADB basic statistics 2006 Figures with ( ) indicates ranking according to Spearman method. For practical reason Ranking in unemployment provides reverse situation with Worst being 1.

Table 27.2: Differential Ranking in Human Geographical Indicator

Nations	*Annual Population Growth Rate*	*Age Dependency Ratio*	*% of Population < Poverty Line*	*Share of Poorest Quantile in National Income*
Indonesia	1.3(5)	52(5)	10.2(5)	8.4(3)
Malaysia	2.1(1.5)	59(2.5)	7.5(6)	4.4(5)
Myanmar	2.0(2.5)	59(2.5)	20.6(2)	Ab
Philippines	2.1(1.5)	67(1)	30.4(1)	14.1(1)
Singapore	2.0(2.5)	39(7)	Ab	5.0(4)
Thailand	0.8(6)	43(6)	9.8(4)	0.7(6)
Vietnam	1.4(4)	56(4)	19.5(3)	9.7(2)

Source: As for Preceding Table.

The result of correlation between selected indices according to Spreaman Method show following outcome:

- GDP Growth Rate and Annual Population Growth Rate
  Calculated Value r = – 0.41.
- Inflation and % of Persons below Poverty Line
  Calculated Value r = + 0.74
- Annual Production Growth Rate and Unemployment Rate
  Calculated Value r = + 0.45

Inflation, Unemployment Rate and per cent of persons below Poverty Line—are the three critical factors that combine in different proportions to surge social unrest.

Therefore, from this perspective labour intensive production system requires to be encouraged. With acquiring of farm land for factories appearing as a burning issue, emphasis on industries with good downstream potentialities rooted to farm products and household productivity, can check the apprehensions of local inhabitants.

Signals from Market: In the GDP Perspective

Driven by tremendous liquidity and robust Economic Growth the MSCI Asia—Pacific Ex. Japan Index gained >25 per cent in USD terms beating the Global Index by 700 basis. It was the emerging markets in the region that delivered the most stunning returns as follows:

1.	Indonesia	64.5%	For Reference:	
2.	Philippines	45.6%	India	42%
3.	Singapore	37.7%	China	65%
4.	Malaysia	29.9%	USA	13.6%
5.	Thailand	08%	Japan	4.5%

According to Economic Survey 2006-07 the ongoing financial and regulatory reforms for the capital market, together with accelerated economic growth and macro-economic stability, sustained the investor's confidence in the country's capital market.

India with a market capitalization of 91.5 per cent of GDP compared favourably not only with emerging markets but also with economies like Japan (96%) and South Korea (94.1%). The market value of Indian stocks was second highest among all emerging markets, surpassing those of markets like Thailand, Malaysia, South Korea and Taiwan at the end of 2006. In comparison, China's market cap was just 33.3 per cent of GDP at the end of 2006.

The Challenges Ahead: Competition from China

But in the era of market driven economy controlling the state economy in one form or other, it is extremely difficult to be certain whether this ideal model can really find the ground for being materialized.

And taming the Chinese Dragon: Post-reform India has emerged as a growing power of soft skills mainly in the Service Sector whereas China's Hard Skill in manufacturing provides preliminary advantage to China.

But India's strength is rooted to its R&D sector which has been awarded with global recognition in terms of FDI flow. Of the 5567 FDI Projects into China between 2003-06 R&D segment received only 7.9 per cent share. In contrast FDI flows into R&D in India accounted for 25.9 per cent. The performance of Indian Corporate Sector aided by steadily expanding domestic and external markets have laid the foundation for new challenges.

According to Prof. Sushil Khanna, 50 per cent of FDI in China is merely "Round Tripping" that is illegal Chinese money taken out of the country and brought back through proper channel from countries such as Taiwan and Hong Kong and only about $15 billion is actual foreign investment.

Industrialist Sanjeev Goenka believes that China is moving from Pro-FDI Policy to a Neutral FDI situation. Without these FDI flows Chinese growth rate could well have slowed down by 3.5 per cent to Indian level.

India is steadily gaining the status of a dependable partner of ASEAN nations for its growth model incorporating soft infrastructure like regulatory frameworks, financial markets and recognized and transparent property right.

The Great Green Expectation in the Perspective of Emerging Reality

The Budget 2007-08 remaining silent on drawing guideline for the implementation of Look East Policy and incentives for industries in North East India, there is nothing but expectations.

If labour intensive industries can find the scope to be promoted then food processing and other agro-based and aquaculture based production system can be encouraged. This recommendation can catalyze growth in North East if a Trans Border R&D and Marketing Network for farm products can be developed. Asia Pacific Association of Agricultural Association (APAARI) has prepared a concept paper on Linking Farmers to Market (LFM). Access to information, capacity building of farmers and partnership of producers as stakeholders are the principal thrust areas of LFM. Necessarily LFM requires greater R&D effort and this is the model that can create the foundation for Agro-based Industry expanding through ASEAN countries from North East.

With Public Private partnership modern terminal marketing centres can be raised maintaining a hub and spoke system. With hub being the marketing centre the spokes would serve as links to collection centres. These collection centres will help in establishing backward linkages with the grassroots producers so that they need not go beyond from the farms to disperse their products. Thus both perishable and non-perishable agricultural and horticultural products can be sent to the market directly by the producers eliminating middleman.

Similarly other non-farming rural products can also be brought under this system. North East having a heritage of renowned Cottage Industry products, the emerging urbanization of ASEAN nations can provide multiple outlets.

Direct and indiscriminate marketing of natural resources particularly vegetative products is to be discouraged if not restricted, to secure the tender eco-system balance of North East

India. However, eco-tourism has great potentiality. Even rural tourism has substantial scope because of the diverse mosaic of socio-ethnic cultural kaleidoscope.

This endeavour can be tested with Malaysia and Singapore. Malaysia with rich bio-diversity can be a promising field for generating agro-based production. A reliable communication and marketing linkage with North East India would allow the farm growers of North East to attain access to ASEAN and East Asian production system as also Malayan farmers to growing Indian domestic market. Moreover Singapore with its reputation as global nodal business point would act as the catalyst for the regional production network. Gradually in association with ASEAN, such a symbiotic collaboration can also be procured.

REFERENCES

Lockwood, William: *The State and Economic Enterprise in Japan.*
Mahatir, Md.: *The Voice of Asia: Two Leaders discuss the Coming Century.*
Noordin, S.: *Towards A New Asia.*

In addition to above books, various editions of *The Indian Express, The Statesman, Yojana* contributed in writing this article.

28

New Economic Policy and its Impact on Traditional Skills of Women in North East India

Dolly Phukon

In order to cope up with the mounting burden of debt leading to a balance of payment crisis, the Government of India launched the New Economic Policy (NEP) in 1991 and adopted a Structural Adjustment Policy (SAP) involving privatization, liberalization, opening of doors to foreign trade of all kinds and reforms in the economic structures in the name of efficiency hoping to provide buoyancy to the stagnating economic, social and cultural levels.

The emerging new world order under globalization is being controlled by the IMF-World Bank which represents a purely monetary model of growth in which everything is subject to free competition under the impetus of market forces undermining the grievous hurt that it causes to the fundamental needs of large segments of population. The New Economic Policy under globalization is basically based on the survival of the fittest logic.

In India, due to the existing gender inequalities, women require active governmental support for their social and economic upliftment and empowerment. Socially the majority of Indian women are still tradition bound and it is a disadvantageous position. After the New Economic Policy in 1991, the Indian economy was opened up suddenly without the required economic and social policies to provide the required safety net to women. Though the New Economic Policy led to prospects of higher education, employment in technology and advanced sectors, changing attitude towards women, integration of world's women's movement etc., still these benefits are enjoyed only by the women belonging to the affluent class of the society. Majority of women in India and other developing countries find themselves stripped off the benefit of social security, government protection of labour rights etc. Any reduction in governmental expenditure involving the public distribution system, education, health care and other infrastructural supportive activities, is bound to have an adverse effect on the quality of their life. Moreover the most negative impact of the NEP falls upon the rural women as almost about 80 per cent of our population reside in the rural areas. These rural women are the preserver of our rich cultural heritage and are the backbone of our economy.

This paper tries to give an overview of the impact of the New Economic Policy on the rural women of North East India with special reference to their traditional skills. The North East India is characterized by diverse ethnic, cultural and linguistic groups. It may be noted here that women's status in the North East is much better and they enjoy greater mobility and visibility compared to the other regions of the country. The women of the North East are well-known for their hardworking nature. They are expert weavers and farmers in addition to being the carrier of North East's rich culture. But still like women of other regions, women of North East have also encountered some specific problems over ages such as—patriarchal culture, inadequate access to productive resources, non-accounting of women's domestic works, insufficient advancement facilities, powerlessness etc. Thus women in this region, though handworkers and experts in many fields, are still a subjugated and dominated social group. But with introduction of NEP and the SAP for globalization, women's status became more vulnerable in North East India. Thus a proper analysis of differential impact of globalization on different sections of women residing in various regions is needed to see how the general thrust of globalization is felt by women of the North East. However, the paper would confine to the impact on the traditional skill of women of Assam such as agriculture, weaving, food preparation and alienation of women from the society and reducing them to mere consumers rather than active producers.

The North East region was well known for its food self-sufficiency and its rich natural resources. The natural resources of the region was harnessed sustainably by the indigenous people. Wood gathering, livestock and animal husbandry, handicrafts, handlooms, fishing and agricultural activities such as sowing, weeding, transplanting, harvesting and post-harvesting activities like thrashing, husking, grinding etc. were undertaken by our rural women. After the liberalization of economy and in the new circumstances created by SAP for globalization, the traditional role of women is being undermined whereas mechanization and automation is becoming prevalent in the market based economy which has adversely affected the village based traditional economy. The opening of markets led to the commercialization of agriculture and new technologies penetrated into our agricultural lands. But in this context too regarding upgradation of agricultural development tools women were neglected. The transmission of knowledge about the new technologies like use of tractors, high quality fertilizers, selection of HYV seeds, pesticides etc. became man-to-man affair. Men were increasingly drawn into the modernizing agriculture sector while women stayed in subsistence agriculture with no access to credits, training and technologies. The agricultural develoment has normally and almost entirely been manned by men right from the decision-making to implementation. Again women have also been excluded from owning or controlling land, the most crucial productive resource in agricultural economies. Earlier women and men were equal partners in agriculture. Their knowledge and contribution and participation in decision-making were recognised. But with the commercialization of agriculture, women's job is taken up by men and mechanization has displaced a large segment of agricultural workforce which performed the traditional agricultural work. In this context, it may be referred that as women do not belong to a homogeneous category, the impact of new technology was different among different segments of women. To the women of middle class agrarian family, tasks like preparation of food for farm labour, caring for livestock, post-harvest tasks and supervision of labour from within the household have increased significantly. This led to the extra agricultural work participation of women which are more invisible works and are not accounted. Improvement of agriculture has also had its effect on the most marginalized segment of women who have lost a large number of their specialized tasks and uses from agricultural waste which provide them subsistence. The process of shaving off already beaten rice, gleaning the grains etc. were the specialized tasks performed by these women and have been replaced by masculinisation of modern chemical intensive and mechanized capital-intensive agriculture.

Thus it could be seen that with the NEP, commercialization of agriculture was encouraged with the use of new technologies for more production. But the process was not properly planned to offer "gender friendly" work environment. The new technologies favoured the men for it opened their horizons and interactions in a wider world. It means a close interaction with the market in relation to the buying and selling of produce, the purchase of fertilizers, pesticides etc., interaction with government personnel for loans, hiring of tractors, threshers, combines, payment of electricity bills etc.—all making the entire process male-centred, thus leading to a certain extent the withdrawal of women from agricultural process in general (Gill, Rajesh, 2005).

Another implication of the NEP is the undermining of women's traditional knowledge of food preparation, weaving, dyeing, fishing etc. In rural areas of Assam, weaving was the common cottage industry in which women were mainly engaged. Its importance was attached to the war victory also. In the traditional Ahom society women believed that the garments woven in one night would lead her husband to victory. Till recently women had woven all her requirements. It is traditional in the sense that the primary qualification of a young girl for her eligibility for marriage was determined by whether she had the skill to weave or not. As there was lack of industrial infrastructure in Assam and also in the North East, weaving provided employment opportunity or earning opportunity to the women. But the advent of the NEP and liberalization of trade made a very adverse effect in our domestic market. In fact, weaving which was primarily known as women's occupation got gradually eroded with most of the tasks being carried out by the males equipped with the knowledge of new technology. Thus in the production process women worked as part-time helpers, unskilled workers, ordinary helpers and the males undertake the responsibility of mechanized weaving and marketing the latter workers in the industry enjoying a higher status and predominant earning. Assam was known for its *gamocha* woven by women the presentation of which was a sign of respect towards the elders. The same could now be pruchased at a cheap rate from Kolkata factories.

Moreover lives of women are changing rapidly along with the process of globalization in North East India. They are no more dependent totally on traditional and handloom dresses, rather they have started depending more on readymade garments. This happened because of the high propaganda in favour of the market forces creating new and artificial wants among the people and forcing their mind to look down upon tradition as ridiculous and backward as opposite of modernity.

But it may be mentioned here that since time immemorial due to our socialization, women were always assigned the private sphere that is the domestic sphere. As a result, women became experts in their own fields and were able to maintain their own identity. The expertise and skill could be harnessed and be made the main tools of empowerment of women and their self-sufficiency but it didn't happen as women's works were never accounted as productive works. But with the advent of globalization and liberalization under the NEP, the same works which were women's exclusive domain came to be undertaken by men and women's works which determined their identity were snatched away reducing women to mere consumers rather than producers.

Again in the case of food preparation too during the festive occasions, village women used to gather and prepare festive food together. But with the advent of modernity, new wants and aspirations were created among the people. This resulted in a spirit of consumerism for the middle class families such as TV, ovens, gas, grinders, mixies creating an active consumer culture. These products, of course, have lessened the burden of women but it has tended to largely erode women's autonomy and life style.

Another important twist that took place in our state under the NEP is that in the name of giving free hand to the market forces, the state has withdrawn from the welfare and public distributive spheres. Consequently, women have become the worst victims. In this context, the privatization of educational system under globalization has further deprived women from accessing to the educational facilities. The study of traditional disciplines in science, humanities, has etc. become less important in relation to new professional courses like fashion designing, hospitality and hotel management with specialization in cookery or catering services etc. The courses like fashion designing, cookery etc. have slowly snatched away women's traditional skills and expertise in traditional colourful textile designs and ethnic wears and native food products. These courses are imparted in exchange of a high cost. The privatization of educational institutions has made education expensive for the poorer household who are now disinclined to send their girls to pursue higher education and have forced them to join cheap labour force of the global market. Thus under the circumstances women are slowly relegated from their traditional identities and works. The cosmopolitan food products and dresses have intruded our markets undermining the role of rural women as the preserver of rich traditional culture and identity, food habits, rich ethnic dresses, customs, etc., in the face of the march of the market forces.

The new structural adjustment policies under the NEP to usher in globalization in traditional economies like the North East India will be able to reach the expected goal only if the process of globalization is well backed by properly planned gender friendly policies in a conducive social and economic environment. The NEP has marginalized majority of women in North East through reduction of employment opportunities and exclusion from the modernized production process due to lack of education and training. No doubt there are some positive sides of globalization and the NEP which have contributed to bring about welcome changes in the lives of women but the gains are attained by those women who can afford them both economically and socially. But as we all know, about 80 per cent of the population of our region stay in the rural areas and are mostly poor and hence the true character of the current globalization and its negative impacts are borne by the weak, the poor and the backward. There must be equitable distribution of technological progress keeping in view the fact that the human development must be strengthened in order to achieve social and gender justice.

REFERENCES

Abbi Kumool, 'State, Market and Gender in India' in Gill, Rajesh (ed.), *State, Market and Civil Society: Issues and Interface*, Rawat Publication, New Delhi, 2005.

Bhagawati Dhiren, *The State of Higher Education in the Age of Liberalization and Globalization: A dialogue in many voices,* Centre for Political Studies, Dibrugarh University, 2005.

Dasgupta Kalpana, *Globalization and Indian Women: Problems, Possibilities and Information Needs—An Overview,* Presented at The World Library and Information Congress: 69th IFLA General Conference and Council, 31 July, 2003.

Dutta, R. Akhil, 'Empowerment and Women Empowerment: A Critique of Neo-Liberal Political Economy Paradigm' in Dutta, Anuradha (ed.) *Journal of Politics,* Vol. 3, Deptt. of Political Science, Gauhati University, 2003.

Phukon Dolly, 'Globalisation and its emerging challenges to the status of women in the Third World', in Adil Ul Yasin (ed.), *Journal of Poliics,* Vol. XII, Department of Political Science, Dibrugarh University, 2005.

Vibhuti Patel, *Women's Challenges of the New Millenium,* Gyan Publishing House, New Delhi, 2006.

29

The Renewable Energy Policy
Issues and Prospects

D.R. Das

Introduction

An increasing share of global energy needs is expected to be met by renewable in the years ahead. Energy policy of the European Union and United States indicates this share to reach about 12 per cent by the year 2010. International estimate suggests that renewables would contribute about one-quater to one-half of the world`s primary energy supply by 2050 and by that year, two of the world's largest petroleum companies expect renewables to account for over 50 per cent of their turnover. Renewables have enormous potential to meet the growing energy requirements of the increasing population of the developing world, while offering sustainable solutions to the global threats of climate change.

In India there has been a growing expansion of use of commercial energy about more than ten fold during the last fifty years. There has been faster growth in economy, i.e. 6.4 per cent GDP growth and subsequent increase in energy demand. India's energy development pogramme has been put to severe pressure with the ever-increasing demand-supply gap and it has been estimated that there is energy shortage of about 7.3 per cent and peak load shortage of 11.7 per cent and there is mismatch of resources coupled with non-uniform growth curve. The challenges faced by India in the management and development of the power sector are multi-dimensional which is primarily form the two broad factors—increasing demand for energy due to rapid industrialazation and growing population and limited reserves of coal and fossil fuels and consequent burden on foreign exchange due to increasing imports.

The Renewable Energy policy has identified the following thrust areas:

- Renewable policy envisages development of all forms of non-conventional energy forms.
- Conservation and effecient management of demand.
- Energy security and sustainable development.
- Development of decentralized energy system based on renewable especially for use in rural areas.

During the 10th and 11th Plan, it is envisaged to achieve capacity addition of 1,00,000 mw through renewable energy (2002-2012) which is very challenging task. The achievement in the Renewable Energy sector is as follows:

Fig. 29.1: Power from Renewables: Progressive Power Generation from Renewables (4.99% of the installed power generation from Renewables)

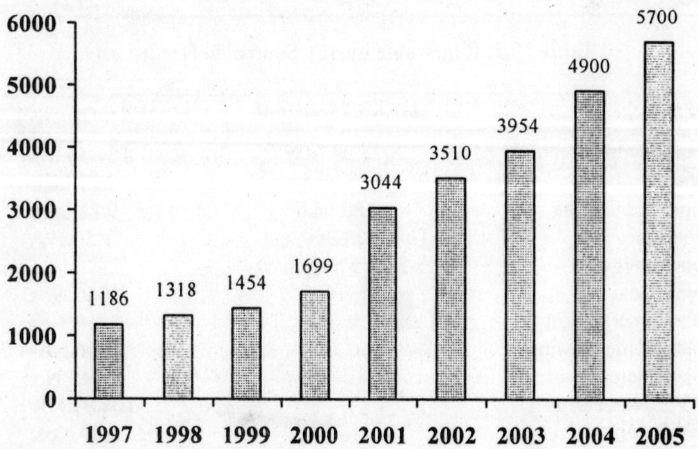

Capacity from All Sources:

Wind	:	2980
Biomas	:	722
Small Hydro	:	1693
Others	:	305
Total	:	5700 MW

Another aspect of Indian energy scenario is marked disparity between consumption pattern in Urban and Rural segments. Only 44 per cent of the rural households have electricity connections compared to 83 per cent urban households. More than 80,000 villages are yet to be electrified out of which nearly 18,000 villages are extremely remote and isolated.

Table 29.1: Renewable Energy Potential and Utilization (Power Generation)

Sources/Systems	*Potential (MW)*	*Harnessed (MW) So far*
Biomass Power	19,500	484
Gasifier		53
Wind Power	45,000	1870
Small Hydro Power	15,000	1519
Waste to Energy	1,700	26
Solar Power		2
Total	81,200	3954

Table 29.2: Renewable Energy Sources in North-East

Sector	*Surveyed Potential*	*Achievement*
Small Hydro (Up to 25 MW)	2028.34 MW	157.50 MW
Biogas	4.22 lakh	0.71 lakh
Improved Chulha	50.80 lakh	9.81 lakh
Biomass	Under assessment	1.5 MW
Solar energy	4.5-5.2 kwh/sq.m/day	
Solar cooker		2350 Nos
Solar street lighting		3416 Nos
Solar Home lighting		8896 Nos
Solar Lanterns		41043 Nos
SPV Power Plants		104.97 KWp
SPV Pumps		109 Nos
Aero Generators and Hybrid		16 KWp
Solar Shops		6 Nos
Battery Operated Vehicles		2 Nos
Energy parks		53 Nos

Renewable Energy Plan 2012

The Government of India has proposed the draft renewable energy policy and programme interventions required to achieve the goals of meeting the minimum rural energy needs, providing decentralized off-grid energy supply and generating grid quality power based on renewables. The mid-term goals of the policy are as follow:

- Achieving a 10 per cent share for renewables in the new power capacity projected upto 2012. In absolute terms, this would translate to setting up of about 12,000MW renewables.
- Providing 10 million homes with solar hot water systems.
- Electrification by renewables of at least one quarter of 18,000 unelectrified remote villages.
- Deployment of 5 million solar lanterns and 2 million solar home lighting systems.
- Coverage of 30 million households through improved chulhas (wood stoves).
- Setting up of further 3 million family size biogas plants.

Conclusion

In order to achieve the goal of energy security for the country through large scale use of renewable energy for power generation, road map is to be prepared for development of the various sources of renewable energy so as to make them commercially viable and acceptable to the common people at large. The road map also suggests suitable pathways including mission mode projects that would help the industry, government, reserch organizations, academia, non-govermental organizations, and other stakeholders to achieve the national goals for achieving 10 per cent capacity addition of power generation through renewables. A key trend in global electrification over the next few decades will be the shift in technology dominance from supply side to demand side as the electricity delivery system becomes integrated with communications to from a new mega-infrastructure with new functions. A balanced focus on the technologies of supply and the technologies of demand will be needed to meet global electrification goals. Sustainable growth of the global economy as it becomes increasingly reliant on quality electricity.

Inaugural Speech by Shri M.M. Jacob, Former Governor of Meghalaya

It gives me profound pleasure to associate myself with the National Seminar on "North East India of New Economic Policy" organized by the North East India Council for Social Science Research. It is in fitness of things that the North East India Council for Social Science Research, Shillong has organized this National Seminar to focus attention on the New Economic Policy of the North East India. I thank the Indian Council of Social Research for inviting me to inaugurate the seminar.

The North Eastern Region has all along been facing various challenges towards its all-round development. These challenges cut across the spheres of economy, society and polity. Their resolution, as a result, requires a holistic and comprehensive approach that can unify the interest of various ethnic groups, and synergize the strengths that are inherent in the society, polity and economy.

The New Economic Policy (NEP) launched by Government of India, in 1991 has the clear objective of integrating the Indian economy with the rest of the world. The main instruments of New Economic Policy are liberalization, privatization and globalization. The policy instruments consisted mainly of providing all facilities to the private sector for starting new industrial ventures, by removing all types of Government restriction, which had been a characteristic feature of the Indian economy right from the First Five Year Plan period. Dismantaling the public sector through disinvestment and denationalization and providing encouragement to the private sector, have been the main focus of the New Economic Policy. Raising competitiveness of the economy through quality productivity, cost and price efficiency, so that Indian products become globally competitive, have been the major objectives of these policy issues. In an effort to create global demand for our products, India not only had to make serious efforts to explore the international markets, but it also had to open up its own markets to encourage international. Trade restrictions have to be liberalized to encourage international trade as one of the policy instruments related to the New Economic Policy.

India has now travelled the path of New Economic Policy for 15 years, numerous hurdles an obstacles notwithstanding. In fact, the nation has also launched the second phase of Economic Reform after the completion of the first decade of New Economic Policy. In the second phase, along with concerted effort at the economic front, the social sector of the economy has been given adequate importance. This is because no policy in economic development particularly in an overpopulated nation can be successful without taking into consideration the deprived and the poorer section of the society. All these features are addressed directly by state intervention in the second phase of economic reform. The policy, it appears, leaves higher education and specialized health sectors to the private players.

The crucial issue therefore that needs to be addressed here is the position of North East India *vis-a-vis* the New Economic Policy. It is an already accepted fact that the socio-cultural and economic environment of the states of North East India is in wide divergence with the rest of the country. The issue that is of concern is to what extent the states of North East Region are prepared to accept and implement the policies having significance to a region, which had hardly witnessed any form of industrialization worth mentioning? It also needs to be examined the difference the New Economic policy had made to the economy and quality of life of the people of the region. Whether the economy of the region had the same competitive strength as other regions of the country so as to enable her to proceed ahead with the policy reforms at the same pace.

Any attempt at understanding the relevance of New Economic Policy in the context of North East of India requires a holistic view and an understanding of the economic history of the region, as well as sociological, psychological and political economy of the various states of the region. Policies of liberalization, privatization and globalization cannot be taken as a single programme of economic development, but a means of transformation of the quality of life of the people of the region. Historically, the tribals who from a significant section of the population of the region are characterized by !ack of competitive spirit. The success of New Economic Policy depends crucially on the presence of this feature. The development experience of the region has revealed that injection of financial aid into the economy of the region has led to the emergence of a financially strong middle class, whose demand for foreign products has been increasing limitlessly. This has resulted in flooding the markets of the region with products produced in other parts of the country. We should also produce quality products and utilize the world market.

The structural transformation of our economy that is being engineered will be meaningful for North East India if it brings better life for the people. What will be the likely implications of the programmes of New Economic Policy for North East India? Can we think of an alternative policy frame in the form of production, co-operation to bring new change? North East India economy should be directed to the maximum use of local resources and renewable form of energy for sustainable privatization and liberalization affecting the traditional economy of North East India which has no industrial base. Has globalization provided a level playing ground for North East India? We are witnessing the emergence of economic patriotism. There is an urgent need to review the operation and impact of New Economic Policy since 1991 on North East India.

Meghalaya is a peaceful State. A pre-condition to development which is peaceful society is herein Meghalaya. Tourism industry has to develop. For that, the road from Gauhati to Shillong and beyond should be 4-lane road. The runway of Shillong Airport has to be extended. More good hotels should come up without yielding to certain pressures of few individuals. Major decisions have to be implemented for the good of all. Essential goods will become cheaper if a Railway line is allowed to pass through. The farmers can get more lucrative price for their products, if Railway transportation is encouraged.

I am sure the deliberations in this seminar will throw many more valuable ideas which can be of interest to the Government of India, the State Governments of the North East and various organizations interested in the development of the States of North Eastern India.

With these few words, I have great pleasure in inaugurating this seminar. I wish the deliberations all success.

Index